Absolute Beginner's Guide

to WordPerfect X3

Laura Acklen

800 East 96th Street,
Indianapolis, Indiana 46240

Absolute Beginner's Guide to WordPerfect® X3

Copyright © 2006 by Que Publishing

All rights reserved. No part of this book shall be reproduced, stored in a retrieval system, or transmitted by any means, electronic, mechanical, photocopying, recording, or otherwise, without written permission from the publisher. No patent liability is assumed with respect to the use of the information contained herein. Although every precaution has been taken in the preparation of this book, the publisher and author assume no responsibility for errors or omissions. Nor is any liability assumed for damages resulting from the use of the information contained herein.

International Standard Book Number: 0-7897-3425-7

Library of Congress Catalog Card Number: 2005925006

Printed in the United States of America

First Printing: December 2005

09 08 07   4 3 2

Trademarks

All terms mentioned in this book that are known to be trademarks or service marks have been appropriately capitalized. Que Publishing cannot attest to the accuracy of this information. Use of a term in this book should not be regarded as affecting the validity of any trademark or service mark.

WordPerfect is a registered trademark of Corel Corporation.

Warning and Disclaimer

Every effort has been made to make this book as complete and as accurate as possible, but no warranty or fitness is implied. The information provided is on an "as is" basis. The author and the publisher shall have neither liability nor responsibility to any person or entity with respect to any loss or damages arising from the information contained in this book.

Bulk Sales

Que Publishing offers excellent discounts on this book when ordered in quantity for bulk purchases or special sales. For more information, please contact

    U.S. Corporate and Government Sales
    1-800-382-3419
    corpsales@pearsontechgroup.com

For sales outside the United States, please contact

    International Sales
    international@pearsoned.com

Associate Publisher
Greg Wiegand

Senior Acquisitions Editor
Stephanie J. McComb

Development Editor
Kevin Howard

Managing Editor
Charlotte Clapp

Project Editor
Tonya Simpson

Indexer
Ken Johnson

Technical Editors
Jan Berinstein
Diana Yarrall

Publishing Coordinator
Sharry Lee Gregory

Interior Designer
Anne Jones

Cover Designer
Anne Jones

Page Layout
Toi Davis

Table of Contents

Introduction 1

Some Key Terms 1

Things to Keep in Mind 2

How to Use This Book 2

Conventions Used in This Book 3

I Learning the Basics 5

1 Getting Started and Finding Help 7

What Is WordPerfect? 8

Getting WordPerfect Up and Running 8

Exploring the WordPerfect Screen 8

Working with the Property Bar and Toolbars 11

Using the Menus 13

Getting Help 13
    Getting "Quick and Easy" Help 14
    Accessing the Help Topics 15
    Getting Help on the Web 16
    Helping Microsoft Word Users Make the Transition 18

2 Creating, Saving, and Printing Documents 21

Creating Documents 22
    Typing Text 22
    Erasing Text 23

Moving Around in a Document 24
    Using the Mouse to Get Around 25
    Using the Keyboard to Get Around 26

Printing a Document 28

Saving Documents 29
    Saving and Closing Documents 29
    Saving to a Different File Format 30
    Closing Documents 33

3 Finding and Opening Documents 35

Getting Familiar with the Open File Dialog Box 36
Opening a File 36
Customizing the View 37
Rearranging the File List 38

Navigating Through Drives and Folders 39

Searching for a File 40
Listing Files by Type 40
Listing Files by Modification Date 41
Searching by Filename or Content 42

Converting Documents on Open 43
Installing Additional Conversion Filters 44
Using the WordPerfect Office Conversion Utility 44

Organizing Files in Folders 46
Creating New Folders 46
Moving and Copying Files 47
Renaming Files 48
Deleting Files and Folders 49

4 Revising Documents 51

Selecting Text 52
Selecting Text with the Keyboard 52
Selecting Text with the Mouse 52

Moving and Copying Text 53

Using Undo to Fix Your Mistakes 55

Using the Zoom Feature 56
Zooming In with the Mouse 57
Zooming In on a Specific Area 58

Switching to 5.1 Classic Mode 59
Switching to the Blue Screen 60
Switching to the WordPerfect 5.1 Keyboard 61

Working with More Than One Document 62

Previewing and Printing Documents 63
Switching to Print Preview 64
Changing the Number of Copies 65
Printing Specific Pages 66
Faxing Documents from WordPerfect 66
Sending Documents via Email 67

5	**Learning Basic Formatting**	71
	Emphasizing Important Text	72
	Choosing the Right Font	73
	Selecting Fonts and Font Sizes	73
	Choosing a Font from the QuickFonts List	75
	Using Other Font Effects	76
	Changing Margins	77
	Using the Guidelines to Adjust Margins	78
	Adjusting the Left and Right Margins Using the Ruler	79
	Using the Page Setup Dialog Box	80
	Creating an Envelope	81
	Inserting Symbols	83
	Using the Symbols Dialog Box	83
	Using the Symbols Toolbar Button	84
	Using QuickCorrect	85
	Working in Reveal Codes	86
	Turning on Reveal Codes	86
	Printing the Codes	88
6	**Using the Writing Tools**	91
	Recognizing WordPerfect's Automatic Proofreading Features	92
	Spell Checking a Document	94
	Checking for Grammatical Errors	96
	Looking Up Words in the Thesaurus	98
	Using the Dictionary	100
	Switching to a Different Language	101
	Searching and Replacing Text and Codes	103
	Searching for Text	103
	Searching for Codes	105
	Discovering the Power of QuickCorrect	107
	Adding and Deleting QuickCorrect Entries	108
	Customizing Format-As-You-Go	109
	Inserting SpeedLinks	111
	Creating QuickWord Entries	112

II Making It Look Nice 115

7 Working with Paragraphs 117

Aligning Text 118
    Using Center and Flush Right 118
    Justifying Text 119

Setting Tabs 121
    Turning on the Ruler 122
    Clearing the Default Tabs 122
    Setting New Tabs 123
    Changing the Tab Type 123
    Editing Tab Settings 124

Indenting Text 125

Adjusting the Spacing Between Lines and Paragraphs 127
    Adjusting the Line Spacing 128
    Adjusting the Spacing Between Paragraphs 129

Keeping Text Together 129
    Enabling Widow/Orphan Protection 130
    Using Block Protect 130
    Setting a Conditional End of Page 131

8 Working with Pages 133

Inserting a Page Break 134

Changing Paper Size and Orientation 135

Subdividing Pages 136

Adding Page Numbers 138
    Inserting Page Numbers in a Preset Position 139
    Inserting Page Numbers Manually 141

Adding a Header or Footer 142
    Creating a Header or Footer 142
    Working with Headers and Footers 144

Suppressing and Delaying Formatting 146
    Using the Suppress Feature 146
    Inserting a Delay Code 147

Adding Borders Around Pages 149

Using the Make It Fit Feature 152

9 Using Styles for Consistency 155

Understanding Styles 156
- Open Styles 156
- Paired Styles 156

Using QuickStyle to Create Your Own Styles 157

Using WordPerfect's Existing Heading Styles 158

Building Your Own Styles 159

Editing Styles 161
- Revising Your Styles 161
- Customizing the Default Settings 162

Using QuickFormat 163

III Organizing Information 167

10 Creating and Formatting Tables 169

Creating Tables 170

Working with Tables 172
- Typing in Tables 172
- Adjusting the Column Widths 172
- Adding Rows and Columns 174
- Deleting Rows or Columns 175
- Joining and Splitting Cells 175

Formatting Tables, Columns, and Cells 177
- Formatting the Entire Table 177
- Formatting Text in Columns 178
- Formatting Rows 179
- Formatting Cells 181

Changing Lines, Fills, and Borders 184
- Using SpeedFormat 184
- Changing the Lines 185
- Changing the Fill Pattern 187
- Choosing a Table Border 188

Using WordPerfect Tables for Calculations 189
- Using QuickSum 189
- Inserting Formulas 191
- Inserting Functions 193

Converting Text to a Table, or a Table to Text 194
    Converting Tabular Columns to Tables 195
    Converting Tables to Other Formats 196

11 Creating Lists and Outlines 199

Working with Lists 200
    Creating Bulleted Lists 200
    Creating Numbered Lists 202
    Editing Lists 203
    Changing the Bullet or Numbering Style 204

Working with Outlines 205
    Creating Outlines 206
    Using the Outline Property Bar 207
    Editing an Outline 207
    Collapsing and Expanding Outlines 210
    Changing the Outline Style 211

IV Adding Visuals 213

12 Working with Graphics 215

Working with Graphic Lines 216
    Inserting Standard Lines 216
    Customizing Graphic Lines 218

Inserting Graphic Images 220
    Inserting Clip Art 221
    Moving and Sizing an Image 222
    Importing Graphics 224

Creating Text Boxes 228

Setting Border, Wrap, and Fill Options 229
    Wrapping Text Around Graphics Boxes 229
    Adding Borders to Graphics Boxes 230
    Adding Fills to Graphics Boxes 232

Adding Watermarks 233

Inserting Shapes 236
    Adding Line Shapes 237
    Adding Closed Object Shapes 238
    Adding Callout Shapes 240

Layering Graphics 240

CONTENTS ix

13 Sharing Data 243

    Copying Data from Other Programs 244

    Using Corel's Clipbook 245
        Loading the Clipbook Program 245
        Using the Clipbook 246

    Using OLE to Link and Embed Data from Other Programs 247
        Using OLE to Create a Link to Existing Data 248
        Creating a New OLE Object 249

    Opening (or Importing) Files from Other Programs 250
        Saving (or Exporting) to Other File Formats 251
        Installing Additional Conversion Filters 252
        Using Data from Unsupported Formats 253

    Publishing Documents to PDF 254

    Publishing Documents to XML 255

V Automating Your Work 257

14 Using the Merge Feature 259

    Working with Data Files 260
        Creating a Data File 260
        Importing Data into Merge Data Files 264

    Creating Form Files 265

    Merging the Data and Form Files Together 269
        Creating Envelopes 271
        Creating Labels 272

    Creating Fill-in-the-Blank Forms 274

15 Using the Address Book 279

    The Address Book 280
        Starting the WordPerfect Address Book 280
        Adding Entries to an Address Book 281
        Creating New Address Books 283

    Working with Address Book Entries 284

    Customizing the Address Book Window 286

    Integrating with Outlook and WordPerfect Mail 288
        Opening the Outlook Address Book 289
        Opening the WordPerfect Mail Address Book 290

| Routing Documents | 291 |

Using Address Books with Merge	293
Associate a Form File with an Address Book	293
Edit an Association to an Address Book	294

| Importing and Exporting Address Books | 294 |

16 Working with Templates ... 297

Using WordPerfect's Templates	298
Filling in Personal Information	299
The Disable Macro Message	300
Using the PerfectExpert Panel	300

Customizing WordPerfect's Templates	302
Backing Up the Default Template	302
Editing the Default Template	303
Editing the WordPerfect Templates	304

| Downloading and Installing Templates | 306 |

| Converting an Existing Document to a Template | 307 |

| Working with WordPerfect OfficeReady Browser | 309 |

17 Creating and Playing Macros ... 313

| What Is a Macro? | 314 |

| Playing Macros | 314 |

| Running WordPerfect's Shipping Macros | 315 |

| Creating Macros | 319 |

| Editing Macros | 320 |

Recording Several Sample Macros	321
Creating a Signature Block Macro	322
Creating a Document Identification Footer	322
Creating a Fax Cover Sheet	323

18 Using WordPerfect's Legal Tools ... 327

Creating a Table of Contents	328
Marking the Entries	328
Defining the Table	330
Generating the Table	333

Creating a Table of Authorities 333
Marking the First Authority 334
Marking Subsequent Authorities 336
Defining the Table 337
Generating the Table 338

Using Document Map to Navigate Long Documents 339

Reviewing Documents 340
Making Comments As a Reviewer 340
Responding to Comments As the Author 342

Comparing Documents 344
Highlighting Changes in a Document Automatically 344
Applying Redline and Strikeout Manually 345
Removing Revision Marks 346

Creating Pleading Documents 346
Creating and Editing Cases 347
Creating and Editing Pleading Styles 349
Publishing Pleadings to EDGAR Format 351
Saving Documents Without Metadata 351

Index 355

Contents at a Glance

About the Author

Laura Acklen has been writing books about WordPerfect since 1993 when she wrote her first book, *Oops! What To Do When Things Go Wrong with WordPerfect*. She contributed to three versions of Que's *Special Edition Using WordPerfect* (6, 6.1, and 7) and co-authored Que's *Special Edition Using Corel WordPerfect 9*, *Special Edition Using Corel WordPerfect 10*, *Special Edition Using WordPerfect 12*, and *Special Edition Using WordPerfect Office X3* books with Read Gilgen. She also wrote the *Absolute Beginner's Guide to WordPerfect 10*, *Absolute Beginner's Guide to WordPerfect 11*, and *Absolute Beginner's Guide to WordPerfect 12*.

Laura writes articles for Corel's wordperfect.com website and their monthly e-newsletter, The WordPerfect Expert. She is a moderator at WordPerfect Universe (www.wpuniverse.com) and maintains a presence on the Corel newsgroups. She is also the Webmistress of wpwriter.com, a website devoted to WordPerfect.

Dedication

To my friends and colleagues at WordPerfect Universe and on the WordPerfect newsgroups. I'm honored to be part of such a friendly and supportive community.

Acknowledgments

For this book, I was lucky enough to able to enlist some of the incredible talent at WordPerfect Universe. Jan Berinstein, the administrator of WordPerfect Universe, graciously agreed to serve as the technical editor, so I'm very confident that we have the most comprehensive and technically accurate book to offer WordPerfect X3 users.

I am thrilled to have another opportunity to work with Stephanie McComb, senior acquisitions editor at Que Publishing. I'm very grateful for her faith in me and in what I wanted to do with this book. Thanks also to Sharry Gregory, team coordinator, for attending to all the details, even at a moment's notice. Thanks to my development editor Kevin Howard and project editor Tonya Simpson; their work is gratefully appreciated. Our collaborative effort produced a great book.

I would especially like to thank Cindy Howard, product manager for WordPerfect

Office, and Mark Rathwell, product manager, Office Productivity. They took time out of their busy days to quickly and thoughtfully respond to my requests. Your support and encouragement is greatly appreciated!

We Want to Hear from You!

As the reader of this book, *you* are our most important critic and commentator. We value your opinion and want to know what we're doing right, what we could do better, what areas you'd like to see us publish in, and any other words of wisdom you're willing to pass our way.

As an associate publisher for Que Publishing, I welcome your comments. You can email or write me directly to let me know what you did or didn't like about this book—as well as what we can do to make our books better.

Please note that I cannot help you with technical problems related to the topic of this book. We do have a User Services group, however, where I will forward specific technical questions related to the book.

When you write, please be sure to include this book's title and author as well as your name, email address, and phone number. I will carefully review your comments and share them with the author and editors who worked on the book.

Email: feedback@quepublishing.com

Mail: Greg Wiegand
Associate Publisher
Que Publishing
800 East 96th Street
Indianapolis, IN 46240 USA

For more information about this book or another Que Publishing title, visit our website at www.quepublishing.com. Type the ISBN (excluding hyphens) or the title of a book in the Search field to find the page you're looking for.

Introduction

If you are new to WordPerfect X3 or to word processing in general, this is the book for you. With clear, concise explanations and a lot of numbered steps, you will quickly learn everything you need to get the most out of the WordPerfect application. We assume that you have no previous experience with a word processor, so you can start from the very beginning and work up to some pretty advanced features.

If you've used WordPerfect before, you will be pleased to discover that version X3 retains the features that made previous versions so user friendly—including Reveal Codes and fully customizable toolbars, keyboards, and menus. At the same time, this latest version does a better job of converting Microsoft Word files and provides additional tools for working with Word, as outlined below.

Owners of new computers from Dell and other large computer companies will be pleased to find a free copy of the WordPerfect Productivity Pack, which includes WordPerfect X3 (and, in some cases, Quattro Pro X3), on their computers. Certain models will come with a copy of the standard edition of WordPerfect Office X3, which includes WordPerfect X3, Quattro Pro X3, and Presentations X3.

WordPerfect is classified as a word processor but in reality, it is much, much more. The majority of users find that even though they have the whole suite of applications from which to choose, they spend most of their time in WordPerfect. From writing a simple letter, to creating presentation materials, to using tables to perform calculations, WordPerfect can do it all. What does this mean to you? Quite simply, it means that you don't need to learn two or three applications to get your job done. You can do most, if not all, of your tasks in WordPerfect.

WordPerfect X3 has several new features designed to make it easier for users to move between WordPerfect and Microsoft Word. Besides improved file compatibility, WordPerfect X3 includes toolbars and menus that imitate those found in Microsoft Word. The familiar look of the screen elements helps to ease the transition from Word to WordPerfect. There is also an option to use Word's keyboard shortcuts. In addition, a floating Microsoft Word compatibility toolbar makes common tasks, such as saving files in Word format and converting multiple documents to WordPerfect format, a cinch.

Some Key Terms

To use WordPerfect, you need to know the basic terminology used for common mouse actions:

- **Point**—Move the mouse on the desk to move the pointer onscreen. The tip of the arrow should be on the item to which you are pointing.
- **Click**—Press and release the left mouse button once. You use a click to select commands and toolbar buttons, as well as perform other tasks.

- **Double-click**—Press and release the left mouse button twice in rapid succession.
- **Right-click**—Press and release the right mouse button once. You can right-click to display a QuickMenu just about anywhere in the program.
- **Drag and drop**—Hold down the mouse button and drag the pointer across the screen. Release the mouse button. Dragging is most often used for selecting and moving text and objects.

Things to Keep in Mind

You can customize many features of WordPerfect so that it is set up the way you like to work. That's one of the major benefits of using WordPerfect. For consistency, though, this book makes some assumptions about how you use your computer. When working through steps and especially when viewing the figures in this book, keep in mind the following distinctions:

- WordPerfect gives you many different methods to perform the same task. For example, for commands, you can select a command from a menu, use a shortcut key, use a toolbar button, or use a QuickMenu. This book usually mentions one or two methods (the most common for that particular task) and then includes other methods in a tip.
- Your WordPerfect screen might not look identical to the one used in this book's figures. For example, if you use the ruler, you see that. (Most of the figures in this book don't show the ruler.) Don't let these differences distract you; the figures might look different from what you see on your computer, but it works the same way.
- Your computer setup is most likely different from the one used in the book. Therefore, you will see different programs listed on your Start menu, different fonts in your font list, different folders and documents, and so on. Again, don't be distracted by the differences.

How to Use This Book

This book is divided into five parts, each part focusing on a different theme. The book builds on the skills you need, starting with the basics of formatting and then moving to more complex topics such as templates and macros. You can read the book straight through, look up topics when you have a question, or browse through the contents, reading information that interests you. Here is a quick breakdown of the parts.

Part I, "Learning the Basics," covers the essentials for creating and editing documents. Everything you need to know to create, edit, spell check, print, and apply basic formatting is in this section. Chapter 1 is an introduction to WordPerfect X3. Chapter 2 covers creating and saving documents. Chapter 3 focuses on locating and opening documents. In Chapter 4, you learn editing techniques. Chapter 5 covers basic formatting techniques and working in Reveal Codes. Chapter 6 explains how to use the writing tools.

Part II, "Making It Look Nice," explains how to apply formatting to paragraphs (Chapter 7) and pages (Chapter 8). Chapter 9 covers the use of styles for consistency and flexibility when you format your documents.

Part III, "Organizing Information," focuses on ways to organize information. Chapter 10 shows you how to use the Tables feature to organize and format information in columns. Chapter 11 shows you how to quickly create bulleted and numbered lists, as well as how to organize information in an outline format.

Part IV, "Adding Visuals," explains how to add graphics and other elements to improve the appearance of your documents. Chapter 12 shows you how to add graphic lines and images to your documents. Chapter 13 explains how you can copy or link information from another program into a WordPerfect document.

Part V, "Automating Your Work," covers the tools that you can use to automate repetitive tasks. In Chapter 14, you learn how to use the Merge feature to generate documents, such as form letters with envelopes and labels. In Chapter 15, you learn how to manage contact information with the WordPerfect Address Book and how to work with the Outlook Address Book, including how to route documents for review. Chapter 16 shows you how to use templates to automate the creation of frequently used documents. In Chapter 17, you learn how to create and play macros, which are capable of automating virtually every process in WordPerfect. Finally, in Chapter 18 you learn how to use WordPerfect's legal tools to create pleadings, tables of contents, and tables of authorities, as well as how to use the compare and review features to collaborate on documents.

I hope you enjoy your WordPerfect learning experience!

Conventions Used in This Book

You will find cautions, tips, and notes scattered throughout this book. Don't skip over these; they contain some important tidbits to help you along the way.

caution

A *caution* tells you to beware of a potentially dangerous act or situation. In some cases, ignoring a caution could cause you significant problems—so pay particular attention to them!

note

A *note* is designed to provide information that is generally useful but not necessarily essential for what you're doing at the moment. Some are similar to extended tips—interesting, but not essential.

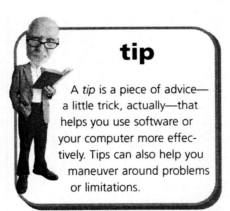

tip

A *tip* is a piece of advice—a little trick, actually—that helps you use software or your computer more effectively. Tips can also help you maneuver around problems or limitations.

There are some other helpful conventions in the book to make your learning experience as smooth as possible. Text that you are going to type looks like this: **type a filename**. Buttons you click, menu commands you select, keys you press, and other action-related items are in **bold** in the text to help you locate instructions as you are reading. New terms being defined in the text are in *italic*. Keep these conventions in mind as you read through the text.

PART 1

LEARNING THE BASICS

Getting Started and Finding Help 7

Creating, Saving, and Printing Documents . . . 21

Finding and Opening Documents 35

Revising Documents 51

Learning Basic Formatting 71

Using the Writing Tools 91

IN THIS CHAPTER

- Get WordPerfect up and running and learn your way around the screen.
- Find out how to work with the toolbars that hold all those buttons.
- Learn how to make selections from the WordPerfect menus using both the mouse and the keyboard.
- Discover all the ways you can get help if you're stuck.
- Learn how to ease the transition from Microsoft Word to Corel WordPerfect.

GETTING STARTED AND FINDING HELP

The *Absolute Beginner's Guide* books are designed for users who are new to WordPerfect (but not necessarily computers in general), so the first section starts at the very beginning. Whether you purchased WordPerfect Office X3 separately or bought a new computer with WordPerfect pre-installed, this book makes it easy for you to get started using WordPerfect right away. Some basic information, such as the steps to start and exit WordPerfect, how to use the mouse or keyboard to select from menus, and other basic computing techniques are covered—just in case you need them.

If you've been working with computers for a while or have used another word processor before, you can skim through most of this chapter and just pick up what you need to get started. When you complete this first section, you will be ready to jump to whatever chapter interests you.

What Is WordPerfect?

Whether you've just purchased your first computer and found this program called WordPerfect installed, or you know how to use your computer but just purchased WordPerfect, this book is for you.

If this is the first time you've ever used WordPerfect, you're in for a real treat. You will soon see that WordPerfect is the most intuitive software application you've ever used. Whether you are self-employed, work for someone else, or use WordPerfect at school, you will be pleasantly surprised at how easy it is to create and edit documents. Here are just a few things you can do with WordPerfect:

- Write a letter or memo
- Create a simple newsletter or brochure
- Write a report, thesis, or resume
- Create a list or outline
- Create tables with built-in calculations
- Prepare a mass mailing with envelopes and labels

Getting WordPerfect Up and Running

The fastest way to start WordPerfect is to double-click the program shortcut on the desktop. If you don't have the shortcut, you can use the Start menu instead by clicking the **Start** button, pointing to **All Programs**, sliding over to **WordPerfect Office X3**, and opening the submenu. Click **WordPerfect X3** to start the program.

note

If you don't see the WordPerfect Office X3 or WordPerfect Productivity Pack folder on your Start menu, the program hasn't been installed on your system yet. Insert the WordPerfect Office X3 CD #1 in the CD drive. If the Setup program doesn't start in a minute or two, choose **Start**, **Run**; browse to the CD drive; and then double-click setup.exe to start the setup program.

Exploring the WordPerfect Screen

You might be new to WordPerfect, but if you've used another Windows program, you will recognize most of the screen elements. There is always a title bar, menu bar, toolbar, and control buttons. This is one of the nice things about Windows: Learning one application puts you ahead of the game when you need to learn another.

When you start WordPerfect X3, the first thing you see is the Workspace Manager. This screen lets you choose from several different work environments, or "modes":

- WordPerfect Mode (the standard or typical view)
- Microsoft Word Mode (with menus and keyboards similar to those in Word)
- WordPerfect Classic Mode (the blue screen and white letters familiar to users of WordPerfect 5.1 for DOS)
- WordPerfect Legal Mode (which displays a special toolbar to help you format legal documents)

FIGURE 1.1
The Workspace Manager lets you choose one of four different modes, or work environments.

Show at startup

The four modes have their own distinctive look and feel. In particular, they display different menus and toolbars and activate different keyboard shortcuts.

If you prefer not to see the Workspace Manager every time you open WordPerfect, click to uncheck the **Show at Startup** checkbox in the lower-left corner of the Workspace Manager screen.

After you close the Workspace Manager, a blank document appears (see Figure 1.2), so you can start typing immediately. The insertion point shows you where the text will appear. The shadow cursor shows you where the insertion point will be if you click the mouse button.

tip
You can change modes at any time by clicking **Tools**, **Workspace Manager**.

FIGURE 1.2

The WordPerfect screen has the same elements you have seen in other Windows applications.

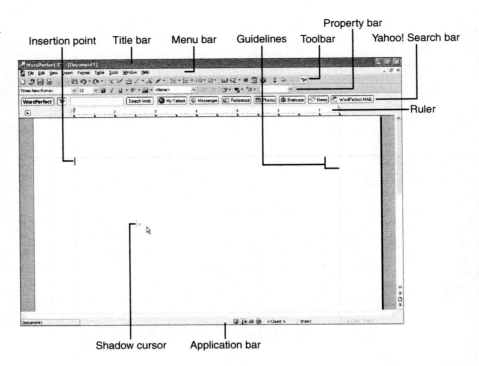

> The Yahoo! Search bar is a new addition to WordPerfect X3. The buttons on this bar take you to specific locations on the Yahoo! site. Clicking the WordPerfect button takes you to Corel's Wordperfect.com website. You can paste text into the text box and either press **Enter** or click the **Search Web** button for a quick online search using Yahoo!. You can turn off the Yahoo! Search bar with the **Show/Hide Yahoo! Search** button on the toolbar.

tip

Clicking and dragging the guidelines is a quick and easy way to change the margins. The visual nature is helpful when you aren't sure exactly what setting you need.

You might also notice some gray lines on your screen. These are called *guidelines*. They help you see the text area of your page by marking the top, bottom, left, and right margins.

If you find the guidelines distracting, you can turn them off by choosing **View**, **Guidelines** from the menu. In the Guidelines dialog box, remove the check mark next to **Margins**; then click **OK**.

Working with the Property Bar and Toolbars

The property bar is located right underneath the toolbar. This bar can morph into something else, depending on what you are doing at the time. You might start out with the text property bar, but as soon as you create a table, it switches to the table property bar. When you create an outline, you get the outline property bar, and so on. It's *very* cool. The buttons you need automatically appear, and you get your work done twice as fast because you aren't searching through the menus for a command.

The toolbar is different from the property bar; it doesn't change unless you tell it to. The toolbar you see in Figure 1.2 is called the WordPerfect toolbar and has buttons for general editing tasks. There are 22 other toolbars from which to choose, including WordPerfect 7, Microsoft Word 2002, Microsoft Word 97, Compatibility, Hyperlink Tools, and Legal toolbars. The availability of toolbars from two versions of Microsoft Word lets you use the latest version of WordPerfect while retaining the look and feel of the word processor you're most familiar (and comfortable) with. The WordPerfect toolbar in versions 8, 9, 10, 11, and 12 was unchanged, but they did include the toolbar from WordPerfect 7 to help those users who might be upgrading from that version. Other toolbars contain buttons for working with fonts, outlines, graphics, tables, macros, and so on.

> **tip**
>
> Trying to figure out what a button does? Point to the button and pause for a second. A QuickTip appears to describe the function of that button.

> **caution**
>
> If you don't see the toolbar or the property bar, it might have been moved to another part of the screen. Look on the left and right sides of the document window. Also, look at the bottom of the screen, just above the application bar. If you don't see the bars at all, they've probably been turned off. Choose **View**, **Toolbars**. Place a check mark in the box next to **Property Bar** and/or **WordPerfect**.

To see a list of toolbars

1. Right-click the toolbar to open the toolbar QuickMenu (see Figure 1.3). You will see that the WordPerfect toolbar already has a check mark next to it. If a check mark appears next to the name, it means that the toolbar is already on.
2. Click the toolbar you want to turn on. Clicking an *unchecked* toolbar name turns it on; clicking a *checked* toolbar name turns it off.
3. To see a complete list of available toolbars, click **More**.
4. Click anywhere in the document to close the toolbar QuickMenu.

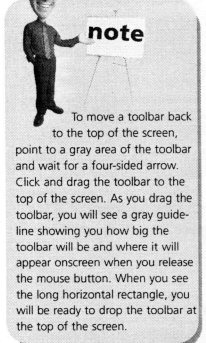

note

To move a toolbar back to the top of the screen, point to a gray area of the toolbar and wait for a four-sided arrow. Click and drag the toolbar to the top of the screen. As you drag the toolbar, you will see a gray guideline showing you how big the toolbar will be and where it will appear onscreen when you release the mouse button. When you see the long horizontal rectangle, you will be ready to drop the toolbar at the top of the screen.

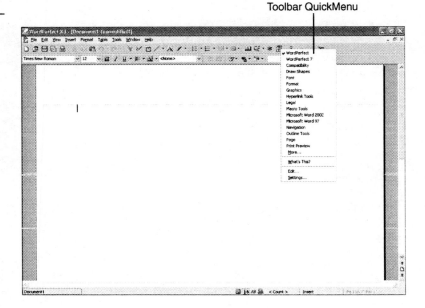

FIGURE 1.3
Right-click a toolbar to open the QuickMenu, where you can switch to another toolbar or turn off the toolbar(s).

Using the Menus

The menus in WordPerfect work the same way as in any other Windows program, so if you've been working with a computer for more than a few days, you've probably already figured this out. However, for those of you who have just purchased your first computer and might need a little help with this, I'm including a short section.

In a Windows application, menus are called *pull-down menus* because when you open a menu, it cascades down into the window. In WordPerfect, they open up into the white workspace. You can use the mouse or the keyboard to select from the menus.

Working with the mouse:

- To open a menu with the mouse, click the menu name.
- To open a submenu, point to an item with an arrow next to it.
- To select an item, click it.

Working with the keyboard:

- To open a menu with the keyboard, hold down **Alt**, and then press the underlined letter. For example, to open the File menu, press **Alt+F**.
- To open a submenu or select an item, press the underlined letter (this time, without the Alt key).
- To move around in the menus, use the arrow keys. Press **Enter** to choose a highlighted command.

In Windows XP, you can hide the underlined letters that show you which key to press (also called hotkeys) in menus and dialog boxes. This setting may be enabled on your system, so you might not see any hotkeys until you press the Alt key. This applies for both menus and dialog boxes. As a long-time WordPerfect user and one who prefers to use keyboard shortcuts whenever possible, I would prefer to see the hotkeys.

To display the underlined letters in your menus and dialog boxes in Windows XP, right-click the Windows desktop and choose **Properties**. Click the **Appearance** tab, and then choose **Effects**. Remove the check mark in the **Hide Underlined Letters for Keyboard Navigation Until I Press the Alt Key** check box.

Getting Help

WordPerfect X3 offers an amazing amount of support to get you up and running as quickly as possible. Even if you're not sure exactly what you're looking for, you can still find the help you need. The nice thing is that after you've found the information you need, you can quickly get right back to where you were and continue working.

Getting "Quick and Easy" Help

The best place to start is with techniques that give you just enough help to get you started. Sometimes all you need is a little hint to get you pointed in the right direction. The first two items show you how to display QuickTips for screen elements and menu items. This is a great way to get acquainted with the toolbars and menu commands.

- You can find out the name of a toolbar button by pointing to it with the mouse and pausing. A QuickTip appears and tells you either the name or a brief description of the button. You can use this on all types of screen elements, not just toolbar buttons.

- You can get descriptions of commands in the drop-down menus by pointing to the command and pausing. A QuickTip appears with a description.

- You can press **Shift+F1** to change the mouse pointer into a What's This pointer. Click on a screen element for a description.

- In dialog boxes, click the **What's This** button, and then click the dialog box option on which you want help. A QuickTip appears with a description for that option (see Figure 1.4). For more help, click the **Help** button in the lower-right corner of the open dialog box. This opens a Help window with the help topic for that dialog box or feature.

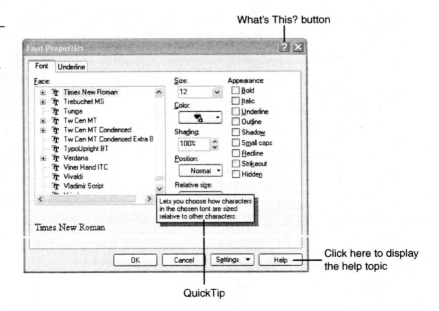

FIGURE 1.4
Most dialog boxes have a What's This button next to the Close button.

Accessing the Help Topics

QuickTips are great when you need a little push in the right direction. For more details, including many numbered steps and links to related items, go to the Help Topics:

- Choose **Help**, **Help Topics**. If necessary, click the **Contents** tab. The Contents section is more task-oriented, so you will find the features organized into projects, such as adding images to your documents or using Internet tools. Double-click the book icons to open up the category. Help topics have a question mark icon next to them (see Figure 1.5). Click these icons to display a help topic.

- Choose **Help**, **Help Topics**. Click the **Index** tab. The Index is great when you want to search for a subject and get a list of help topics to choose from. Type a keyword (or just the first few letters) to jump down through the index (see Figure 1.6). Double-click an index entry to display the help topic, or in some cases, a list of possible help topics from which to choose.

> **note**
> A significant percentage of the computer user population has trouble with tiny print on Web pages and in help screens. Corel has addressed this problem with new Zoom buttons in the WordPerfect Help dialog box (see Figure 1.5). These buttons let you zoom in on the help topic information to make it easier to read. When you are finished reading, you can zoom back out to see more of the topic.

FIGURE 1.5
The Contents tab of the Help Topics dialog box organizes help topics using a book-and-chapter model.

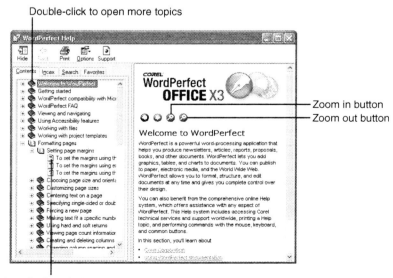

Double-click to open more topics

Zoom in button
Zoom out button

Click to display a help topic

FIGURE 1.6
The Index tab of the Help Topics dialog box displays the help topics alphabetically.

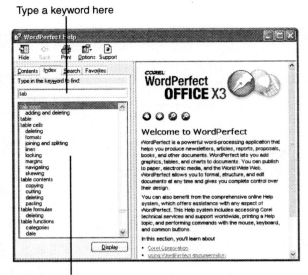

Type a keyword here

Double-click an entry to display the help topic

Getting Help on the Web

If you have an Internet connection, there are several ways to access Corel websites for support:

- Choose **Help**, **Corel on the Web**; then choose an item from the list. WordPerfect launches your default web browser and takes you to the selected page. Figure 1.7 shows Corel's Support page, which has links to newsgroups, Corel's Knowledge Base, and downloadable patches and updates.

- Corel also maintains an online searchable knowledge base. Choose **Help, Help Topics;** then click the Corel Knowledge Base button (on the toolbar). Type a keyword, and then click **Search** to search through thousands of technical information documents (TIDs) created by Corel's Technical Support department. You can also go directly to the knowledge base at http://support.corel.com (see Figure 1.8). (There is a separate knowledge base available for help with earlier versions of WordPerfect at http://kb.corel.com.)

> **tip**
>
> If you find yourself looking up the same topics over and over again, you can add them to a Favorites list. With the help topic displayed, click the Favorites tab. The name of the help topic will appear in the Current Topic text box. You can edit it if you like. Choose Add to add it to the Topics list. From now on, you can get to that topic in just one click, instead of drilling down through the Contents list, or searching in the Index tab.

CHAPTER 1 GETTING STARTED AND FINDING HELP 17

FIGURE 1.7
The Technical Support option on the Help menu takes you to Corel's Support page.

FIGURE 1.8
You can search the Corel Knowledge Base for how-to and troubleshooting articles.

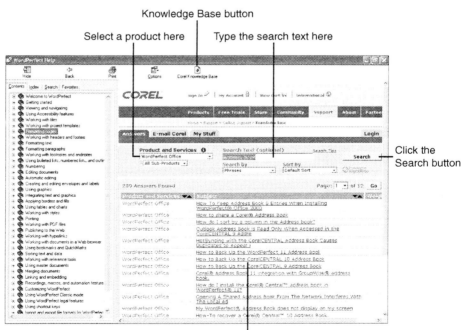

Helping Microsoft Word Users Make the Transition

For those making the transition from Microsoft Word, there is a special help section just for you. Choose **Help**, **Microsoft Word Help** to display the WordPerfect Compatibility with Microsoft Word help topic (see Figure 1.9).

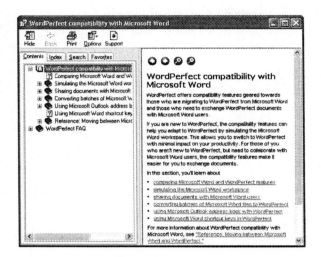

FIGURE 1.9
A special section in Help assists Word users when they make the transition to WordPerfect.

In this section of help topics, you will learn how to

- Compare WordPerfect and Word features so that you can match up similar features.
- Simulate the Microsoft Word workspace by turning on the Word toolbar and menu so that you can find familiar buttons and commands.
- Open Microsoft Word documents in WordPerfect.
- Save documents in Microsoft Word format so that you can easily share documents with clients and associates who use Word.
- Convert multiple Microsoft Word documents to WordPerfect.
- Integrate the Microsoft Outlook address book with WordPerfect.
- Compare the Word shortcut keys to WordPerfect shortcut keys so you can see the differences. A link takes you to a help topic that explains how to customize the shortcut keys to reflect Microsoft Word or WordPerfect settings.

Using familiar toolbars, menus, and keyboard shortcuts will go a long way toward easing your transition to WordPerfect.

Word users also will benefit by reading the FAQ (Frequently Asked Questions) section of the WordPerfect Compatibility with Microsoft Word Help. The FAQ section includes tips about opening and saving Word documents in WordPerfect, copying and pasting formatted text from Word files into WordPerfect, and using

WordPerfect's reviewing documents feature (the equivalent of Track Changes/Compare Documents in Word).

Most importantly, Word users should review the section on Reveal Codes in Chapter 5, "Learning Basic Formatting." Reveal Codes, a powerful feature of WordPerfect for which there is no true equivalent in Word, gives you an easy and intuitive way to troubleshoot unexpected problems. Mastering this feature will help you gain control over your documents.

THE ABSOLUTE MINIMUM

- You learned how to start WordPerfect with a desktop shortcut or through the Start menu.
- You got acquainted with all the elements on the screen and learned what they do.
- You saw how to use the toolbars and property bar. You now know that there are more than 20 different toolbars to pick from, including a toolbar that has the same buttons as the toolbar in Microsoft Word 2002 and a Compatibility toolbar.
- You used the mouse or the keyboard to choose commands from the menus.
- When you got stuck, you got help right away in the Help Topics and on the Web. Thank goodness they are all inside WordPerfect, so you didn't have to stop and launch another program.

In the next chapter, you will learn how to create, save, and print documents.

In This Chapter

- Identify the default settings for all new documents.
- Learn how to insert and delete text.
- Use the mouse and keyboard to move around and to reposition the insertion point.
- Learn how to save and print a completed document.
- Discover how to save documents in a different format so that they can be opened in other programs.

Creating, Saving, and Printing Documents

So, you've started WordPerfect and now you're staring at a blank document, wondering what to do next. It's easier than it looks—click where you want to start typing, and then start pressing keys. When you're done, you will want to know how to save it so that you can come back to it later.

Right away, you will learn about one of WordPerfect's biggest advantages—the capability to save documents in a different file format so that you can share them with people who use other programs. It really doesn't matter what applications your co-workers use because WordPerfect has the most comprehensive set of conversion filters available. You simply save your files to their preferred format and send them off.

Creating Documents

When you start WordPerfect, you can immediately start typing in the blank document. The new document that you are creating comes with standard settings already in place. Because of these default settings, you can create and save many types of documents without making any adjustments at all. Table 2.1 lists some of these settings.

Table 2.1 WordPerfect's Default Settings

Element	Default Setting
Font	Times New Roman 12 point
Margins	1 inch at the top, bottom, left, and right
Line spacing	Single-spaced
Tabs	Every 1/2 inch
Paper size	8 1/2 inches × 11 inches
Automatic backup	Every 10 minutes

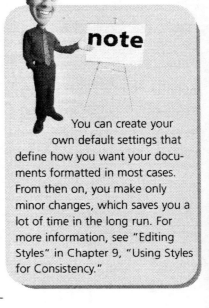

You can create your own default settings that define how you want your documents formatted in most cases. From then on, you make only minor changes, which saves you a lot of time in the long run. For more information, see "Editing Styles" in Chapter 9, "Using Styles for Consistency."

See the sidebar titled, "Backing Up Your Work Automatically," in the "Saving and Closing Documents" section later in this chapter for more information on the Automatic Backup feature, including how to adjust the save interval.

Typing Text

One of the many features built into WordPerfect X3 as a result of user feedback is the click-and-type feature. Quite simply, you click anywhere in a document window and start typing. You don't have to press Enter to insert blank lines or Tab to move over on the line.

To type text in a document

1. Click anywhere in the document window (the white page). The insertion point moves to the new place (see Figure 2.1).
2. Begin typing text.
3. When you are ready to start a new paragraph or insert a blank line, press **Enter**.

If you're working in one document and you want to create a new document, click the **New Blank Document** button on the toolbar. You can also choose **File, New (Ctrl+N)**.

FIGURE 2.1
In WordPerfect, you click where you want to insert text and start typing.

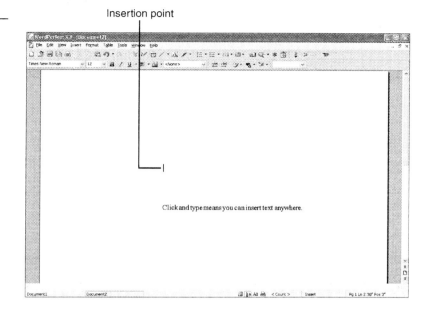

As you type along, you might notice that things happen automatically. For example, if you forget to capitalize the first word in a sentence, WordPerfect corrects it for you. This is the Format-As-You-Go feature working for you. Format-As-You-Go fixes common mistakes as you type. For more information on customizing Format-As-You-Go, see Chapter 6, "Using the Writing Tools."

Erasing Text

The beauty of using a word processor is that no matter how many mistakes you make when you type, you can correct them all before anyone else sees the document. There are several ways to erase text; you are probably familiar with some of them.

caution

It's important that you do not press Enter at the end of every line (as you would with a manual typewriter). This causes all sorts of formatting problems when you edit the text or change the formatting.

- The Backspace key is the most popular method because most mistakes are seen right away. Backspace moves backward, deleting text as long as you hold down the key.
- If you happen to be in front of the problem, click right before the text you want to delete, and then press **Delete**. If you hold down the key, you can delete bigger chunks of text. The longer you hold down the key, the faster the text disappears.
- Select the text with either the mouse or the keyboard, and then press **Delete**.

caution

Be careful with Backspace and Delete! It's easy to get in a hurry and delete more text than you intended. If it's too late and you've deleted too much text, you can bring it back with Undo. You can either click the **Undo** button or choose **Edit**, **Undo** (Ctrl+Z).

INSERTING TODAY'S DATE

If you stop and think about it, you might be surprised at the number of times a day you type in the date. In WordPerfect, you can insert the current date in just one keystroke. Simply click in the document where you want the date to appear and press **Ctrl+D**. Choose **Insert**, **Date/Time** if you want to customize the date or insert the time instead.

WordPerfect gets the current date and time from Windows. If the date or time that you insert is wrong, you need to reset the Windows date/time. Double-click the time on your taskbar to open the Date and Time Properties dialog box, where you can make the necessary changes.

Moving Around in a Document

To make changes to your document, you have to move the insertion point to the section of text that you want to edit. When you click in the document window, you move the insertion point to the place where you want to insert text. The same thing is true for text that you want to delete. You must move the insertion point to that text to remove it.

Both the mouse and the keyboard can be used to move the insertion point in a document. I'll cover the mouse first because it's a bit more straightforward.

Using the Mouse to Get Around

To move the insertion point with the mouse

- **Point and click**—Point to the location in the text where you want to place the insertion point, and then click (the left mouse button).
- **Scrollbars**—All Windows applications use scrollbars, so you might have seen these before. Click the **up** and **down** arrows on either end of the vertical scrollbar to scroll a line at a time. To scroll faster, click and drag the scroll box on the vertical scrollbar. When you drag the scroll box, WordPerfect displays a QuickTip with a page number to show you where you are in the document. The horizontal scrollbar appears only if the document is too wide to fit in the document window. To scroll from side to side, click the **scroll arrows** or click and drag the scroll box.
- **Browse buttons**—These buttons are located at the bottom of the vertical scrollbar (see Figure 2.2). They allow you to jump back and forth between specific items. By default, you browse by page, so you click the **double up arrow** to go to the previous page, and click the **double down arrow** to go to the next page. To switch to another method of browsing, click the **Browse By** button, located between the double up and down arrows.

FIGURE 2.2
You can scroll through a document by pages, headings, footnotes, and other elements by using the Browse By button.

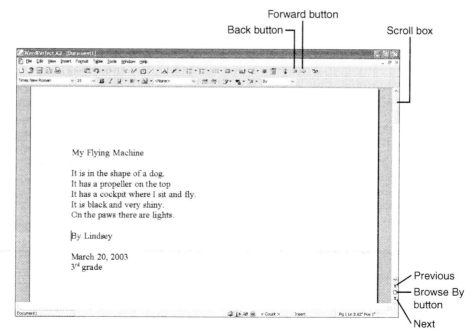

- **Back and Forward buttons**—These two buttons are located on the right side of the toolbar (see Figure 2.2). The Back button takes you backward through a list of previous insertion point locations. The Forward button moves you forward through the list of insertion point locations. If the Back button isn't available, you haven't moved the insertion point yet. If the Forward button isn't active, you haven't used the Back button to go back to a previous location yet.

- **Autoscroll button**—The Autoscroll button is located right next to the Back button. Click the **Autoscroll** button on the toolbar to turn on "automatic scrolling." The cursor shows up in the middle of the screen and changes to a dot with up and down arrows (see Figure 2.3). To scroll upward, move the mouse up; the pointer changes to a dot with an upward arrow. To scroll downward, move the mouse down; the pointer changes to a dot with a downward arrow. To speed up scrolling, move the mouse pointer to the left or right side of the screen. Move back toward the center to slow down. To turn off Autoscroll, click in the document window or click the Autoscroll button.

note

If you have previous experience with a computer, the information in the next couple of sections will be completely familiar to you, and you can skip to the next major section on printing. For those who might be starting out with their first computer, the information is provided as a reference.

Using the Keyboard to Get Around

If you prefer to keep your hands on the keyboard, there are quite a few ways to move around in a document. Some people feel that moving the insertion point using the keyboard is quicker and more accurate. Table 2.2 contains a list of WordPerfect keyboard shortcuts.

tip

The list of keyboard shortcuts might look a bit intimidating, but don't worry. There are only a couple of different ways to move around; it's just that each method can be used in more than one direction (that is, up, down, left, right). Try one or two at first; then add others as you become more comfortable.

FIGURE 2.3

The Autoscroll feature is helpful when you're working in lengthy documents.

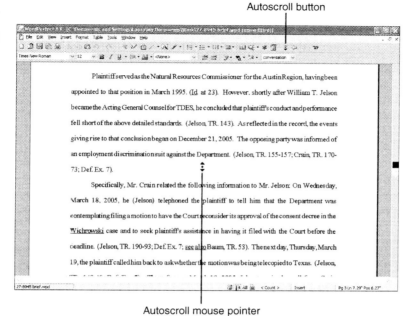

Autoscroll button

Autoscroll mouse pointer

Table 2.2 WordPerfect's Keyboard Shortcuts

Keystroke(s)	Insertion Point Moves
Right arrow	One character to the right
Left arrow	One character to the left
Down arrow	One line down
Up arrow	One line up
Ctrl+Right arrow	One word to the right
Ctrl+Left arrow	One word to the left
Ctrl+Down arrow	One paragraph down
Ctrl+Up arrow	One paragraph up
Home	To beginning of current line
End	To end of current line
Page Down (PgDn)	To bottom of current screen
Page Up (PgUp)	To top of current screen
Alt+Page Down	To top of next physical page
Alt+Page Up	To top of previous physical page
Ctrl+Home	To beginning of document
Ctrl+End	To end of document

Printing a Document

When you're ready to print, it can be done in as little as two keystrokes. This shortcut works only if you want to print the entire document and you don't need to switch to a different printer.

To quickly print the entire document, press **Ctrl+P** and then press **Enter**.

The Print dialog box shown in Figure 2.4 has options to change the number of copies, switch to a different printer, print only specific pages, and much more. Choose **File**, **Print (Ctrl+P)** to open the Print dialog box. Make your choices, and then click **Print**. See "Previewing and Printing Documents" in Chapter 4 for more information.

> **tip**
>
> WordPerfect has a Print Preview feature that enables you to see exactly how your document will look when it is printed. You can fine-tune the formatting and double-check for consistency without printing a copy that might be discarded. See "Previewing and Printing Documents" in Chapter 4, "Revising Documents," for more information on the Print Preview feature.

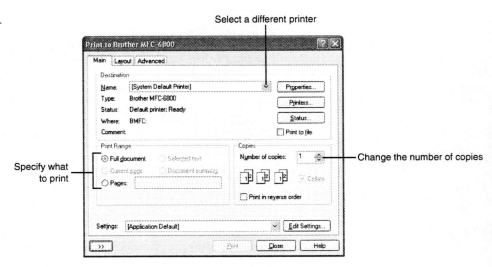

FIGURE 2.4
The quick print method (Ctrl+P, Enter) lets you print your document with just a few keystrokes.

Saving Documents

Electronic copies of documents have virtually replaced paper copies, so even if you don't expect to work with a document again, it's a good idea to save it on disk so that you have a record of it. Bear in mind that because fewer paper copies are kept, the electronic copies need more protection. It's very important that you back up your important files regularly.

Saving and Closing Documents

Until you save your document, it is stored in memory. Memory is a temporary storage location because when you turn off your computer, the memory space is cleared. If a storm comes up and the power is interrupted, or if your system locks up, you will lose everything that you haven't saved.

A nifty feature that was first introduced in WordPerfect 10 is called Auto-Suggest Filename. The first time you save a document, WordPerfect automatically inserts a suggested filename in the File name text box. You can either accept this name or type your own.

Follow these steps to save a document:

1. Click the **Save** button or choose **File**, **Save** (**Ctrl+S**).

    - If you've already named this document, it will seem like nothing has happened. Because the document has already been named, WordPerfect saves the changes without any intervention from you. The only difference you will see is (unmodified) after the filename in the title bar—this is how you know a document has been saved.
    - If you haven't named the document yet, the Save File dialog box appears (see Figure 2.5).

2. Type a filename and press **Enter** (or click the **Save** button).

    - Filenames can be up to 255 characters long and can contain letters, numbers, and spaces. Some symbols can be used, but not others, so to prevent problems, avoid these special symbols: !@#$%^&*()\.
    - You can include the name of the drive and the folder where you want the document to be saved when you type the filename. For example, typing `j:\financials\fy2005` saves the document `fy2005` to drive j: in the `financials` folder.
    - When you type a filename without selecting a location, the document is saved in the default folder if you have just started WordPerfect, or in the last opened folder if you've opened a folder other than the default.

FIGURE 2.5

The Save File dialog box is used when you need to save a new document.

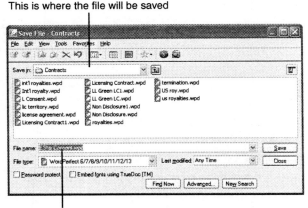

This is where the file will be saved

Auto-suggest filename

BACKING UP YOUR WORK AUTOMATICALLY

WordPerfect has a Timed Document Backup feature that automatically makes a backup copy of your document while you work. It's already turned on and set to make a backup every 10 minutes. You can adjust the interval and take a look at where your backup files are created in the Files Settings dialog box. Choose **Tools**, **Settings**, **Files**. If necessary, click the **Document** tab. First, enable the **Timed Document Backup Every** check box; then you can adjust the Timed Document Backup interval by typing a new value in the text box or by clicking the spinner arrows next to the text box.

Saving to a Different File Format

Let's face it—Microsoft Word users outnumber WordPerfect users. Even though WordPerfect is more flexible, easier to use, and much more powerful, Microsoft products continue to dominate the market.

You probably have friends and business associates who use Microsoft Word for their word processing. You might be thinking that because you use WordPerfect and they use Word, you can't collaborate on documents. That's not a problem! WordPerfect X3 has the most complete conversion filters for Microsoft Word products available today.

All you have to do is save your documents in Microsoft Word format. Your friends and associates can open your documents in Word, make their changes, save the file in Word format, and send it back to you. You can then open the document in WordPerfect without losing anything. You can choose to save the document back to WordPerfect format, or you can keep the file in Word format. Either way, you can continue to use WordPerfect without sacrificing the capability to share documents with Word users.

CHAPTER 2 CREATING, SAVING, AND PRINTING DOCUMENTS

To save a file in a different format

1. Choose **File**, **Save As (F3)**.
2. In the Save As dialog box, click the **File Type** drop-down list arrow to open the list of file types.
3. Scroll through the list to locate the file format that you want to use (see Figure 2.6). As you can see, WordPerfect can save to many different Word formats.

FIGURE 2.6

The Save As dialog box is used when you need to save a document to a different file format.

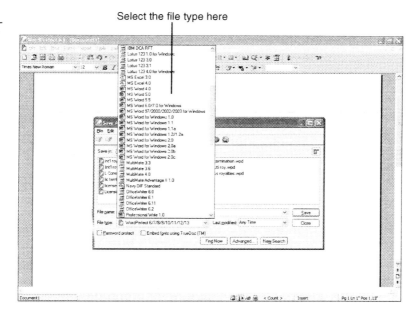

4. Select the format from the **File Type** drop-down list.
5. If necessary, type a filename and select a location for the file.
6. Click **Save**.

WordPerfect X3 provides an even quicker and easier way to save files in Microsoft Word format: the Compatibility toolbar. When that toolbar is displayed, just click the Save as Microsoft Word button. The Save As dialog box opens, suggesting a filename that ends in "doc" (the file extension for MS Word documents) and showing the file type as MS Word 97/2000/2002/2003. If you type a filename and click the Save button, WordPerfect saves your file in MS Word format. It's as simple as that!

To display the Compatibility toolbar, click **View**, **Toolbars** to open the Toolbars dialog box (see Figure 2.7). Click to put a check in the checkbox next to the Compatibility toolbar, and then click OK.

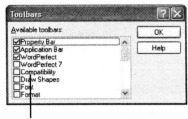

FIGURE 2.7
Enable the Compatibility check box to display the Compatibility Toolbar.

Choose the Compatibility toolbar

The Compatibility toolbar (see Figure 2.8) also lets you save files in several other common file formats, including PDF, HTML, and XML. Saving to PDF (Portable Document Format), a generic file format, is especially handy if you work in a law firm or other business that shares files with clients or colleagues who don't have WordPerfect. Saving to HTML (HyperText Markup Language), the language used to create web pages, lets you create documents that can be opened in a web browser. Saving to XML (Extensible Markup Language) is useful for more advanced web and programming work.

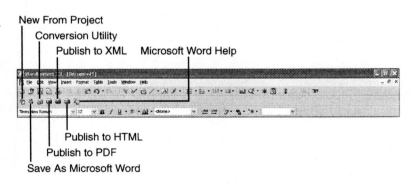

FIGURE 2.8
The Compatibility toolbar makes it easy to save files in Microsoft Word or other common file formats—or to convert Word files to WordPerfect.

New From Project
Conversion Utility
Publish to XML   Microsoft Word Help

Publish to HTML
Publish to PDF
Save As Microsoft Word

Note that the Compatibility toolbar appears automatically (as a floating toolbar) when you choose Microsoft Word mode from the Workspace Manager.

To close the Compatibility toolbar, right-click anywhere in the toolbar, then remove the check mark next to the Compatibility toolbar. If the toolbar is floating, click the X in the upper-right corner.

Closing Documents

When you're finished with a document, clear it off your screen by closing the document window. If you haven't saved it yet, you will get a chance to do so.

To close a document

1. Click the **Document Close** button on the right corner of the menu bar, or press **Ctrl+F4**.

   If you haven't made any changes since the last time you saved, WordPerfect closes the document. If you *have* made some changes, you will be prompted to save the document (see Figure 2.9).

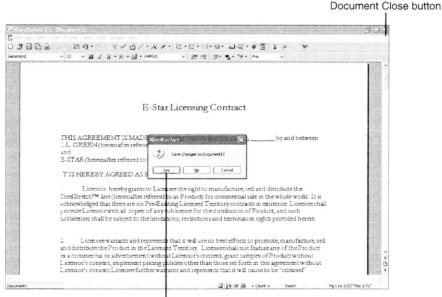

FIGURE 2.9
When you click the Close button, WordPerfect prompts you to save your changes before clearing the document off the screen.

Document Close button

Click Yes to save your changes

2. Click **Yes** if you want to save your work; click **No** if you want to close the document without saving.

   If you click **Yes** and you haven't yet given this document a name, the Save File dialog box appears. This is where you can type a name and location for the file. Otherwise, WordPerfect saves and closes the document.

3. Type the filename and press **Enter**.

The Absolute Minimum

- You learned how to create a new document and how to move around in a document so that you can edit the text.
- When you're finished editing, you save your changes, and if you want a copy, you send the document to the printer.
- It's easy to save documents in a different format so that you can collaborate on documents with people who use other programs.
- When you are ready to move on to something else, you can close a document and clear it off the screen.

In the next chapter, you will learn how to use the file management dialog boxes to navigate through the files on your system and to select and open files when necessary.

In This Chapter

- Learn how to get around in the Open File dialog box.
- See how to navigate through drives and folders and display the files in other folders.
- Learn how to search for a file when you can't remember the name or where it is located.
- Convert documents from a different format so that you can work with documents created in other programs.
- Learn how to organize your files into folders so that you can locate them later.
- Learn how files can be moved, copied, renamed, and deleted—all from within the file management dialog boxes.

Finding and Opening Documents

In Chapter 2, "Creating, Saving, and Printing Documents," you learned how to create a document from scratch and save it to a disk. In many situations, you can use an existing document to help get you started on a new document. For example, suppose you create a newsletter for your company for the month of June. When July rolls around, you don't have to create another newsletter from scratch. You can just open the June newsletter, revise it, and save it as the July newsletter. You leverage the time and energy you spent on the June newsletter to simplify the creation of the July newsletter. The key to making this work is being able to find the file you need when you need it. After all, what good is that well-researched, carefully planned, professionally designed document if you can't find it later?

Getting Familiar with the Open File Dialog Box

When you're ready to open a file, you will use the Open File dialog box. You will spend more time in this dialog box than in almost any other dialog box in WordPerfect, so it's important to spend a few minutes getting familiar with it.

To display the Open File dialog box

1. Click the **Open** button, or choose **File**, **Open** (**Ctrl+O**). The Open File dialog box appears (see Figure 3.1).

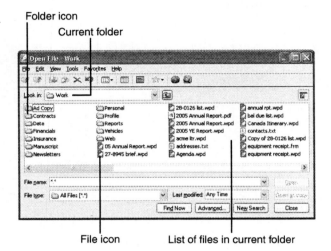

FIGURE 3.1
Use WordPerfect's Open File dialog box to locate and open documents.

Opening a File

When you open the Open File dialog box, WordPerfect automatically displays the contents of the default or the most recently used folder. The section "Navigating Through Drives and Folders," later in this chapter, covers switching to a different drive or folder.

To open a file

1. Click the file you want to open.
2. Click **Open**. You can also double-click the file to select and open it at the same time.

> **tip**
> WordPerfect maintains a list of the previous nine documents that you've opened. They appear at the bottom of the File menu. To choose one of these documents, open the **File** menu and either click the filename or press the underlined number next to the filename. WordPerfect opens the file into a new document window, and you are ready to go.

Customizing the View

There are several different ways to display files and folders in the Open File dialog box. It could be personal preference, or it could be that a different view makes it easier to locate a file. Whatever the reason, it's a snap to switch to a different view with the Views button.

You can click the **Views** button to cycle through the different views, or you can click the **drop-down arrow** to the right of the Views button to choose from the following options:

> **tip**
>
> In WordPerfect, you can open as many as nine documents at once. To select more than one document, click the first document and hold down the **Ctrl** key as you click the others. When you're finished selecting files, click **Open**.

- **Thumbnails**—Shows each file with a large icon. In the case of photos, you'll see a small picture.
- **Tiles**—Displays the files and folders in two columns with large icons. The type and size of the document are also shown.
- **Icons**—Displays the folders and files with an identifying icon. Only the folder or filename is shown.
- **List**—Displays the names of the folders and files with small icons.
- **Details**—Displays the names of the folders and files with small icons. The size, type, and creation/modification date and time are also shown (see Figure 3.2).

FIGURE 3.2
The Details view provides the most information about the files and folders.

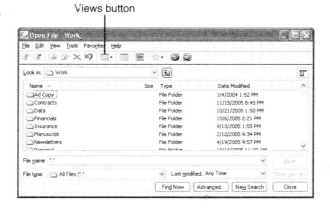

Views button

Different types of files have different file icons. For example, a WordPerfect document has an icon of a pen on a blue background. The icon for a Word document has a blue W on a white page. Application files usually have a smaller version of the icon that appears on the desktop. The icons can help you zero in on the file you want.

Rearranging the File List

The Details view has an added advantage. Because you now have columns for each item of information, you also have column headings that identify the item. Clicking these column headings enables you to sort the file list by the creation/modification date, the size, or the type.

Let's say you are looking for a particular file that you edited yesterday. Sort the file list by the creation/modification date to group the files by date and scroll down the list to see the files that were saved on that date (see Figure 3.3).

> **tip**
> You can enlarge the Open File dialog box and display more files and folders at one time. This trick is especially helpful when you are using the Details view. Point to a side or corner of the dialog box and wait for the two-sided arrow. Click and drag the dialog box border. Release the mouse button when you're satisfied with the new size. You can use this same method to make the dialog box smaller. You also can click the Maximize button (the square button in the top-right corner of the dialog box) to expand the dialog box to full screen. Click the Restore button, which replaced the Maximize button, when you are ready to switch back to a dialog box.

FIGURE 3.3
Arranging the file list by date or by type can help you locate a specific file.

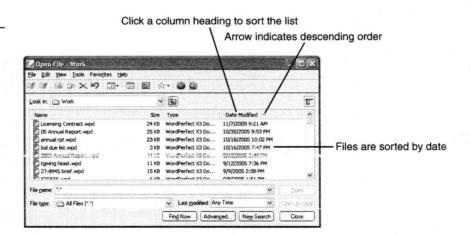

To rearrange the file list

1. Click a column heading that you want to sort by, such as **Type**.
2. Click the column heading again to arrange the list in reverse order. You will notice an arrow next to the column heading. This arrow indicates a descending or ascending sort order.

Navigating Through Drives and Folders

At first, you might choose to save all of your documents in the same folder. When you are just starting out, it's easier to keep everything in one place. However, the more documents you create, the more difficult it becomes to locate the one you want. The "Organizing Files in Folders" section, later in this chapter, covers file management strategies to help you get your files organized.

Moving around in the drives or folders on your system is easily done thanks to the tools in the Open File dialog box. Try these techniques to look through the drives and folders:

- Double-click a folder icon to open the folder and display the list of files and folders in that folder.
- Click the **Go Back One Folder Level** button to move up a level in the folder list or to move back to the previous folder.
- Click the **Look in** drop-down list arrow and choose another drive (see Figure 3.4).

If you like the way the Windows Explorer looks, you can make the WordPerfect Open File dialog box look just like it. Click the Folders button (refer to Figure 3.4) to split the file list in two. The left side (or pane) has a list of drives and folders. The right side doesn't change. It still has the list of folders and files in the current folder.

> **tip**
> To create a new folder from within the Open File dialog, first use the drop-down arrow to the right of the Look in box to make sure the correct drive or folder is showing. Then click **File**, **New**, **Folder**. When the icon appears with the words "New Folder" highlighted, type a name for the folder and press the **Enter** key. If you press Enter before typing a new name, simply right-click the words **New Folder**, click **Rename**, type a folder name, and press **Enter**.

> **note**
> When you open a different folder in the Open File dialog box, that folder becomes the new default folder. The next time you open the Open File dialog box, you will see the list of files in that folder. However, when you close WordPerfect and start it again, the list of files reverts back to the folder specified in Tools, Settings, Files as the default document folder.

FIGURE 3.4
You can navigate through the drives and folders on your system and on your network in the Open File dialog box.

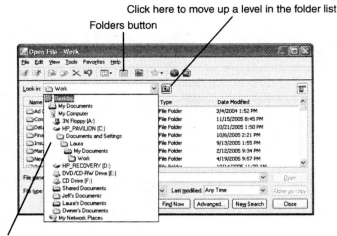

Searching for a File

With the size of the hard drives installed in computers today, you can store literally thousands of files on one disk. Even with the best file management system, locating a single file can be daunting. Learning how to use the tools that help you locate files is one of the most important skills you can master. WordPerfect has a great collection of tools that can help you locate files so that you don't have to start another program to do a search.

Listing Files by Type

When you have a lot of different types of files in a folder, limiting the number of files in the list can be a big help. One way to accomplish this is to display only a specific type of file in the list. For example, if you display only WordPerfect documents in the list, it's easier to find the file you are looking for.

By default, the file type is set to All Files, so you will see every file saved in that folder, whether or not you can work with that file in WordPerfect.

To display only a particular type of file

1. Click the **File Type** drop-down list arrow to display the list of file types (see Figure 3.5).

FIGURE 3.5

After you select a particular file type, only those files appear in the file list.

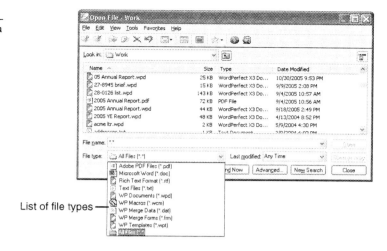

List of file types

2. Choose the type of file you want displayed in the list, such as WP Documents (*.wpd) or Microsoft Word (*.doc).

3. When you are ready to see all the files again, select **All Files (*.*)** from the **File Type** drop-down list.

Listing Files by Modification Date

One of most popular methods is grouping files by modification date. Most people can remember *when* they worked on a document faster than they can remember the name of the file. The fact that you don't have to be exact about the time frame helps. The list of options includes This Week, This Month, Last Week, Last Month, and so on.

To display a list of files by modification date

1. Click the **Last Modified** drop-down list arrow to display a list of general time frames (see Figure 3.6).

2. Either type a specific date in the **Last Modified** text box or select an option from the list.

3. When you are ready to display the complete list of files again, open the **Last Modified** drop-down list and select **Any Time**.

FIGURE 3.6
Grouping files by modification date is a popular way to locate files.

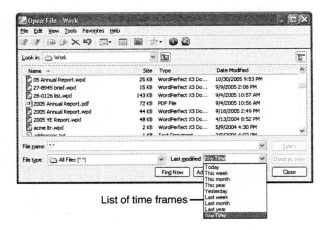

List of time frames

BACK UP IMPORTANT FILES REGULARLY
If you have ever suffered through a hard disk crash, you don't need to be told how important it is to back up your data. Imagine how you would feel if all of a sudden, you couldn't get to any of the files on your computer. Avoid a potential disaster by backing up your important files on a regular basis. Use the **Last Modified** option in the Open File dialog box to display only those files that you have modified within a certain time frame, and then copy those files onto an external hard drive or a CD for safekeeping.

Searching by Filename or Content

Last, but certainly not least, is the capability to search for files by the filename or by the file's contents. Some of us can remember a filename, or at least a part of the filename, but almost everyone can remember something about the contents of a file. Whether it's a client name, a project name, a technical term, or a phone number, all you need is a piece of information that can be found in the file.

To search for files by filename

1. Type the filename, or a portion of the filename, in the **File Name** text box.
2. Click **Find Now**. WordPerfect searches through the files and builds a new list based on the search. When the search is complete, the **Find Now** button changes to a **Back** button (see Figure 3.7).

> **tip**
> You can also search for text *in* a document by typing the word or phrase in the **File Name** box and following the steps provided. This is a bit confusing, I know. Just remember that you can search for text in a filename, or text in the document itself, using essentially the same steps.

FIGURE 3.7
When you search for files, WordPerfect builds a new list of files that fit the search criteria.

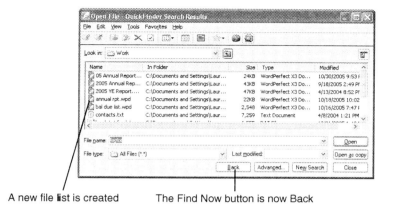

A new file list is created   The Find Now button is now Back

3. When you are ready to switch back to the full list of files, or if you want to start another search, click **Back**.

If you start a search in a particular folder, WordPerfect searches through the files and the subfolders in that folder. This is especially helpful when you can't remember exactly where you stored a file.

Converting Documents on Open

Because WordPerfect isn't the only word processing application available, you're likely to need to share documents with someone using another application such as Microsoft Word. Thankfully, WordPerfect X3 includes the most comprehensive set of conversion filters available for Microsoft Word documents.

You might also be surprised at how many WordPerfect users are still using older versions of the program. Some companies are resistant to change, and others are limited by the computing power of their systems. Thousands, if not millions, of local government employees are quite happily using WordPerfect 10 and 11.

Thanks to WordPerfect's built-in file conversion feature, you can open nearly every kind of word processing document. All you have to do is open the file and let WordPerfect's conversion filters do all the work. Bear in mind that if your copy of WordPerfect was free with a new computer, you might not have the full-blown set of filters found in the full versions of the WordPerfect Office X3 suite.

> **tip**
> I want to draw your attention to the fact that WordPerfect hasn't changed its file format since version 6. If you are working with files from WordPerfect versions 6, 7, 8, 9, 10, 11, or 12, no conversion is necessary. Minor formatting changes in the converted document are usually traced back to the change of printer driver.

When you save a converted document, WordPerfect asks whether you want to save it in the latest WordPerfect format (WordPerfect 6–X3) or in the original format from which it was converted. If you are returning the document to someone who isn't using WordPerfect, select the original format and click **OK**.

Installing Additional Conversion Filters

If you get an "Invalid format" error message when you try to open a file in a different format, you might need to install additional conversion filters. The complete set of filters is not installed with the Small Business, Standard and Professional editions of the suite because of space considerations. The OEM and Productivity Pack versions install everything by default, so if you are getting this error message, you will need to upgrade to the full suite to get the conversion filters you need.

To install additional conversion filters

1. Insert the CD in the drive.
2. When the Setup program starts, choose **WordPerfect Office X3**.
3. Select **Change which Program Features Are Installed**, then choose **Next**.
4. In the list box, scroll down, and then click the plus sign next to Filters.
5. Click the drop-down arrow next to Word Processor Conversions and choose **This Feature Will Be Installed on the Local Hard Drive.**
6. Click **Next**, **Begin**.

When the install is finished, the new filters are integrated into WordPerfect, and they are ready to use.

Using the WordPerfect Office Conversion Utility

One of the most useful components in WordPerfect Office X3 is a conversion utility that lets you convert batches of files, instead of opening them one at a time. You can convert files to a variety of different WordPerfect formats, including early DOS and Macintosh versions. The conversion utility is a separate program from WordPerfect, so you start it from Windows.

To run the conversion utility and convert a batch of files

1. Choose **Start**, **(All) Programs**, **WordPerfect Office X3**, **Utilities**.
2. Click **Conversion Utility** to start the program. The WordPerfect Office Conversion Utility dialog box opens (see Figure 3.8).

FIGURE 3.8
Use the WordPerfect Office Conversion Utility to convert batches of files to WordPerfect formats.

3. Click the **Add** button to browse your system and create the list of files to convert. You can select files from different folders to build the list.
4. If necessary, open the **Convert to** drop-down list and choose another WP file format.
5. If necessary, click the **Options** button and make your selections.
6. Choose **OK** to convert the files.

> **caution**
> Be sure your older WordPerfect files have a .wpd extension, or they might not convert properly.

 In WordPerfect X3, the conversion utility is also available from within WordPerfect—via a button on the Compatibility toolbar (see Figure 3.9).

FIGURE 3.9
The Conversion Utility button makes it easy to convert multiple files to WordPerfect.

Organizing Files in Folders

One nice thing about WordPerfect is that you can do all your file management tasks from within the program. You don't have to start Windows Explorer to create new folders and move files around. Also, you can work with virtually any file on your system, not just WordPerfect files.

The file management tools are available in every file-related dialog box, such as Save As, Insert File, Insert Image, and Select File. Because the Open File dialog box is used more often, it is used here in the examples.

Creating New Folders

Setting up an electronic filing system is just like setting up a filing system for your printed documents. Just as you take out a manila folder and attach a label to it, you can create a folder on your hard disk and give it a name. Organizing files into folders by account, subject, project, or client helps you locate the files you need quickly and easily.

To create a new folder

1. Open the drive or folder where you want to create the new folder.
2. Right-click in the file list and choose **New**, **Folder**. You can also choose **File**, **New**, **Folder**. A new folder icon appears in the file list with a temporary name of New Folder (see Figure 3.10).

FIGURE 3.10
When you create a new folder, you replace the temporary name of New Folder with a name you choose.

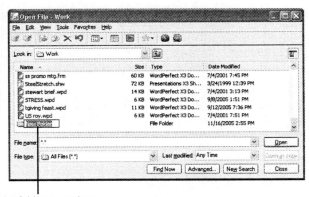

Type the folder name here

3. Type a name for the folder. Because the temporary name New Folder is selected, the name you type automatically replaces it.

Moving and Copying Files

If you accidentally save a file to the wrong folder, it's not a disaster. You can always move it to another folder later. Just be sure to *move* the file rather than copy it because you don't want two copies in two different places. Things can get pretty confusing when you are trying to figure out which copy is the most recent.

On the other hand, there are good reasons why you would want to copy a file rather than move it. Backups come to mind. If you've been working on an important document all day, make a copy of the file onto a floppy disk or CD when you're finished. You will sleep better at night knowing that you have a backup copy in case something happens to the original. Likewise, if you want to share a file with a co-worker on your network, you want to copy the file to his folder on the network. This way, you still have your original, and he has a copy that he can freely edit.

Remember, if you want to move or copy more than one file, you need to click the first file to select it. Then hold down the **Ctrl** key and click the others. Continue to hold down the **Ctrl** key until you are finished selecting the other files.

To move files

1. Select the file(s) that you want to move.

2. Click the **Move To** button or choose **Edit**, **Cut**, or choose **Edit**, **Move To Folder**.

3. Navigate to the folder where you want to store the files.

4. Click the **Paste** button or choose **Edit**, **Paste**, or, in the Move Items dialog box, click **Move**.

To copy files

1. Select the file(s) that you want to copy.

2. Click the **Copy To** button or choose **Edit**, **Copy**, or choose **Edit**, **Copy To Folder**.

3. Switch to the folder where you want to store the files.

4. Click the **Paste** button or choose **Edit**, **Paste**, or, in the **Copy Items** dialog box, click **Copy**.

I like using the Move To and Copy To buttons because I can pick a folder from the list instead of navigating to the destination folder and then navigating back to where I was.

The instructions to move and copy files work on folders, too, so if you want to work with all the files in a folder, you don't have to select them all. Just select the folder and work with it instead.

> **tip**
>
> Keyboard shortcuts make the process of moving and copying files even easier and faster. After selecting a file, you can use Ctrl+X to cut (move) the file or Ctrl+C to copy it. Then navigate to a folder, click to select it, and press Ctrl+V to paste the file into that folder.

Renaming Files

When you save a file (or create a folder), you try to give it a descriptive name. Later, however, that name might no longer seem appropriate. It could be as simple as a misspelling in the name or a case in which the content of the file changes and the name needs to reflect that change. Regardless of the reason, you can quickly rename a file or folder in just two steps.

To rename a file or folder

1. Click the file or folder that you want to rename.
2. Wait a second and click the file or folder name again. An outline appears around the file or folder name, and the name is selected (see Figure 3.11). You can also right-click the file and choose **Rename**.

FIGURE 3.11
When an outline appears around the filename and the text is selected, you can edit the name.

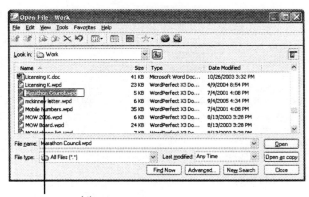

An outline appears around the name

3. Edit the name as necessary.
4. Either press **Enter** or click in the file list when you are finished.

Deleting Files and Folders

If you decide that you no longer need a folder, you can delete it. Before you do, open the folder and make sure there are no folders or files that you need to keep. Deleting a folder automatically deletes the contents.

To delete a file or folder

1. Select the file or folder.

2. Click the **Delete** button or choose **File**, **Delete**. Usually—but not always—a Confirm File Delete message box appears, asking if you're sure you want to send the file to the Recycle Bin. If you do, click **Yes**. If not, click **No**.

> **tip**
>
> Clicking, pausing, and clicking again can be a little tricky, especially if you inadvertently move the mouse between clicks. You might find it easier to choose **File**, **Rename** to rename a selected file.

Mistakes can happen to anyone, which is why we all love the Undo feature. If you accidentally delete a file or folder, you can quickly restore it by clicking the **Undo** button (see Figure 3.12).

FIGURE 3.12
The Open File dialog box has a Delete and an Undo button.

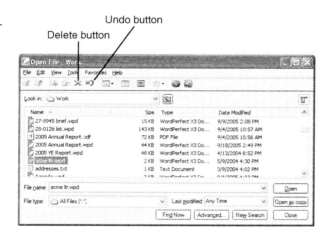

The Absolute Minimum

- You learned how to use the Open File dialog box, so you can now comfortably work in all the file management dialog boxes in WordPerfect.
- You became skilled at navigating through the drives and folders on your system so that you can work with files in another folder.
- Searching for a file is easy, even if you don't remember the name or where the file is located.
- Converting documents from a different format is as easy as opening them in WordPerfect. The built-in conversion filters do all the work for you.
- Anything you can do in Windows Explorer, you can do in WordPerfect. You saw how to move, copy, rename, and delete files from within a file management dialog box.

In the next chapter, you will learn how to select text so that you can act on it independently. You will also see how you can customize the screen to help you revise documents. You will also learn how to fax and email documents straight from WordPerfect.

IN THIS CHAPTER

- Learn how to select text, and move and copy selected text so you can quickly edit your documents.
- Bail yourself out of trouble with the Undo feature.
- Adjust the zoom setting to make it easier to inspect small details in a document.
- Switch to the popular WordPerfect 5.1 Classic Mode complete with blue screen, gray text, and familiar keystrokes.
- Open multiple documents at the same time and preview a document before printing.
- Learn how to fax a document directly from WordPerfect, and use your email program to attach a document to an email message.

REVISING DOCUMENTS

The most important skill for you to learn at this point is how to select text. You will use the techniques over and over as you revise documents. Think about it—if you want to make a sentence bold, you have to select it first. If you want to move a paragraph, you have to select it first.

The second most important skill? How to fix your mistakes with the Undo feature. It reverses the last action, so it's as if it never happened. Other features make it easier than ever to review and revise documents: Zoom, 5.1 Classic Mode, Print Preview. And when you're finished, you can email or fax the document instead of printing it.

Selecting Text

The Select feature is a powerful tool. Whenever you just want to work with a section of text, you can select that portion and work on it independently from the rest of the document. Selecting text is flexible, and, because of the visual nature, it's easy to comprehend. When you edit documents, you will do a lot of selecting, so it's worth a few minutes to learn some shortcuts.

Selecting Text with the Keyboard

You can use either the mouse or the keyboard to select text. Let's first look at selecting text using the keyboard. You might want to review the navigation techniques in Table 2.2 in Chapter 2, "Creating, Saving, and Printing Documents," because you will use those same techniques to select text with the keyboard.

To select a portion of text

1. Position the insertion point at the beginning of the area you want to select.
2. Hold down the **Shift** key.
3. Use the arrow keys, or any of the navigation shortcuts that you learned about in Chapter 2, to move to the end of the selection. For example, to select text a word at a time, hold down the **Shift** key while pressing **Ctrl+right arrow**. To select everything from the cursor to the end of the line, hold down the **Shift** key and press **End**.

WordPerfect highlights the selection as seen in Figure 4.1. You can now work with this area of the document as a single unit.

Selecting Text with the Mouse

Selecting text with the mouse is also easy, although it might take a bit of practice before you get really good at it. Table 4.1 shows several methods of using the mouse to select text.

Table 4.1 Selecting Text with the Mouse

Mouse Action	What It Selects
Drag across text	One whole word at a time
Double-click	Entire word
Triple-click	Entire sentence
Quadruple-click	Entire paragraph
Single-click in left margin	Entire sentence
Double-click in left margin	Entire paragraph

> **note**
> Notice that when you move the mouse pointer into the left margin, the pointer reverses direction and points to the right (instead of the regular left-facing pointer). When you see this special pointer, you can click to select a line or double-click to select a paragraph.

FIGURE 4.1

Selected text is displayed with a different background color.

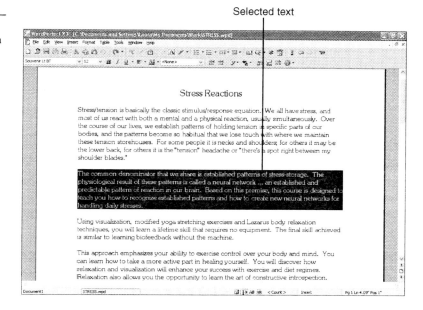

Moving and Copying Text

Now that you have text selected, you're probably wondering what to do with it. As you read through this book, you will learn dozens of things that you can do with selected text. One of the most basic functions is to move or copy text. If you move the text, deleting it from the original location, you are *cutting and pasting* text. When you make a copy of the text, leaving a copy in the original location, you are *copying and pasting* text.

One thing that makes WordPerfect unique is that you can choose from a number of different methods to accomplish the same result. The program conforms to your working style, not the other way around. There are several different ways to cut/copy and paste selected text. The different alternatives are listed here. Generally, the steps to move and copy are

1. Select the text you want to copy or move.
2. Copy (or cut) the selected text.
3. Reposition the insertion point at the target location.
4. Paste the text you copied (or cut).

Some methods for copying, cutting, and pasting text work better in certain situations. For example, if your hands are already on the keyboard, the keyboard methods might be more convenient. Others prefer to use the mouse. Experiment with the different methods and find your favorites.

This list contains the multiple methods for copying text:

- Click the **Copy** button.
- Choose **Edit**, **Copy**.
- Right-click the selected text and choose **Copy**.
- Press **Ctrl+C**.
- Press **Ctrl+Insert**.

This list contains the multiple methods for moving text:

- Click the **Cut** button.
- Choose **Edit**, **Cut**.
- Right-click the selection and choose **Cut**.
- Press **Ctrl+X**.
- Press **Shift+Delete**.

This list contains the multiple methods for pasting text:

- Click the **Paste** button.
- Choose **Edit**, **Paste**.
- Right-click in the document and choose **Paste**.
- Press **Ctrl+V**.
- Press **Shift+Insert**.

If you prefer, you can also use the mouse to drag selected text from one location and drop it in another. The drag-and-drop method works best when you are moving or copying text within the document window. When you have to scroll up or down, things get a little tricky.

To drag and drop text

1. Select the text you want to move or copy.
2. Position the mouse pointer on the highlighted text. The pointer changes to an arrow.
3. If you want to move the text, click and hold down the mouse button; if you want to copy the text, hold down the **Ctrl** key before you click and hold down the mouse button.

> **tip**
> If you can remember the Shift key, you can use a series of keyboard shortcuts to move and copy text— Shift+arrow keys to select the text, Shift+Delete to cut the text, and then Shift+Insert to paste the text. Practice this technique and see how much time you save!

4. Drag the mouse to the target location. The mouse pointer changes to an arrow along with a small rectangular box (see Figure 4.2). An insertion point also appears showing you exactly where the text will be inserted when you release the mouse button.
5. Release the mouse button.

FIGURE 4.2
You can use the mouse to quickly drag and drop text.

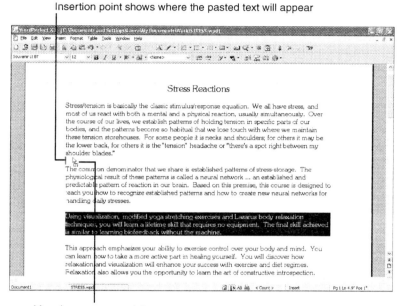

Insertion point shows where the pasted text will appear

Move/copy mouse pointer

The text is still selected, so if you didn't get the text right where you wanted it, click and drag it again. When you have the selection where you want it, click in the document window to deselect the text.

Using Undo to Fix Your Mistakes

WordPerfect has the ultimate "oops" fixer, and it's called Undo. Essentially, Undo reverses the last action taken on a document. For example, if you delete selected text, Undo brings it back. If you change the margins, Undo puts them back the way they were. It's as if you never took the action.

Undo has a twin feature called Redo. Redo reverses the last Undo action. If you accidentally Undo too many things, Redo puts them back.

To use the Undo feature, use one of the following options:

- Click the **Undo** button on the toolbar.
- Choose **Edit**, **Undo**.
- Press **Ctrl+Z**.

To use the Redo feature, use one of the following options:

- Click the **Redo** icon on the toolbar.
- Choose **Edit**, **Redo**.
- Press **Ctrl+Shift+Z**.

The Undo and Redo buttons have drop-down arrows next to them. Click the arrow to display a list of the 10 most recent actions (see Figure 4.3). Instead of repeatedly clicking the Undo or Redo buttons, you can choose an action from one of the lists. Stay with me now because this gets a little tricky. If you choose an action from this list, all the actions up to and including that selected action will be reversed, not just the selected action.

> **note**
>
> By default, WordPerfect remembers the last 10 actions you took on the document. You can increase this amount to a maximum of 300 actions. Choose **Edit**, **Undo/Redo History**, **Options**, and change the Number of Undo/Redo Items.

FIGURE 4.3
Use the Undo and Redo history lists to select which action to undo/redo.

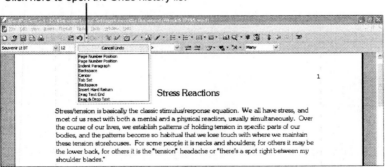

Using the Zoom Feature

Zoom controls the magnification of the document onscreen. It doesn't affect the printed copy, so you can freely use whatever zoom setting you prefer. By default, WordPerfect displays documents at a zoom ratio of 100%, which displays the text and graphics in approximately the same size that they will be when printed. A zoom setting of 50% displays the document at half the printed size. A zoom setting of 200% displays the document twice as large as the printed copy.

To adjust the zoom setting

1. Click the drop-down arrow next to the **Zoom** button on the toolbar (or on the Print Preview toolbar). A pop-up menu of zoom settings appears (see Figure 4.4).
2. Select a zoom setting.

FIGURE 4.4
Hovering over a Zoom setting activates RealTime Preview, which shows you how the document will look at each zoom setting.

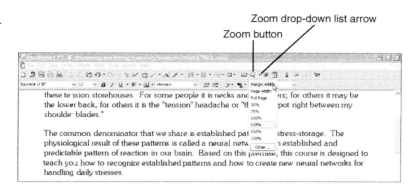

RealTime Preview can show you a preview of each zoom setting before you choose it. Simply point to and hover over any of the zoom settings. This activates RealTime Preview, which shows you how each setting will look. As you read through the book, you will see other ways that RealTime Preview helps you make decisions.

If you have a Microsoft IntelliMouse or other type of mouse with a scroll wheel, you can adjust the zoom ratio by holding down the **Ctrl** key and rotating the wheel. Notice that the wheel has small notches. WordPerfect zooms in or out at intervals for each notch on the wheel.

You might decide that you don't like any of the preset zoom settings. If so, choose **Other** from the Zoom pop-up menu, or choose **View**, **Zoom**. This opens the Zoom dialog box, where you can type the preferred zoom ratio.

Zooming In with the Mouse

The Zoom feature can be turned on, and you can zoom in and out of a document by clicking the left and right mouse buttons. This method works well when you're going back over a document and you need to be able to zoom in on small details and then zoom back out to scroll down.

To zoom in and out with the mouse

1. Click the **Zoom** button on the toolbar. The mouse pointer changes to a magnifying glass (see Figure 4.5).

FIGURE 4.5
The Zoom feature can be turned on, and you can zoom in and out with the mouse.

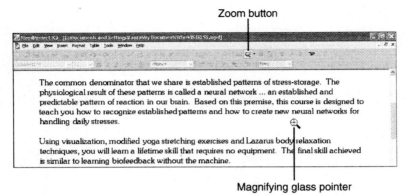

Zoom button

Magnifying glass pointer

2. Click in the document window to start zooming in.
3. Continue clicking the left mouse button to zoom in on the document.
4. Click the right mouse button to zoom out.
5. Continue clicking the right mouse button to zoom all the way out.

6. Click the **Zoom** button again to turn off the Zoom feature.

Zooming In on a Specific Area

At times, you will want to zoom in and out of a specific area of a document. For example, if you are working with a lot of graphics and graphics captions, you might want to zoom in on each graphic so you can proofread the caption.

To magnify a specific section of a document

1. Click the **Zoom** button on the toolbar. The mouse pointer changes to a magnifying glass.
2. Click and drag the area of the document you want to magnify (see Figure 4.6). WordPerfect adjusts the zoom ratio to display the selected text as large as possible.
3. Click the **Zoom** button again to turn off the magnification feature.
4. If necessary, click the **Zoom** button drop-down arrow and choose a normal zoom ratio once again.

FIGURE 4.6

Using the Zoom pointer, you can click and drag across an area to enlarge it.

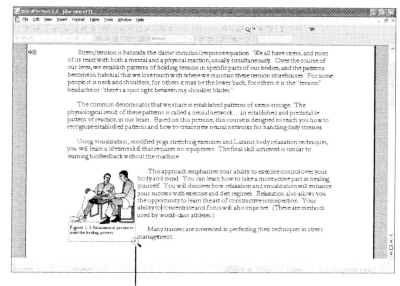

Click and drag the area to enlarge

Switching to 5.1 Classic Mode

In response to thousands of user requests, Corel has incorporated the popular WordPerfect 5.1 Classic mode into WordPerfect X3. So, what is this Classic mode, you ask? Simply put, it's a simpler interface that is much easier on the eyes. Early DOS versions of WordPerfect displayed white text on a blue background. There were no toolbars or scrollbars to take up space, so the screen is much cleaner, with more room for the document text, and less distracting for those of us who don't use all those buttons!

The DOS versions were written before Windows and the mouse gained popularity. Those of us who learned on these versions could make menu selections at the speed of light using keyboard shortcuts. Classic mode combines the easy-on-the-eyes blue background with the speed of keyboard commands. You activate the blue screen and keyboard separately, so I'll show you how to do both.

Switching to the Blue Screen

You won't believe how soothing a blue background with gray text is until you've seen it. It's very simple to switch back and forth, and you might find yourself going back and forth depending on what you are working on.

To switch to the 5.1 Classic mode

1. Choose **Tools**, **Settings** (or press **Alt+F12**) to open the Settings dialog box.
2. Choose **Environment** to display the Environment Settings dialog box.
3. Click the **Theme** tab to display those options (see Figure 4.7).

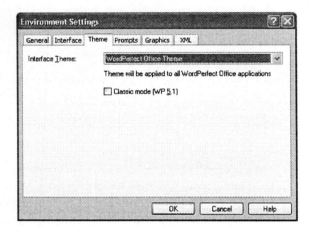

FIGURE 4.7
Switch to the WordPerfect 5.1 Classic mode in the Environment Settings dialog box.

4. Enable the **Classic mode (WP 5.1)** check box.
5. Click **OK** to close the Environment Settings dialog box.
6. Click **Close** to return to the document. The screen now shows the Classic mode (see Figure 4.8).

After you switch to Classic mode, you can selectively turn screen elements on and off as you need them:

- To turn on the horizontal scrollbar, choose **Tools**, **Settings**, **Display**. Click the **Document** tab. In the Scrollbars section, select the **Horizontal** check box.
- To display the ruler, choose **View**, **Ruler** (Alt+Shift+F3).
- To display the toolbar, choose **View**, **Toolbars**. Select the **WordPerfect** check box.
- To display the property bar, choose **View**, **Toolbars**. Select the **Property Bar** check box.

You can also select Classic mode from the Workspace Manager—either when you first start WordPerfect or at any time—by clicking **Tools**, **Workspace Manager**.

FIGURE 4.8
Classic mode doesn't display the toolbars or scrollbars, so the screen is less cluttered.

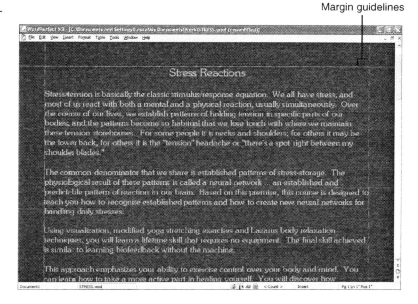

Margin guidelines

Switching to the WordPerfect 5.1 Keyboard

Heavy production work is hampered when you have to reach for the mouse to do something other than type text. The popularity of DOS programs, even today in a Windows world, can be explained by the large number of users who want to be able to work without moving their hands off the keyboard. The WordPerfect 5.1 keyboard feature in WordPerfect X3 contains most of the keyboard commands used in that version. It offers a solution for people who have resisted upgrading from the DOS version because they would have to relearn keystrokes, but it also offers a heavy keyboardist an alternative to using the mouse.

To switch to the WordPerfect 5.1 keyboard

1. Choose **Tools**, **Settings**, **Customize** to open the Customize Settings dialog box.
2. Click the **Keyboards** tab to display the list of keyboards (see Figure 4.9).
3. Select the **<WPDOS 5.1 Keyboard>** entry.
4. Choose **Select**, then **Close**.
5. Choose **Close** again to dismiss the Customize Settings dialog box.

To switch back to the standard WordPerfect X3 keyboard, simply open the Customize Settings dialog box again (**Tools**, **Settings**, **Customize**), click the **Keyboards** tab, select the <WPWin Keyboard> keyboard, choose **Select**, click **Close**, and then click **Close** again to exit the dialog box.

FIGURE 4.9
Select the WordPerfect 5.1 keyboard to use your favorite WP 5.1 keyboard shortcuts.

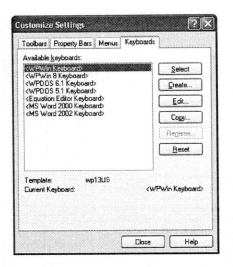

Working with More Than One Document

Think of how you use your computer. On a typical day, you probably have two or three applications running at once—WordPerfect, your email application, several Web browser windows, a scanner or digital camera program, and so on. Your taskbar has buttons for every program you are running so that you can quickly switch back and forth between programs.

In that same spirit, WordPerfect lets you work on up to nine document windows at once. Each document has a button on the application bar (at the bottom of the screen), so you can quickly switch back and forth between documents (see Figure 4.10).

You already know how to open a document. You might not realize that when you open a document, WordPerfect automatically places it in a new document window. So, if you are already working on something, you can open other documents without disturbing anything. Also, you can open more than one file at a time while you're in the Open File dialog box. Simply click the first file, and then hold down the **Ctrl** key to click the other files.

caution

Depending on your WordPerfect installation, the Classic mode environment and keyboard features might not be installed on your system. You can install them at any time by running the setup program. Choose **Start**, **(Settings)**, **Control Panel**, **Add or Remove Programs**. Choose **WordPerfect Office X3** in the list, and then choose **Change**. In the Installshield wizard, choose **Change which program features are enabled**, then choose **Next**. In the Select Features list, click the plus sign next to **WordPerfect Office X3**, click the plus sign next to **WordPerfect**, and then select the **WordPerfect Classic Mode** option. Choose **This Feature Will Be Installed on the Local Hard Drive**. Follow the rest of the instructions to complete the installation. Be ready to insert the WordPerfect Office X3 CD if you are prompted for it.

FIGURE 4.10

Each open document has a button on the application bar.

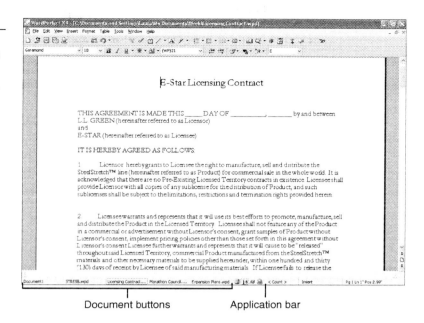

Document buttons   Application bar

 To start a new document, you need a blank document in a new document window. Click the **New Blank Document** icon on the toolbar; choose **File**, **New**; or press **Ctrl+N**.

You can switch from one document to another with any of the following methods:

- On the application bar, click the name of the document you want to work on.
- Open the **Window** menu, and then click the document you want.
- Press **Ctrl+F6** (Previous Window) repeatedly until WordPerfect displays the document you want to work on.

Multiple document windows make it a snap to cut, copy, and paste between documents. Simply cut or copy while viewing one document, and then switch to another document and paste.

Previewing and Printing Documents

In Chapter 2, you learned how to do a quick print of a document. With the quick print method, you skip over the Print dialog box and send the entire document to the default printer.

What if you want to print to a different printer? Or maybe you need five copies of a document. Let's cover some of the most frequently used options. You can tackle the rest when a situation arises and you need the other tools.

Switching to Print Preview

The Print Preview feature shows you exactly what your document will look like when you print it. Use it as often as possible. You will save time, paper, and printer resources, not to mention your frustration when you notice a tiny mistake.

Earlier versions of WordPerfect included a Print Preview feature, but you couldn't make any changes while in it. In WordPerfect X3, you can freely edit the text, reposition graphics, change the margins, and so on.

Using buttons on the Print Preview toolbar, you can switch to a Two Page view, or you can use the Zoom feature to adjust the size of the page. Other buttons give you access to the Spell Checker, the Make It Fit feature, and both the Page Setup and the Print dialog boxes.

To use the Print Preview feature

1. Choose **File**, **Print Preview** from the menu. The current page is displayed (see Figure 4.11).
2. To zoom in on the text, click the Zoom arrow and select a different option, or click the **Zoom** button, left-click the document to zoom in, then right-click the document to zoom back out.
3. Make any necessary adjustments. If you clicked the Zoom button in step 2, click it again to turn off the Zoom feature.
4. When you are finished, click the **Print Preview** button (on the Print Preview toolbar) to switch back to the document window.

FIGURE 4.11
Print Preview displays a fully editable representation of how the document will look when printed.

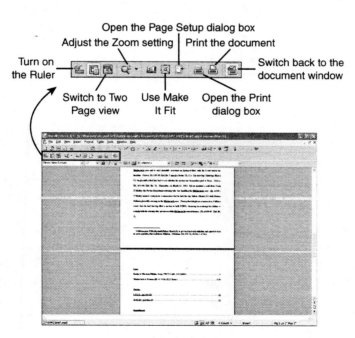

For more information on magnifying specific areas of your document, see the "Using the Zoom Feature" section in this chapter.

Changing the Number of Copies

The cost of printing multiple copies on a laser printer is virtually identical to the cost of running copies on a copier. It's much faster just to print three copies of a document than it is to print a copy, walk to the copier, punch in your account number, figure out which buttons to press to get three copies, and wait for them to be finished.

To change the number of copies

1. Click the **Print** button (**Ctrl+P**) to display the Print dialog box (see Figure 4.12).

   If necessary, click the **Main** tab.

2. Change the number in the **Number of Copies** text box.

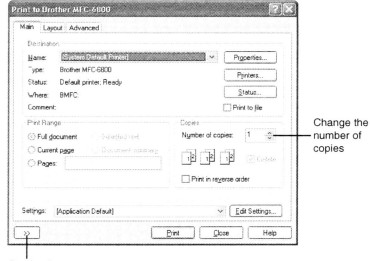

FIGURE 4.12
Adjust the number of copies to print more than one original.

Layout Preview button

Change the number of copies

If you choose to print more than one copy, WordPerfect groups the copies as illustrated in the Copies area of the dialog box. You can collate the copies by enabling the **Collate** check box. If you do this, the copies will be printed in page number order. In other words, three copies of three pages will print out 1, 2, 3 then 1, 2, 3 then 1, 2, 3 instead of 1, 1, 1 then 2, 2, 2 then 3, 3, 3.

Printing Specific Pages

When you're revising a multipage document, it doesn't make sense to print the whole thing when you need to check only a few pages. Save trees and print just the pages you need to proofread.

- To print the current page, choose **Current Page**.
- To print multiple pages, type the page numbers you want to print in the **Pages** text box. For example, if you need to print pages 3 through 9, type **3-9**. If you also want to print page 15, type **3-9, 15** in the text box. Finally, if you type a page number followed by a dash, WordPerfect prints from that page number to the end of the document. For example, **13-** prints page 13 and everything that follows it.
- To print selected text, select the text before you open the Print dialog box. Then click **Selected Text**.

When you choose to print selected text, the text appears on the printed page in the same location in which it would have appeared had you printed the surrounding text. For example, if you select the last paragraph on the page, the paragraph prints by itself at the bottom of the page.

If you click the **Advanced** tab of the Print dialog box, you see options for printing multiple pages or labels, secondary pages, chapters, and volumes. However, under the Main tab, you can indicate only page numbers.

caution
The numbers you enter in the **Pages** text box must be in numeric order; otherwise, all the pages might not print. For example, if you specify **12-15, 4**, only pages 12–15 print. To print these specific pages, you must enter **4, 12-15**.

note
There is a button in the WordPerfect X3 Print dialog box called the Layout Preview button. Located in the lower-left corner, this button expands the dialog box to include a preview page. When you make selections in the Layout tab, those changes are reflected on the preview page. For example, if you choose to print thumbnails (small images) of your document, the preview page will illustrate how the thumbnails will be laid out on the paper.

Faxing Documents from WordPerfect

How many times have you printed a document, fed it into a fax machine, and then put the printout in the recycle bin? You can save time, paper, and printing resources by faxing directly from WordPerfect. Several items must be in place first:

- A fax board must be installed in your computer (or connected to your network). Most modems come with faxing capabilities built in, so if you have a modem, you probably already have the hardware needed to fax. Check your modem manual for more information.
- A Windows-based fax program must be installed on your computer. When fax software is installed, a fax printer is added to your list of available printers. You can check this by opening the Print dialog box in WordPerfect and looking at the Name drop-down list. Many modems also ship with fax software. Check your modem documentation for more information.
- The person to whom you send the fax must have a fax machine or a computer-based fax program and a fax/modem to receive the fax.

To send a fax from WordPerfect

1. With the document that you want to fax in the active window, click the **Print** button or choose **File**, **Print**.
2. On the Main tab, click the **Name** drop-down list arrow and choose the fax printer from the list.
3. Make other changes to the print setup as desired (for example, which pages to print).
4. Click **Print** to fax the document. WordPerfect prepares the document and hands it off to the fax software.
5. Your fax software displays a dialog box that enables you to designate where to send the fax. If the dialog box doesn't appear, click the fax software icon on the Windows taskbar.
6. Fill in the destination information in the fax program's dialog box, and then send the fax.

After the document is scheduled for sending, you can use the fax program's software to monitor the fax status, check the fax logs, or even cancel the fax if it hasn't been sent yet.

Sending Documents via Email

If you can send an email message, you can send documents via email. There are two options: A selected portion of the document can be sent as a part of a message, or the entire document can be sent as an attachment to the message.

To determine whether your mail program has been installed and is integrated with WordPerfect, choose **File**, **Send To**. Supported mail programs are listed on the menu, as is a Mail Recipient option (see Figure 4.13).

FIGURE 4.13

If your mail program is installed and recognized by WordPerfect, it appears on the File, Send To menu.

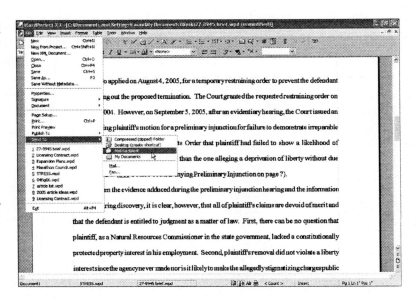

 To send the entire file as an email attachment, click the **Mail** button or choose **File, Send To, Mail Recipient**. Windows switches to your email program, which then adds the document as an attachment and enables you to send a message with the attachment (see Figure 4.14).

FIGURE 4.14

If you send your document as an attachment, the receiver can then download the attachment and open it in WordPerfect.

Attached filename in the subject line

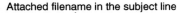
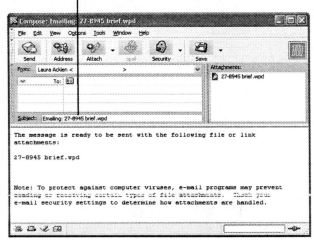

You can also send just a portion of the document as part of the body of your message. In WordPerfect, select the text you want to mail; choose **File**, **Send To**, **Mail**. The mail program is launched, and the selected text is added to the body of the message. You provide an address, edit the text, and send the message.

If your email program doesn't work well with WordPerfect, you still have these options:

- You can save the document and open your email program separately. Compose a message and attach the document.
- You can copy text from a WordPerfect document and paste it in the body of the email message. Bear in mind that this method removes most, if not all, of WordPerfect's formatting.

THE ABSOLUTE MINIMUM

- Selecting text is one of those skills that you will use over and over again. Now that you've learned how to select text, you can use the same techniques to select items in other applications. From rearranging a list to using an already formatted heading to creating a new one, you will move and copy text frequently in your documents.
- The Undo feature is the ultimate "oops" fixer. Even if you've just accidentally selected the entire document and deleted it, Undo can bring it back.
- You might find your favorite zoom setting and leave it alone from then on, but when you need to read some tiny print or check a detailed graphic, you will be able to quickly switch to a different setting and then back again.
- The Classic Mode from WordPerfect 5.1 has been brought back from retirement, so now Windows users can enjoy the easy-on-the-eyes gray text on a blue background.
- You can open up to nine documents at once, so you can easily create a new document from pieces of existing documents using the copy and paste methods.
- Before you send a document to the printer, take a minute to preview it in Print Preview. You might be surprised at how many mistakes you can catch.
- Printing and mailing documents are still done, but more frequently, users are faxing and emailing documents directly from WordPerfect.

In the next chapter, you will learn basic formatting techniques so that you can emphasize text, change the margins, create envelopes, insert symbols, and work in Reveal Codes.

IN THIS CHAPTER

- Learn how to use bold, italic, and underline to emphasize important text.
- Select different fonts and font sizes to improve the appearance of your documents.
- Change the margin settings to squeeze more text on a page.
- Create an envelope with the mailing address automatically inserted for you.
- Choose from more than 1,500 symbols and special characters that can be inserted into a document.
- Turn on Reveal Codes and learn how to edit or remove codes.

Learning Basic Formatting

You've learned a lot in the first four chapters, and now it's time to put it into practice. This chapter covers a collection of features that fall into the "basic formatting" category. These are things you will likely want to do right away, such as applying bold, changing to a different font, adjusting margins, printing envelopes, and inserting symbols.

Reveal Codes, a feature that lets you view hidden formatting instructions, is WordPerfect's secret weapon, so don't miss the discussion at the end of the chapter. You will learn how easy it is to adjust formatting and correct conflicts. You can even print a document with the codes embedded in the text so you can troubleshoot a document when you are away from the computer.

Emphasizing Important Text

In an oral presentation, you use different intonations for emphasis. To get an important point across, you might raise your voice and pronounce each word slowly and clearly. Speaking in a monotone will either bore your audience to tears or put them to sleep. Using a different tone of voice and pausing before important points help to hold your audience's attention.

You can do the same thing with a printed document. Judicious use of bold, italic, underline, and other effects can guide a reader through the text and draw attention to key points.

- **Bold**
- *Italics*
- <u>Underline</u>

To apply bold, italic, or underline

1. Select the text.
2. Click the **Bold**, **Italic**, or **Underline** button on the property bar (or any combination of the three).

FIGURE 5.1
Use the Bold, Italic, and Underline buttons on the property bar to emphasize text.

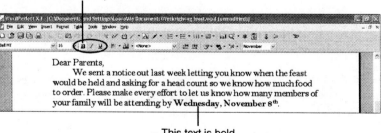

The Bold button is pushed in

This text is bold

When bold, italic, or underline has been applied to a section of text, the buttons on the property bar appear "pushed in" (see Figure 5.1).

Choosing the Right Font

Choosing a font can be intimidating, especially because there are now thousands of fonts to choose from. It's worth the time and effort, though, because the right font can improve the appearance of a document and make it easier to read. Attractive fonts generate interest in your subject. Titles and headings should be larger than the body text so that they stand out a bit. It takes only a few minutes to select the fonts in a document, and the results are well worth your effort.

INSTALLING THE BONUS FONTS
Corel includes 950 fonts with WordPerfect Office X3. Of these, 24 are the character set fonts, which contain the symbols and foreign language alphabets. During a typical installation, a default set of fonts is installed. The rest can be installed separately, using either Corel Setup or the Fonts folder.

You can open the Fonts folder from the Control Panel. Click **Start (Settings)**, **Control Panel**. Select Fonts. In the **Fonts** folder, choose **File, Install New Font,** and then follow the instructions You will need to have the WordPerfect Office X3 CD #2 ready to insert.

Selecting Fonts and Font Sizes

Before we talk about choosing another font or font size, I want to point out the importance of selecting the text that you want to work with first. If you don't, the change will take place at the insertion point and continue until another font or font size is selected.

The quickest way to choose a different font is to click the **Font Face** drop-down arrow on the property bar. A drop-down list of fonts appears, and a large preview window pops up at the top of the document (see Figure 5.2). As you point to a font in the list, the sample text in the preview window changes into that font.

Thanks to Corel's RealTime Preview, the text in the document also changes to reflect that font. You don't have to play guessing games, trying to figure out how a font will look from a tiny piece of sample text—you can see how a whole page of text will look. When you find the font that you want, click it.

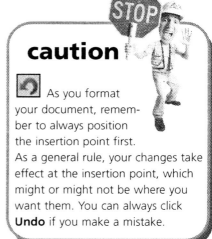

caution

As you format your document, remember to always position the insertion point first. As a general rule, your changes take effect at the insertion point, which might or might not be where you want them. You can always click **Undo** if you make a mistake.

FIGURE 5.2
As you hover over fonts in the drop-down list, the sample text in the preview window and the text in the document change to that font.

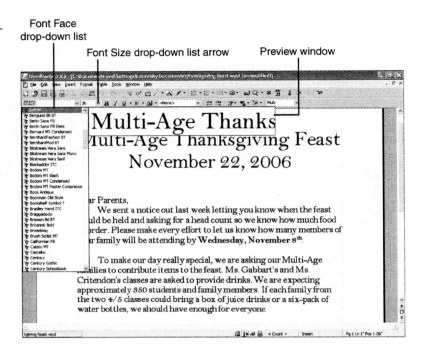

Choosing a different font size works essentially the same way as choosing a different font. Click the **Font Size** drop-down list arrow on the property bar to open a drop-down list of sizes. If you click the scroll arrows, you will see that the list has sizes ranging from 6 to 72 points. A preview window with sample text opens next to the list. As you move the mouse down through the list, the sample text and the document text expand and contract to show the new size.

When you've decided which font you want to use for the body text, set that as the default font for the document, as follows:

tip
If you want to use a font size that isn't shown in the list, click the **Font Size** box (to select the current size), and then type the size you want. Press Enter to change the size.

1. Choose **Format**, **Font** to open the Font Properties dialog box.
2. Make your selections.
3. Click **Settings**.
4. Click **Set Face and Point Size As Default for This Document**.

Likewise, if you select a font that you want to use for most, if not all, of your documents, set that as the default for all *new* documents, as follows:

1. Choose **Format**, **Font** to open the Font Properties dialog box.
2. Make your selections.
3. Click **Settings**.
4. Click **Set Face and Point Size As Default for All Documents**.

SAVING THE FONTS WITH THE DOCUMENT
Have you ever tried to make last-minute changes to a document on a machine that didn't have the same fonts installed? It can be a nightmare. Thanks to font-embedding technology, you can save fonts with a document so that they go where the document goes. When you save a file, choose **Embed Fonts Using TrueDoc (TM)** at the bottom of the Save File (and Save As) dialog box (underneath the File type drop-down list). WordPerfect compresses the fonts and saves them with the file.

Choosing a Font from the QuickFonts List

Let's say that you just finished revising the text in your resume. You're ready to polish the appearance. You're finished experimenting, so you know which fonts you want to use for your headings and job titles. Even with the Font Face and Font Size drop-down lists, reselecting the same fonts and sizes over and over can be tedious.

Thank goodness for the QuickFonts feature, which maintains a running list of the last 10 fonts (with sizes and effects) that you selected. Click the **QuickFonts** button on the property bar (see Figure 5.3), and then click the font you want to reuse. (In case you're wondering, RealTime Preview doesn't work here.)

FIGURE 5.3
Click the **QuickFonts** button to select from the 10 most recently used fonts.

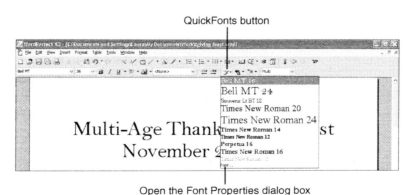

Some good rules of thumb are as follows:

- Don't use more than three or four fonts on a page.
- Don't apply bold *and* italic *and* underline (all at once).
- Don't use a bunch of different font sizes.
- Do choose an attractive font that suits the subject matter.

Figure 5.4 shows the text from two newsletters. The newsletter on the left uses decorative fonts, but they are difficult to read, and the combination of bold, underline, and italic on the date is too "busy." The newsletter text on the right uses an attractive font, the use of bold or italic alone, and a smaller type size. The use of bullets in the list of items also helps the reader follow along.

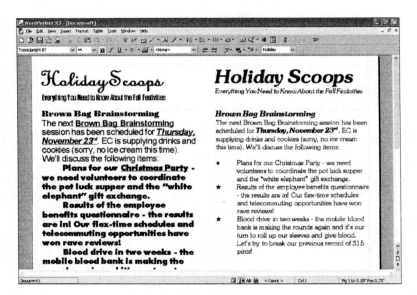

FIGURE 5.4
The newsletter on the right illustrates how different font selections can improve the appearance of the text.

Using Other Font Effects

Bold, italic, and underline all have buttons on the property bar, so they are the most accessible font effects. The other effects, also called *attributes*, are found in the Font Properties dialog box.

To use the other font effects

1. Position the insertion point where you want the effects to start (or select some existing text).
2. Choose **Font** from the **Format** menu (**F9**) or right-click and choose **Font** from the QuickMenu to open the Font Properties dialog box (see Figure 5.5).

FIGURE 5.5
The Font Properties dialog box is helpful when you need to set multiple font options or if you want to preview your changes first.

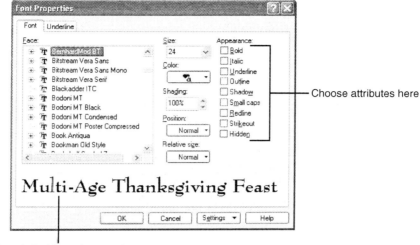

Choose attributes here

Sample text from document

3. Click **OK** when you're finished choosing effects.

The font attributes are listed in the Appearance section. As you select attributes, the sample text in the lower-left corner shows you how the attributes will look when applied to the text. The RealTime Preview feature pops up again here—WordPerfect pulls in a short section of text from your document and uses it as the sample text. (If you're working in a blank document, the sample text is the name of the currently selected font.)

Use the Font Properties dialog box anytime you need to set more than a couple of font options at once. For example, if you need to choose a different font and size, and apply bold and italic, it's faster to do it all at once in the Font Properties dialog box than to choose each one separately from the property bar.

Changing Margins

It isn't something you think about every day, but you can actually make your document easier to read by adjusting the margins. A wider margin creates more whitespace around the text and reduces the number of words on a line. And remember, the shorter the line, the less likely the reader is to lose her place.

On the other hand, if you're trying to keep down the number of pages, you might want to make the margins smaller so that you can fit more on a page. When you use headers and footers, for example, you might want to cut down the top and bottom margins to 1/2 inch. In WordPerfect, the margins are set to 1 inch on all sides by default, a standard widely used for formatting business letters. This differs from

Microsoft Word, where the default left and right margins are 1.25 inches and the top and bottom margins are 1 inch.

The margins can be adjusted in several different ways. Using the mouse, you can click and drag the guidelines in or out, or click and drag the margin indicators on the ruler. Or, you can open the Margins dialog box and change the settings there.

Using the Guidelines to Adjust Margins

Using the guidelines is a popular choice because most of us leave the guidelines turned on. They don't take up any space in the document window, unlike the ruler.

To adjust the margins with the guidelines

1. Position the mouse pointer over a guideline and wait until the pointer changes to a double arrow.

   - To adjust the top margin, position the mouse pointer over the horizontal guideline at the top of the document window.
   - To adjust the left margin, position the pointer over the vertical line on the left side of the document window.
   - To adjust the right margin, position the pointer over the vertical line on the right side of the document window.
   - To adjust the bottom margin, position the pointer over the horizontal guideline at the bottom of the document window.

> **caution**
> If you don't see the guidelines (as shown in Figure 5.6), someone might have turned them off on your system. Choose **View**, **Guidelines**; place a check mark next to **Margins**; and then click **OK**.

2. Click and drag the guideline. When you click and drag, a dotted guideline and a bubble appear. The dotted guideline shows you where the new margin will be, and the bubble tells you what the new margin will be (in inches) when you release the mouse button (see Figure 5.6).

FIGURE 5.6

Clicking and dragging guidelines is a quick way to adjust the margins.

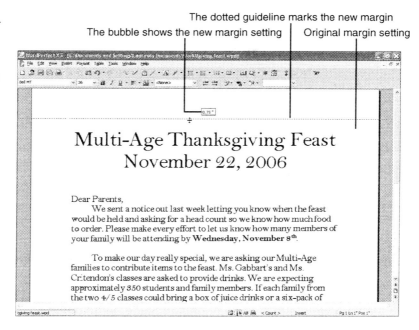

Adjusting the Left and Right Margins Using the Ruler

The ruler is a nice feature for people who use tabs a lot in their documents. With the ruler displayed, it's a snap to add, move, or delete tabs. For more information on setting tabs with the ruler, see Chapter 7, "Working with Paragraphs."

Margin indicators on the ruler show what the current margins are. You can click and drag these indicators to adjust the left and right margins.

To adjust the left and right margins with the ruler

1. If necessary, display the ruler by choosing **View**, **Ruler**. The ruler appears under the property bar.

2. Position the cursor over the left or right edge of the margin indicator and wait for the double arrow.

3. Click and drag the margin indicator to the left or right to adjust the margin (see Figure 5 7).

FIGURE 5.7
It's easy to adjust the left and right margins with the ruler.

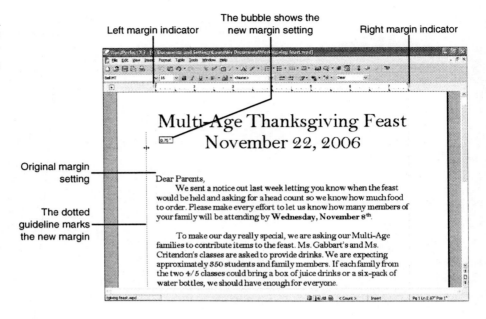

Using the Page Setup Dialog Box

If you're not comfortable with clicking and dragging, or if you just want to be more precise, you can make your changes in the Page Setup dialog box.

To set the margins in the Page Setup dialog box

1. Choose **Format**, **Margins** (**Ctrl+F8**) to open the Page Setup dialog box (see Figure 5.8).
2. Either type the measurements in the text boxes or click the spinner arrows to bump the value up or down—in this case, 0.1 inch at a time.

You can quickly set equal margins by adjusting one of the margins and clicking **Equal**. Also, if you want to set the margins to the bare minimum for that printer, click **Minimum**.

> **caution**
> Certain types of printers are not capable of printing to the edge of the paper. This area is called the *unprintable zone*. The size of this zone varies from printer to printer, so the information is kept in the printer's setup.
>
> If you try to set a margin within the unprintable zone, WordPerfect automatically adjusts it to the printer's minimum margin setting.

FIGURE 5.8
Use the Page Setup dialog box to adjust the margin settings.

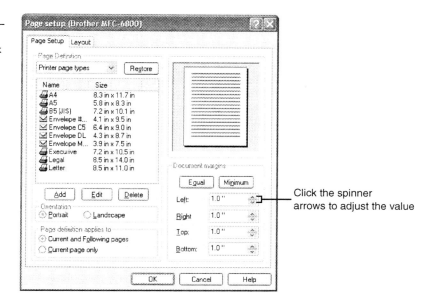

Click the spinner arrows to adjust the value

Creating an Envelope

We spend a lot more time emailing documents back and forth, and we don't need to print as many envelopes as we used to. Still, it's fast and easy, so the next time you reach for a pen to address an envelope, why not let WordPerfect do the work?

WordPerfect figures out where the mailing address is in the document and pulls it into the envelope dialog box, so you don't even have to retype it. You may wonder how this is done. The program looks for three to six short lines of text followed by a blank line. If two address blocks are in a letter, such as a return address followed by a mailing address, WordPerfect uses the second address.

ENTERING YOUR PERSONAL INFORMATION

When you choose **Format**, **Envelope**, you might see the following message (instead of the Envelope dialog box): "The Template feature allows you to enter information about yourself that will personalize your templates. You need only enter this once." Creating an envelope is one area in the program where your personal information is used.

You have a choice: You can either create a record in the Address Book with your personal information now—in which case WordPerfect automatically inserts your return address—or you can skip this step and manually type your return address in the envelope. Keep in mind that if you skip the step of entering your personal information, you will be prompted to do it every time you try to do something that involves a template or your personal information. For more information on entering the personal information, see "Filling in Personal Information" in Chapter 16, "Working with Templates."

To create an envelope

1. Choose **Format**, **Envelope** to display the Envelope dialog box (see Figure 5.9).

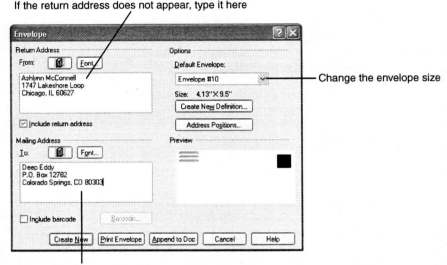

FIGURE 5.9
WordPerfect locates the mailing address and inserts it in the Envelope dialog box so that you don't have to type it twice.

2. If there isn't a return address in the **From** text box, or if you want to revise the address, you have a couple options:
   - Click in the **From** text box and enter the information.
   - Click the **Address Book** icon if you want to select an address from one of the available address books. (The type and number of available address books will vary depending on your email capabilities.)

3. If necessary, you can do the following:
   - You can either manually replace the mailing address or click the **Address Book** icon and choose a mailing address from one of the available address books.
   - Click the **Font** button to change the font or font size for the return address and mailing address.
   - Enable the **Include Barcode** check box; click the **Barcode** button, then type the recipient's ZIP Code and choose a position for the bar code.
   - Click the **Address Positions** button, and then adjust the placement of the return and mailing addresses.
   - Click the **Default Envelope** drop-down list arrow, and then choose a size from the pop-up list.

4. When you're finished, choose from the following:

   - Click the **Create New** button if you want to place the envelope in a new document.
   - Click the **Print Envelope** button to send the envelope directly to the printer.
   - Click the **Append to Doc** button if you want to place the envelope at the bottom of the current document.

Inserting Symbols

The capability to insert symbols is one area in which WordPerfect stands head and shoulders above the competition. WordPerfect Office X3 comes with fonts for more than 1,500 special characters and symbols, including entire foreign language alphabets. You can insert the characters anywhere in your document.

Using the Symbols Dialog Box

The Symbols dialog box has a complete list of all the character sets and special characters. You can switch to a different character set and quickly insert any symbol from the list.

To insert special characters with the Symbols dialog box

1. Click in the document where you want the special character to appear.
2. Choose **Insert**, **Symbol** (**Ctrl+W**) to open the Symbols dialog box (see Figure 5.10). You might need to scroll down to see the symbol you want.

caution
Some printers have a large unprintable zone on the left side, which interferes with printing the return address on the envelope. A macro that comes with WordPerfect X3, called `flipenv`, is used to create an envelope that is rotated 180 degrees (the text is upside down) so that you can get around the problem. See Chapter 17, "Creating and Playing Macros."

note
Not all special characters are available in every font. Depending on the font you have selected, you might see empty boxes instead of special characters, which means that those characters aren't available. On the other hand, certain fonts, such as Wingdings, are composed entirely of special characters.

FIGURE 5.10
Through the Symbols dialog box, you can insert more than 1,500 symbols and characters from foreign language alphabets.

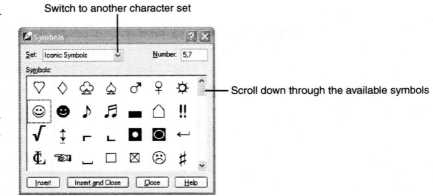

3. If you don't see the character you need, click the **Set** button and select a different character set from the list.
4. Select the symbol, and then click **Insert**, or double-click a symbol in the list to insert it. The dialog box stays open to make it easier for you to insert other symbols. If you only need to insert one symbol, click **Insert and Close** instead.
5. Click **Close** when you are finished.

Using the Symbols Toolbar Button

You can use the Symbols button on the toolbar to open a palette of 16 common symbols. Using the mouse, you can insert one of the symbols in just two clicks.

To select a symbol from the palette

1. Click the **Symbols** button on the property bar to open the palette (see Figure 5.11).

> **tip**
> WordPerfect has a great shortcut for inserting special characters. The next time you select a symbol, jot down the two numbers in the **Number** text box. The next time you need to insert the character, press **Ctrl+W**, type the two numbers (separated by a space or a comma), and then press **Enter**. For example, to insert the smiley face shown in Figure 5.10, press **Ctrl+W**, type **5,7**, and then press **Enter**.

FIGURE 5.11
Select one of the 16 symbols from the Symbols palette.

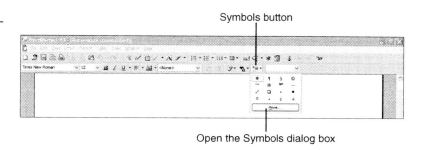

Symbols button

Open the Symbols dialog box

2. Click the symbol that you want to insert.
3. If you don't see the symbol that you want, click **More** to open the Symbols dialog box.

The symbol palette changes as you insert symbols into your documents, remembering up to the last 16 symbols you've used. After you've inserted the symbols that you use most often, they appear on the palette and can be easily inserted with the Symbols button.

Using QuickCorrect

The QuickCorrect feature is designed to automatically correct common spelling errors and typos while you type. The five common symbols that you can insert with QuickCorrect are shown in Table 5.1.

Table 5.1 Inserting Symbols with QuickCorrect

To Insert This Symbol	Type This
Copyright symbol	(c or (c)
Registered trademark symbol	(r or (r)
$\frac{1}{2}$	1/2
En dash	-- or n-
Em dash	--- or m-

If you don't want QuickCorrect to make these automatic replacements, you can take these symbols out of the list. Choose **Tools**, **QuickCorrect**. Select the symbol you want to remove, and then click **Delete Entry**. See "Adding and Removing QuickCorrect Entries" in Chapter 6 for more information.

Working in Reveal Codes

Opening the Reveal Codes window is a lot like raising the hood of a car. You're going under the hood of a document to see exactly how formatting codes control the appearance. There is no comparable feature in Microsoft Word. This is where WordPerfect distinguishes itself from the competition. No other application gives you the same power and flexibility.

Turning on Reveal Codes

When you turn on Reveal Codes, the document window is split in half. The Reveal Codes window takes up the lower half of the screen (see Figure 5.12). In this window, you see a duplicate of the text in the document window with the codes displayed.

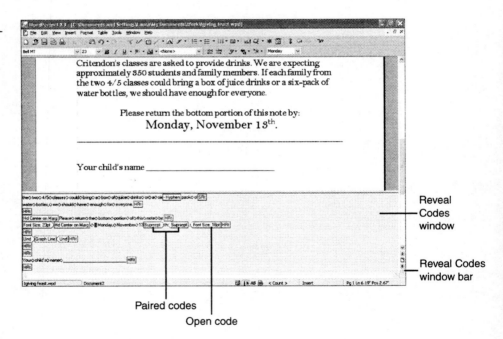

FIGURE 5.12
The Reveal Codes window displays the document text and the formatting codes.

The placement of the codes controls the appearance. You read through the codes just like you read a book—from left to right. A code takes effect where it is placed and remains in effect until another matching code is reached. For example, if you change the top margin, the change stays in effect until the end of the document, or until another top margin code is found.

There are two types of codes: paired and open. *Paired* codes have an On code and an Off code. The On code is at the beginning of the affected text; the Off code is at the end. For example, if you boldface a title, you will see a Bold On code at the beginning of the title and a Bold Off code at the end. An open code, such as a margin change or a hard return, stands alone. If you want to make changes, you simply edit the codes or delete them altogether.

You can use any of the following methods to turn on Reveal Codes:

- Right-click the document window and choose **Reveal Codes** from the QuickMenu.
- Choose **View**, **Reveal Codes**.
- Press **Alt+F3**.
- Click the **Reveal Codes window bar** located at the bottom of the vertical scrollbar (refer to Figure 5.12).
- Drag the **Reveal Codes window bar** up as high as you like (you can drag it back down to close Reveal Codes).

> **caution**
> Be especially careful when you edit a document with Reveal Codes on. If the Reveal Codes window is open, WordPerfect assumes that you see the codes and that you intend to delete them when you use Delete or Backspace.
>
> If you accidentally delete a formatting code, use Undo to restore it. Click the **Undo** button on the toolbar, or press **Ctrl+Z**.

Formatting codes appear in the Reveal Codes screen as buttons mixed in with the text. The insertion point is shown as a small red box. You can click in the Reveal Codes window to move the insertion point, or you can use the arrow keys.

To edit or delete a code

- You can delete codes by clicking and dragging them out of the Reveal Codes screen (see Figure 5.13).
- Alternatively, you can delete a code by positioning the cursor to the right of the code and pressing the **Backspace** key, or by positioning the cursor to the left of the code and pressing the **Delete** key.
- The quickest way to make formatting adjustments is to edit the code. Simply double-click the code in the Reveal Codes window. This opens the corresponding dialog box, where you can make the necessary changes. When you close the dialog box, your changes are saved.

As you work through these chapters, turn on Reveal Codes now and then so you can see that the selections you make in dialog boxes result in the insertion of codes that control the formatting of a document. The order of the codes is important. If you are having trouble figuring out why something is happening, the first thing you should do is turn on Reveal Codes and check the order of the codes. In many cases, all you need to do is rearrange the order of the codes or delete the codes causing trouble. Incidentally, you can select and move or copy codes in the Reveal Codes window using the same techniques that you learned in Chapter 4, "Revising Documents."

FIGURE 5.13

The quickest way to delete a code is to click and drag it out of the Reveal Codes window.

Click and drag a code out to delete it

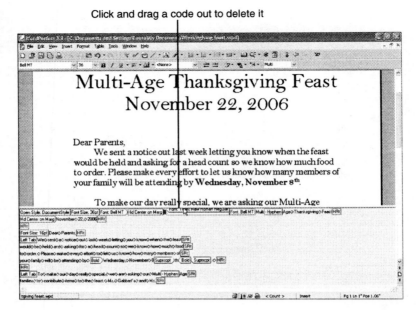

Printing the Codes

Another great troubleshooting tool is a handy feature that was first introduced in WordPerfect 11. You can now print out the codes with the document text. No more scrolling through a document to troubleshoot a problem. Just print out the affected pages and review the codes on paper. They are much bigger on the printed page, and they have a gray background so that they stand out from the rest of the text.

To print codes with the text

1. Choose **File**, **Print** (Ctrl+P) to open the Print dialog box.
2. Select the pages that you want to print.
3. Click the **Advanced** tab.
4. Enable the **Print Reveal Codes** check box.
5. Choose **Print**. Figure 5.14 shows an example of a page printed with the codes.

FIGURE 5.14
Printing the codes makes it easier to troubleshoot formatting conflicts.

[Open Style: DocumentStyle] [Font Size: 36pt] [Hd Center on Marg] [Font: Bell MT] Multi [- Hyphen] Age◊Thanksgiving◊Feast [HRt] [Hd Center on Marg] November◊22,◊2006 [HRt] [HRt] [Font Size: 16pt] Dear◊Parents, [HRt] [Left Tab] We◊sent◊a◊notice◊out◊last◊week◊letting◊you◊know◊when◊the◊feast [Srt] would◊be◊held◊and◊asking◊for◊a◊head◊count◊so◊we◊know◊how◊much◊food [Srt] to◊order.◊Please◊make◊every◊effort◊to◊let◊us◊know◊how◊many◊members◊of [Srt] your◊family◊will◊be◊attending◊by◊ [Bold> Wednesday,◊November◊8 [Suprscpt> th <Bold] <Suprscpt] .◊ [HRt] [HRt] [Left Tab]
To◊make◊our◊day◊really◊special,◊we◊are◊asking◊our◊Multi [- Hyphen] Age [Srt] families◊to◊contribute◊items◊to◊the◊feast.◊Ms.◊Gabbart's◊and◊Ms. [Srt] Critendon's◊classes◊are◊asked◊to◊provide◊drinks.◊We◊are◊expecting [Srt] approximately◊350◊students◊and◊family◊members.◊If◊each◊family◊from [Srt] the◊two◊4/5◊classes◊could◊bring◊a◊box◊of◊juice◊drinks◊or◊a◊six [- Hyphen] pack◊of [Srt] water◊bottles,◊we◊should◊have◊enough◊for◊everyone. [HRt] [HRt] [Hd Center on Marg] Please◊return◊the◊bottom◊portion◊of◊this◊note◊by: [HRt] [Font Size: 23pt> [Hd Center on Marg] ◊Monday,◊November◊13 [Suprscpt> th <Suprscpt] . <Font Size: 16pt] [HRt] [HRt] [Und> [Graph Line] <Und] [HRt] [HRt] [HRt] Your◊child's◊name_____ [HRt] [HRt] [HRt] What◊would◊you◊like◊to◊bring? [HRt] [HRt] [Left Tab] [Hyperlink> ◻ <Hyperlink] ◊◊◊Juice◊boxes [Hd Left Ind] [Hd Left Ind]
How◊many?◊_____ [HRt] [Left Tab] [Hyperlink> ◻ <Hyperlink]
◊◊◊Water◊bottles [Hd Left Ind] How◊many?◊_____ [HRt] [HRt]
Thank◊you◊for◊your◊generosity!

The Absolute Minimum

In this chapter, you learned how to perform basic formatting tasks. You learned how to select fonts, apply attributes, change the margins, create envelopes, and insert symbols.

- You learned the importance of using good judgment when selecting fonts and font attributes to emphasize important sections of text and to improve the appearance and readability of your document.
- There are several methods for changing the margins, and you got a chance to try them all.
- You learned how to create and print an envelope.
- You now know about WordPerfect's unique special character sets. You can insert characters from foreign alphabets, as well as a huge variety of symbols and other special characters.
- Understanding the role of codes helps you maintain total control over the formatting.

In the next chapter, you will learn how to use WordPerfect's writing tools to improve accuracy and ensure consistency in your documents.

In This Chapter

- Learn how to run a spell check and use Grammatik to check documents for grammatical errors.

- Use the 30,000-word dictionary to look up definitions.

- Learn how to switch to a different set of writing tools for other languages.

- Learn how to search (and replace) text, codes, or a combination of both.

- Use QuickCorrect, QuickWords, and Format-As-You-Go to make your typing efficient and accurate.

Using the Writing Tools

Word processors have evolved from glorified typewriters to document production engines. WordPerfect blurs the lines between word processors and desktop publishers by combining features designed for the placement and structure of graphics with features that allow you to manipulate text.

At the same time, the type of worker using word processors has evolved. Not everyone has the luxury of an assistant—most of us produce our own materials. People who have never typed their own documents are learning how to use spelling and grammatical checkers to improve the readability and credibility of their work. WordPerfect has an exceptional collection of productivity tools to help automate many common tasks performed by today's office workers.

Recognizing WordPerfect's Automatic Proofreading Features

You might notice that as you type a document, red underlines appear under some words. This is the Spell-As-You-Go feature working for you. Spell-As-You-Go has marked these words as possible misspellings.

Spell-As-You-Go is one of the two automatic proofreading features in WordPerfect—the other is Grammar-As-You-Go, which checks for grammatical errors. The theory behind these two features is that it's faster to correct errors while you are typing than to go back and fix them later. If Grammar-As-You-Go is activated rather than Spell-As-You-Go, you might see blue dashes in the text as well.

To correct a word with Spell-As-You-Go

1. Right-click a red underlined word to open a list of suggested replacement words from which you can choose (see Figure 6.1).
2. Click the correctly spelled word in the list.

That's it—you just corrected the misspelled word. Selecting a word from this list automatically replaces the underlined word with the word you chose.

If you find these proofing marks distracting, you can disable the Spell-As-You-Go and Grammar-As-You-Go features. If you opt to disable these features, you can run a spell check and/or grammar check on the entire document when you are finished editing.

You might notice that some menu items have a check mark next to them and other items have a bullet. Besides showing you which item is currently selected, is there any other difference? Yes!

Bullets tell you that only one of the options in the group can be selected at one time. Check marks tell you that more than one option in the group can be selected at one time.

To disable the automatic proofing features

1. Choose **Tools**, **Proofread**. Notice that Spell-As-You-Go has a bullet next to it—this means that it's turned on (see Figure 6.2). Grammar-As-You-Go includes the Spell-As-You-Go feature, so you can select either **Spell-As-You-Go** or **Grammar-As-You-Go**, but you cannot select both from the Proofread submenu at the same time.
2. Click **Off** to turn off both Spell-As-You-Go and Grammar-As-You-Go.

FIGURE 6.1
When you right-click a red underlined word, a list of suggested replacements appears.

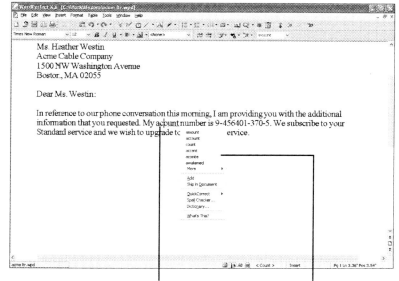

Underlined word   Choose a replacement word from this list

FIGURE 6.2
Choosing Grammar-As-You-Go activates both Grammar-As-You-Go and Spell-As-You-Go.

Spell-As-You-Go is turned on

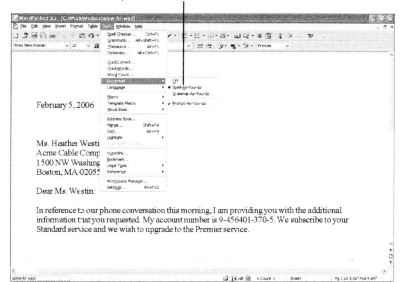

Spell Checking a Document

Who would have thought something as simple as a few misspelled words could undermine all your hard work? They can, and they will. Like it or not, readers will question the credibility of a writer if they find typos in the text. Save yourself the potential embarrassment by running Spell Checker on every document, no matter how short it is, before you send it off.

Develop a habit of saving documents before you run any of the writing tools such as the Spell Checker. This way, if you make some changes that you decide you don't want to keep, you can always go back to the saved copy. Also, the writing tools may occasionally lock up your system, especially with long or complex documents, so it's especially important that you have a good backup that you can revert to after you restart.

To start Spell Checker and correct mistakes in your document

1. Choose **Tools**, **Spell Checker**, press **Ctrl+F1**, or click the **Spell Checker** button on the toolbar. The Writing Tools dialog box with tabs for Spell Checker, Grammatik, Thesaurus, and the Dictionary appears (see Figure 6.3). Spell Checker immediately begins checking the document. A potential error is highlighted, and suggested replacement words appear in the **Replacements** list box.

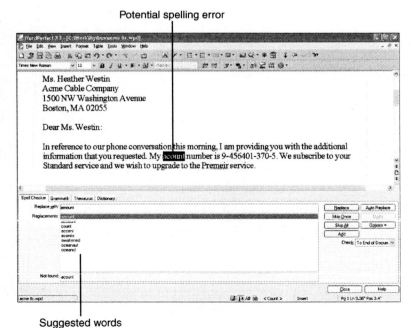

FIGURE 6.3
Spell Checker, Grammatik, Thesaurus, and the Dictionary are all integrated into the same dialog box. Click the appropriate tab to switch to another writing tool.

2. Choose from the following options to correct the misspelled word, add the word to the dictionary, or skip the word:

- To correct a misspelled word manually, click in the document window, correct the problem, and then click **Resume** to continue spell checking.

- To replace a misspelled word with the correctly spelled word, select the correctly spelled word in the **Replacements** list box and click **Replace**. In the case of duplicate words and irregular capitalization, select the single word, or the word with correct capitalization, in the **Replacements** list box. Alternatively, you can double-click the replacement word.

- If this is a frequently misspelled word, select the correct spelling in the **Replacements** list box, and then click **Auto Replace** to add the combination to the QuickCorrect list. (See "Adding and Deleting QuickCorrect Entries" later in this chapter for more information.)

- If the correct spelling doesn't appear in the **Replacements** list, edit the word manually in the **Replace with** box, and then click **Replace**.

- To skip the word here but have Spell Checker stop if it finds the word again, click **Skip Once**.

- To skip the word here and for the rest of the document, click **Skip All**.

- To add this word to the active user word list, click **Add**. A user word list is a list that you can customize to supplement the built-in word list.

- If you accidentally replace the misspelled word with the wrong replacement word, click **Undo**.

> **note**
>
> Choosing **Skip All** adds the word to the document word list, which is saved with the document and doesn't affect other documents. The strength of this feature becomes clear when you work with documents full of complex or technical terms. It takes only a few mouse clicks, and once you've built the list, Spell Checker runs faster because it isn't stopping on those terms anymore.

By default, Spell Checker checks the entire document. If you don't want to check the whole document, select the portion that you want to check first. Also, you can specify which portion of the document you want checked by selecting an option on the **Check** drop-down list.

Checking for Grammatical Errors

Grammatik is WordPerfect's grammar checker. A grammar checker proofs documents for correct grammar, style, punctuation, and word use, and thus catches many errors that get by most spell checkers. Interestingly, Spell Checker is integrated into Grammatik, so you only need to run Grammatik to run both.

Grammatik uses grammatical rules when checking a document for problems. Many good writers, however, often bend these rules to make a point. You shouldn't feel compelled to fix every problem or accept every suggested solution if it changes the meaning of your words.

To start Grammatik and check your document

1. Choose **Tools**, **Grammatik** (**Alt+Shift+F1**) or if you already have the Writing Tools dialog box open, just click the **Grammatik** tab. Grammatik immediately starts checking the document and, like Spell Checker, stops and highlights a potential error (see Figure 6.4).

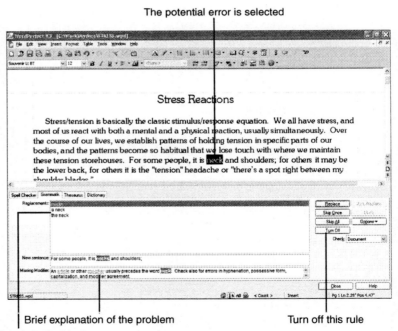

FIGURE 6.4
Grammatik has many of the same options as Spell Checker to correct a potential problem or move past it.

2. Choose from the following options to correct the error, skip the error, or turn off the rule:

   - To correct a writing error manually, click in the document window, correct the problem, and then click **Resume** to continue the grammar check.
   - To fix a writing error, select one of the suggestions in the **Replacements** list box, and then click **Replace**.
   - To skip the writing error here but have Grammatik stop if it finds the error again, click **Skip Once**.
   - To skip the writing error here and for the rest of the document, click **Skip All**.
   - The rules by which Grammatik checks your document are organized into *rule classes*. To disable a particular rule class, click **Turn Off**. This change is temporary, so when you run Grammatik again, the rule will be turned back on.

   - If you correct a problem and then change your mind, click **Undo** to reverse the last action taken by Grammatik.

By default, Grammatik checks the entire document. If you want to check only a portion of the document, click the **Check** drop-down list arrow and select an option.

Depending on the type of document you are working on, you might want to use a different set of grammatical rules to check your document. Grammatik offers 11 predefined checking styles, and if you're really motivated, you can create your own.

By default, Grammatik uses the Quick Check style to check your documents. It's pretty simple to switch to one of the other checking styles.

> **note**
> Because Spell Checker is integrated into Grammatik, when you run Grammatik, you will also correct errors found by Spell Checker.

To select a different checking style

1. Choose **Tools**, **Grammatik** to open the Writing Tools dialog box. If you are prompted that the Grammar check is complete, answer **No** so that you don't close the Grammatik dialog box.
2. In the Grammatik tab, choose **Options**, **Checking Styles** to display the Checking Styles dialog box (see Figure 6.5).

FIGURE 6.5
Choose from one of the 11 predefined checking styles in the Checking Styles dialog box.

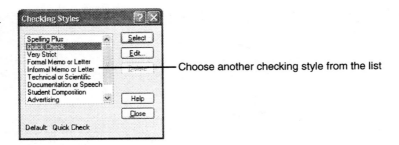

Choose another checking style from the list

3. To choose a checking style, select it in the list, and then click **Select**. Checking styles remain in effect until you choose another.

Looking Up Words in the Thesaurus

A thesaurus helps you find just the right word to describe something. Some concepts are more complex than others, and ideas can be expressed in a number of ways. Using the right words enables you to convey exactly the message you want to the reader.

WordPerfect's Thesaurus looks up synonyms (that is, words with similar meanings), antonyms (words with opposite meanings), and related words. You can start the Thesaurus from a blank screen, but if you click on a word first, the Thesaurus looks up that word.

> **tip**
>
> You can edit the built-in checking styles or create your own custom styles. Simply select a style and choose **Edit**. You will be taken to a dialog box where you can turn rule classes on and off, adjust thresholds, and change the formality level. You can then save that style under a new name, or save the changes, keeping the same name.

To look up a word in the Thesaurus

1. Choose **Tools**, **Thesaurus** (**Alt+F1**) or, if you already have the Writing Tools dialog box open, click the **Thesaurus** tab. The Thesaurus looks up the word and displays a list of synonyms by default and, if available, a list of antonyms and related words (see Figure 6.6).

2. Choose from the following options to look up words in the Thesaurus:

   - If you selected a word in step 1, the Thesaurus looks up the word and displays the results in the window. Otherwise, you need to type the word you want to look up in the text box and then click **Look Up**.

   - To see a list of words within a category, double-click the category or click the plus sign in the box. The left and right arrows on your keyboard can also be used to open and close categories.

CHAPTER 6 USING THE WRITING TOOLS   99

■ To look up one of the words in the list, double-click the word. A new window opens up for that word. If you double-click a word in the second window, a third window opens. When you fill up three windows, more windows are created (to the right). Click the scroll arrows to move one window to the left or right (see Figure 6.7).

FIGURE 6.6
The Thesaurus helps you improve your writing by showing you alternative words to use.

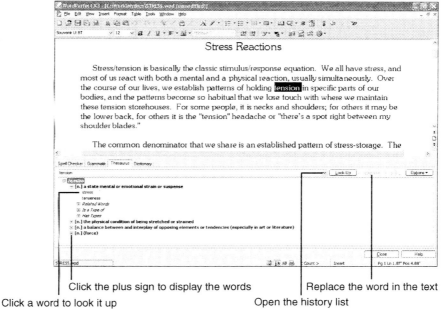

Click the plus sign to display the words
Click a word to look it up
Replace the word in the text
Open the history list

FIGURE 6.7
If you fill up more than three windows, use the scroll arrows to move back and forth in the windows.

Move one window to the right
Move one window to the left

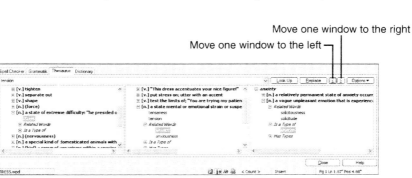

- To replace the word in the document with the word from the Thesaurus, select the word, and then click **Replace**.

- If you change your mind about replacing a word, click the **Undo** button, or choose **Edit**, **Undo** (in the document window) to reverse the change.
- The Thesaurus has a history list, so you can jump back to a word that you typed in and looked up earlier. Click the drop-down list arrow next to the **Look Up** button to select from the history list.

Using the Dictionary

WordPerfect X3 includes an integrated version of the *Oxford English Pocket Dictionary*, which contains more than 30,000 words. You can look up the definition of a selected word in your document, or you can just type in a word.

To look up a word in the Dictionary

1. Select the word in your document.
2. Choose **Tools**, **Dictionary** (**Alt+Ctrl+F1**). Or, if you already have the Writing Tools dialog box open, click the **Dictionary** tab to display the Dictionary dialog box (see Figure 6.8).

FIGURE 6.8
The built-in *Oxford English Pocket Dictionary* contains definitions for more than 30,000 words.

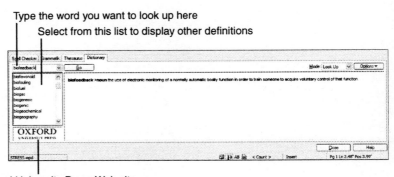

With a printed dictionary, you need to have *some* idea of how to spell the word, or you won't be able to find it. The beauty of an electronic dictionary is that you can locate words by searching through the definitions. For example, you can locate all the terms that have the word "flower" in the definition. Also, if you know how to spell a part of the word, you have a much greater chance of locating it with an electronic search.

To search through the dictionary

1. With the Dictionary dialog box displayed, open the **Mode** drop-down list and click **Search**.
2. Type the word that you want to search for in the text box underneath the writing tools tabs.
3. Click **Go**. A list of terms that contain the search word in the definition appears in the window (see Figure 6.9).

The built-in *Oxford English Pocket Dictionary* can be upgraded to the *Oxford English Concise Dictionary*, which contains 70,000 definitions. The **Upgrade** option on the **Options** menu takes you to the Corel store, where you can download the upgrade for a small fee.

FIGURE 6.9
With an electronic version of a dictionary, it's simple to locate words by searching through their definitions.

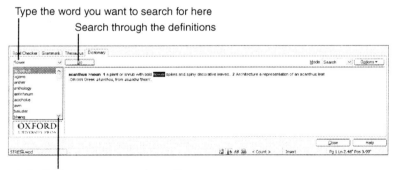

Type the word you want to search for here
Search through the definitions
Scroll down through the list to see more search results

Switching to a Different Language

We are truly working in a global marketplace. It's not unusual to carry on business with companies located all across the globe. When you correspond in a different language, you must be able to do more than just enter, display, and print the non-English characters. You also must be able to correct spelling, check grammar, and look up terms in the Thesaurus in addition to using the proper date conventions and currency symbols. WordPerfect supports multiple languages in three ways:

- You can mark sections of a document as being in one of the more than 30 languages supported by WordPerfect. Additional language modules can be installed that support the Spell Checker, Grammatik, Thesaurus, Dictionary, and Hyphenation.

- A Language Resource File (LRS file), which comes with the program and each language module, contains the information for formatting numbers and footnote-continued messages, among other things. You can edit this file to customize these options.

- You can purchase WordPerfect in a different language so that the menus, prompts, messages, dictionaries, and thesauri are all in that language.

To switch to a different language

1. If you want to mark only a section of text, select it first. Otherwise, click in the text where you want to switch to a different language.
2. Choose **Tools**, **Language**, **Settings**. The Language dialog box appears, with a list of available language modules (see Figure 6.10).
3. Scroll through the list and double-click the language you want.

FIGURE 6.10
You can disable the writing tools for sections of text that need to be checked in a different language.

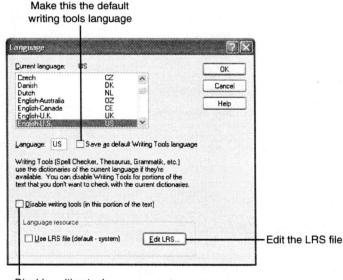

Make this the default writing tools language

Edit the LRS file

Disable writing tools

If you frequently switch back and forth between languages, you will love this feature. You can display the current language in the application bar. Right-click the application bar (at the bottom of the screen) and click **Settings**. Scroll down through the list, enable the check box next to **Language**, and click **OK**. A new Language button appears on the far-right side of the application bar. Click this button to open the Language dialog box, where you can choose another language.

You can switch to a different language when you're using any of the writing tools. In the Spell Checker, Grammatik, or the Thesaurus, choose **Options**, **Language** to open the Select Language dialog box (see Figure 6.11).

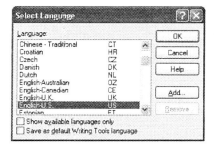

FIGURE 6.11
Use the Select Language dialog box to switch to a different language when you're using the writing tools.

Click **Show Available Languages Only** to display only those languages supported by the current writing tool. Select the language you want. Click **Save as Default Writing Tools Language** if you want the setting to be permanent. If you purchase additional language modules, you can add them in the Select Language dialog box. Click the **Add** button to add a language. Choose **OK** when you are finished.

Searching and Replacing Text and Codes

The Find feature can locate a snippet of text, or a specific code in your document, in just a few seconds. The Replace feature takes the process a step further by allowing you to substitute something else for the search item.

Here's an example of how you might use the Replace feature with Find: Let's say that you accidentally misspelled someone's name throughout a long document. You can search for all occurrences and replace them with the correct spelling. The same thing goes for codes. If you decide you want to search for a particular font and replace it with another one, you can do it with Find and Replace by searching for the code of the unwanted font and replacing it with the code of the desired font.

Searching for Text

Searching for text is fairly straightforward. You can do broad searches by searching for the first several characters in a word, or you can be very specific by searching for a particular sentence or phrase.

For the most part, I use Find to locate a particular word or phrase to quickly jump to the section of text that I need to work on. It's faster than scrolling through a document to find the place where I need to start. With that said, don't underestimate the Replace side of the Find and Replace feature. When it comes to making a global change throughout a document, nothing beats it for speed and accuracy.

To search for (and replace) text

1. Choose **Edit**, **Find and Replace** (**F2**) to open the Find and Replace dialog box (see Figure 6.12).

FIGURE 6.12
With Find and Replace, you can quickly locate a section of text and, optionally, replace it with something else.

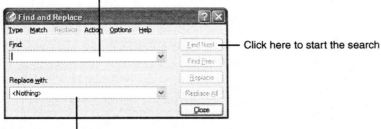

Type the text you want to search for here

Click here to start the search

Type the replacement text here

2. Type the text you want to search for in the **Find** text box. This might be a complete or partial word, phrase, or number.
3. (Optional) Type the replacement text in the **Replace with** text box. The replacement text must be exact because it will be inserted in the document exactly as it appears in the text box.
4. Click **Find Next** to start the search.

If you want to delete selected instances of the search text, leave <Nothing> in the **Replace with** text box (or leave it blank). As you go through the search, you can selectively replace the search text with nothing, deleting it from the document.

When WordPerfect locates the search text, you have the following options:

- Click **Find Next** to continue the search.
- Click **Find Prev** to move back to the previous instance.
- Click **Replace** to replace the search text with the replacement text.
- Click **Replace All** to replace all the rest of the occurrences without further confirmation from you.
- Click **Close** if you're just using Find to locate your place in a document and you want to get to work.

If you've already closed the Find and Replace dialog box, but you need to continue searching, you can use two shortcuts. Press **Ctrl+Alt+N** to find the next occurrence and **Ctrl+Alt+P** to find the previous occurrence. You also can use the QuickFind buttons on the property bar to move to the next or previous instance of the search text.

Searching for Codes

You can extend a search into the document codes to locate a particular code so that you can either edit or delete it. It's much faster and more accurate to let WordPerfect do the searching.

To search for a code

1. Choose **Edit**, **Find and Replace** (**F2**) to open the Find and Replace dialog box.
2. Choose **Match**, **Codes** from the menu in the Find and Replace dialog box. This opens the Codes dialog box (see Figure 6.13).

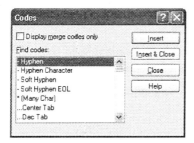

FIGURE 6.13
Using Find and Replace, you can search for virtually any code in a document.

3. When you find the code you want to search for, select it and click **Insert & Close**.
4. Click **Find Next**. When WordPerfect stops, close the Find and Replace dialog box and then turn on **Reveal Codes** (**View**, **Reveal Codes**). The insertion point will be positioned right after the code.
5. At this point, you can either delete or edit the code:
   - To delete the code, press **Backspace** or click and drag it out of the Reveal Codes window.
   - To edit a code, double-click it.

You can also use Find and Replace to replace a certain code with another one. For example, if you often work with converted documents, Find and Replace can be your best friend. After you identify the codes you want to get rid of, you can search for the codes and delete them. Some documents are so poorly formatted that it's quicker to clean out the codes and start over. Although this might take numerous find and replace operations, it's still faster than manually deleting each code.

To find and replace a code

1. Repeat the preceding steps 1–3.
2. Select the **Replace with** text box.

3. Choose **Replace, Codes**. The same Codes dialog box from Figure 6.13 opens. This time, only the codes that can replace the code you are searching for are available. All the others are grayed out. For example, you can't replace a Center Tab code with a Date Format code.

4. When you find the code you want, select it and then click **Insert & Close**.

5. Click **Find Next**. When WordPerfect stops, click **Replace** to replace this code and move on to the next one; click **Replace All** to replace the rest of the codes without further confirmation.

> **tip**
>
> You might not have thought of this yet, but you can combine text and codes in the **Find** text box to look for text followed (or preceded) by a certain code.

I mentioned earlier that you could search for a specific font and replace it with another. This is an example of searching for codes with a specific setting. Margin codes also have specific settings, as do line spacing and styles.

To find and replace codes with specific settings

1. Choose **Edit, Find and Replace**, or press **F2** to open the Find and Replace dialog box.

2. Choose **Type, Specific Codes** to open the Specific Codes dialog box (see Figure 6.14).

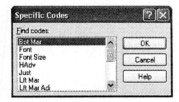

FIGURE 6.14
To search for a code with a specific setting, select the code from the Specific Codes dialog box.

3. Select a code from the list and click **OK**. Based on your selection, a modified Find and Replace dialog box appears with options for you to select the setting that you are searching for. Figure 6.15 shows the dialog box you get after choosing the Font code.

FIGURE 6.15

When you select Font from the Specific Codes dialog box, you get a Find and Replace Font dialog box.

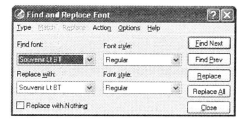

4. Use the Find and Replace Font dialog box options to specify exactly what you want to find (and replace). For example, you could search for Arial Bold and replace it with Tahoma, or you could search for all the 14-point text and replace it with 16-point text. The possibilities are endless.

5. Click **Find Next** to start the search.

> **tip**
>
> In the modified Find and Replace dialog box, put a check mark in the **Replace with Nothing** check box if you want to replace the code with nothing, thus deleting it from the document.

Discovering the Power of QuickCorrect

The QuickCorrect feature is designed to correct common mistakes automatically, without any intervention from you. QuickCorrect cleans up extra spaces between words, fixes capitalization errors, corrects common spelling mistakes and typos, inserts special symbols, and replaces regular straight quotation marks with typeset-quality curly quotation marks. It also helps you create graphic lines, bulleted lists, ordinal numbers, hyperlinks to Internet or intranet addresses, files on your network, or files on a local hard drive. QuickCorrect has a lot to offer, so take a few minutes and learn what it can do for you.

Choose **Tools**, **QuickCorrect** to open the QuickCorrect dialog box (see Figure 6.16). Tabs exist for all the different features that fall under the QuickCorrect umbrella.

FIGURE 6.16
In the QuickCorrect dialog box, you can add, delete, and edit the QuickCorrect entries. You also can disable QuickCorrect so that it won't correct words while you type.

Default QuickCorrect entries

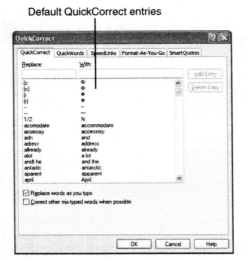

Adding and Deleting QuickCorrect Entries

QuickCorrect comes with a long list of frequently misspelled words and typos. After you add your own common typing mistakes to the QuickCorrect list, you will spend a lot less time proofing your documents.

To add words or phrases to QuickCorrect

1. Choose **Tools**, **QuickCorrect** to open the QuickCorrect dialog box.
2. Type the word or phrase that you frequently type incorrectly in the **Replace** text box.
3. Type the replacement word or phrase in the **With** text box (see Figure 6.17).
4. Click **Add Entry**.

If you would prefer not to use the QuickCorrect feature, you can turn it off completely. Choose **Tools**, **QuickCorrect**, and deselect the **Replace Words as You Type** check box (that is, remove the check mark).

> **tip**
> Think of ways you can use QuickCorrect to insert long or hard-to-type words when you type a few characters. For example, you could add an entry to replace "wpo13" with "WordPerfect Office X3" or "pab7" with "7th period Pre-AP Biology."

A better solution might be to remove the entries that you don't like so that you can continue to take advantage of those that are helpful. To remove an entry, select it in the list and click **Delete Entry**, **Yes**.

FIGURE 6.17
You can add your frequent misspellings and typos to the QuickCorrect list and let WordPerfect fix your mistakes automatically.

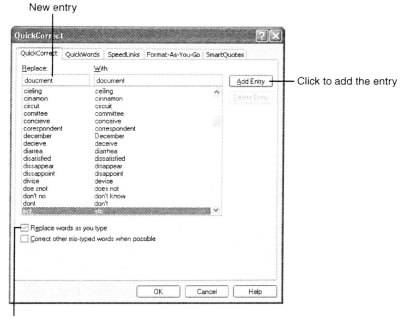

Customizing Format-As-You-Go

The Format-As-You-Go feature is designed to keep sentence structure accurate by cleaning up extra spaces and incorrect capitalization. There also are shortcuts for creating lists, graphic lines, ordinal numbers, and symbols.

To customize the Format-As-You-Go feature

1. Choose **Tools**, **QuickCorrect** to open the QuickCorrect dialog box.
2. Click the **Format-As-You-Go** tab. By default, all the options in the Sentence corrections section are selected, and End of Sentence Corrections is set to None (see Figure 6.18).

In addition to the sentence structure corrections, Format-As-You-Go has a variety of shortcuts for creating lists, lines, and ordinal numbers. A check mark in the box indicates that a tool is enabled. You can turn these tools on and off by enabling (add check mark) and disabling (remove check mark) the check boxes.

FIGURE 6.18
The Format-As-You-Go feature has six different tools to help you quickly create bulleted lists, graphic lines, ordinal numbers, en dashes, and em dashes.

Select from the following options:

- **CapsFix**—Fixes problems with capitalization when Caps Lock is on by mistake and you hold down the Shift key to capitalize the first letter (such as tHIS). CapsFix works only if Caps Lock is on.

- **QuickBullets**—Helps you quickly create bulleted lists. To quickly create a bulleted list or numbered list, you simply type a letter, number, or bullet character, followed by a Tab. Search for "QuickBullets" in the Help topics for a list of bullet characters.

- **QuickIndent**—Pressing **Tab** at the beginning of the first and second lines of a paragraph creates a left indent for that paragraph.

- **QuickLines**—Typing four dashes and then pressing **Enter** creates a single horizontal line from the left to the right margin; typing four equal signs and then pressing **Enter** creates a double horizontal line from the left to the right margin.

- **QuickOrdinals**—Typing ordinal text after a number converts the ordinal text to superscript when you press the spacebar. As a reminder, superscript text is smaller and set higher than the adjacent text.

- **QuickSymbols**—Typing two hyphens followed by a space inserts an en dash; typing three hyphens followed by a space inserts an em dash.

> **caution**
> The QuickBullets feature can be a problem for some users. Not everyone wants a numbered list turned into a code-oriented automatically updated numbered list! It's easy enough to turn off, though—just remove the check mark next to it.

Inserting SpeedLinks

The SpeedLinks feature is designed to automatically generate a hyperlink whenever you type the beginning of an Internet address, such as www, ftp, http, or mailto. You can then give that hyperlink a friendlier name. For example, when you type the URL **http://support.corel.com**, SpeedLinks creates the hyperlink to the Web page. This also works for email addresses such as *yourname@isp.com*.

To create SpeedLinks

1. Choose **Tools**, **QuickCorrect**; then click the **SpeedLinks** tab to display the SpeedLink options (see Figure 6.19).
2. Type the friendlier name that you want to use to activate the hyperlink in the **Link Word** text box (the @ symbol is inserted automatically).
3. Type the location to link it to in the **Location to Link to** text box. If necessary, click the **Files** icon to browse your system (or the network) and select a drive, folder, or file.

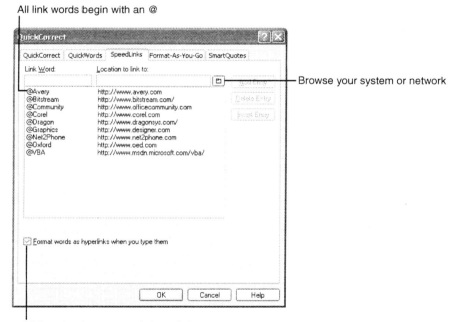

FIGURE 6.19
Using SpeedLinks, you can create a link word that automatically creates a hyperlink to a Web page, email address, document, folder, or drive.

To insert a SpeedLinks entry in a document, type the @ symbol followed by the link word. When you press the spacebar or Enter, WordPerfect creates the hyperlink for you.

Creating QuickWord Entries

As you can see, QuickCorrect is really a collection of powerful features that help you automate your repetitive tasks. The QuickWords feature, which lets you insert frequently used text or graphics (such as a signature block or a logo) with just a few keystrokes, is the hidden jewel of QuickCorrect tools. If you are involved in heavy document production (and who isn't?), you really need to take a look at this time-saving feature.

Here's how it works:

- You assign an abbreviation to a word or phrase.
- You use the abbreviation when typing the document.
- You expand the abbreviation(s) either as you type or all at once.

QuickWords aren't limited to words or phrases. You can create QuickWord text that includes formatting codes, such as font attributes, or graphics that you would use for logos.

You can assign entire paragraphs to a QuickWords entry and then use them to quickly build documents that consist of form paragraphs (such as wills, leases, contracts, and so on).

To create a QuickWord entry

1. Select the text or graphic you want to assign to QuickWords. If you want to insert a graphic or logo with a QuickWords entry, turn on Reveal Codes and position the red cursor to the left of the box code. Press **Shift+→** to select the box code.
2. Choose **Tools**, **QuickWords** to display the **QuickWords** tab of the QuickCorrect dialog box (see Figure 6.20).
3. Type the abbreviation you want to use in the **Abbreviated Form** text box. The abbreviation can be a few letters or a one- or two-word phrase.
4. Click **Add Entry**.

caution

Be sure you use words that won't normally come up in your documents for QuickWords abbreviations. For example, you could use "compadd" to expand your company address, "clogo" for the company logo, or "sigblock" for your signature block. If you accidentally use a word or phrase that comes up naturally, QuickWords will expand the abbreviation and insert information in the wrong places.

FIGURE 6.20
With QuickWords, you can assign an abbreviation to text or graphics, and then simply type the abbreviation to insert it into a document.

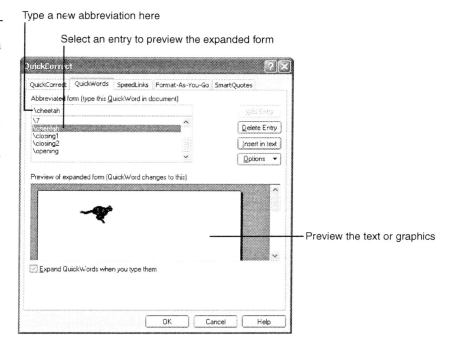

Use one of the following methods to insert QuickWords in a document:

- Type the abbreviation; then press the **spacebar**, **Tab**, or **Enter** key. If this method doesn't work, the **Expand QuickWords When You Type Them** option (in the QuickWords tab of the QuickCorrect dialog box) has been disabled. You can manually expand a QuickWord by pressing **Ctrl+Shift+A**.
- Open the QuickWords dialog box, select a QuickWord from the list, and then click **Insert in Text**.

It's easy to update a QuickWords entry when the form text changes (in the case of form paragraphs) or if you want to insert a different graphic image with a certain QuickWords entry.

To replace a QuickWords entry

1. Select the text or graphic.
2. Choose **Tools**, **QuickWords**.
3. From the list, select the QuickWords entry that you want to assign to the selected text or graphic.
4. Click the **Options** button and click **Replace Entry**.
5. Click **Yes** in the confirmation message box.

If you change the content of a QuickWord, it makes sense that you would want to assign a new QuickWord name.

To rename a QuickWord entry

1. Choose **Tools**, **QuickWords**.
2. Select the QuickWords entry.
3. Choose **Options**, **Rename Entry**.
4. Type the new name, then click **OK**.

Every now and then, it's a good idea to go through the QuickWords entries and remove the ones you aren't using anymore.

To delete a QuickWords entry

1. Choose **Tools**, **QuickWords**.
2. Select the QuickWords entry.
3. Click **Delete Entry**.

If you're creating a QuickWords entry for a graphic image, be sure that **Expand As Text with Formatting** is selected on the **Options** menu. Otherwise, the graphic won't appear in the document.

Finally, you can turn off QuickWords if you don't want to expand the QuickWords as you type. In the QuickWords dialog box, deselect **Expand QuickWords When You Type Them**.

The Absolute Minimum

This chapter focused on the features that help support the job of writing material.

- You learned how to check your documents for spelling and grammatical errors.
- You saw how fast and easy it is to use an electronic Thesaurus and Dictionary.
- Searching and replacing text or codes can save you from long hours of repetitive editing.
- You saw how to incorporate text in other languages into your documents.
- You learned how to take advantage of all the tools in the QuickCorrect collection.

In the next section of the book, you will learn how to make your document look nice through a variety of formatting options.

PART II

Making It Look Nice

Working with Paragraphs 117

Working with Pages 133

Using Styles for Consistency 155

IN THIS CHAPTER

- Learn how to use center and flush right to align text.
- Use the Justification feature to align paragraphs.
- Learn how to work with tabs and how to indent text.
- Adjust the spacing between lines and paragraphs to make long passages of text easier to read.

WORKING WITH PARAGRAPHS

This is the first in a series of three chapters on formatting documents. This chapter covers formatting paragraphs, the second covers formatting pages, and the third explains how to use styles for consistent formatting.

Because this chapter discusses how to format paragraphs, now is a good time to clarify the definition of a paragraph as WordPerfect sees it. At first glance, you might think of a paragraph as several lines of text all together in one chunk. You're right—that is a paragraph, but so is a single line. In fact, anything that ends with a hard return is considered to be a paragraph. (As a reminder, a hard return is inserted into the document each time you press the Enter key.) The hard return ends the current line and moves the insertion point down to the next line.

Aligning Text

One of the most common formatting tasks is centering a line of text. When you center text on a line, WordPerfect does the math and makes sure there is an equal amount of space on either side of the text. If you add or remove text, WordPerfect automatically adjusts the position of the text so that it is at the exact center of the page. Flush right is a little less common, but it still has an important place, especially in legal documents. Text that is flush right is aligned against the right margin, so it extends out to the left.

The Justification feature is also used to align text. In addition to Center and Flush Right, you can also justify text so that the left and right margins are smooth. Justification is used in situations in which a series of paragraphs needs to be aligned to either the left margin, the right margin, or both margins (full justification).

Using Center and Flush Right

When you issue the command to center or flush right text, the command works for only a single line. Pressing Enter after you type the text turns Center or Flush Right off, so the next line is aligned against the left margin. For this reason, the Center and Flush Right commands are well suited for aligning one or two lines at a time. If you need to align multiple lines or several paragraphs, you're better off using the Justification feature, which is discussed next.

- To center a line of text, press **Shift+F7** and type the text. If you've already typed the text, click at the beginning of the line, and then press **Shift+F7**.
- To align text against the right margin (flush right), press **Alt+F7**, and then type the text. If you've already typed the text, click at the beginning of the line, and then press **Alt+F7**.
- To center or flush right more than one line of existing text, select the text first; then press **Shift+F7** for center or **Alt+F7** for flush right.

You can also find Center and Flush Right commands in the menus. Choose **Format**, **Line** (see Figure 7.1). Note the keyboard shortcuts listed next to the commands on the menu.

FIGURE 7.1
The Line menu has commands to make lines of text centered and flush right.

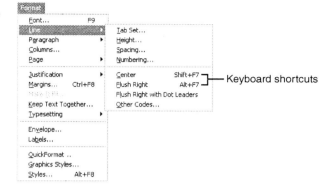

Justifying Text

Justification controls how text flows between the left and right margins. The Justification feature continues to center or flush right text, even after you press Enter. For this reason, it's a better choice when you need to align multiple paragraphs. To use Justification, turn it on at a specific point in the document. It stays in effect until the end of the document or until you switch to a different justification setting.

The default setting in WordPerfect is left justification, which creates a smooth left margin and a ragged right margin. The result is an open, informal appearance that is accessible and easy to read. For that reason, this book has been formatted with left justification.

There are four other justification options that you might be interested in, especially if you work with columns, newsletters, and formal documents (see Figure 7.2).

What's the difference between Center and Justify Center? When you change the justification to Center, every line you create from then on is centered, until you change the justification to something else. This works great for title pages, where you have an entire page of centered text. It's not the most efficient option for one or two lines. In this situation, the Center feature is the best choice.

FIGURE 7.2
This sample document illustrates the different justification settings.

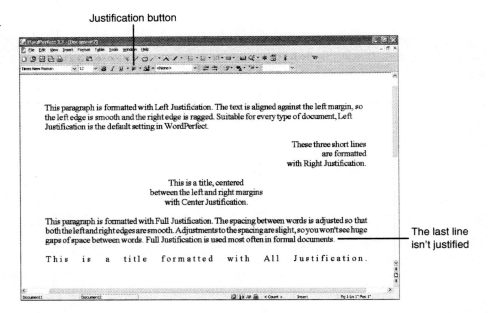

WordPerfect offers the following justification options:

- **Left**—Text is aligned against the left margin so that the left margin is smooth and the right is ragged. It's suitable for almost every type of document, especially those with long passages of text. To apply left justification, choose **Format**, **Justification**, **Left** (**Ctrl+L**).

- **Right**—Text is aligned against the right margin so that the right side is smooth and the left is ragged. The unique placement draws attention, but because it's difficult to read, you might not want to use it on more than three or four lines unless you are using it to align a column of numbers. To apply right justification, choose **Format**, **Justification**, **Right** (**Ctrl+R**).

- **Center**—Text is centered between the left and right margins. Headings in contracts and other legal documents often are formatted using center justification. To apply center justification, choose **Format**, **Justification**, **Center** (**Ctrl+E**).

- **Full**—Text is aligned against the left and right margins, so both edges are smooth. Full justification gives documents a more formal and organized appearance. To apply full justification, choose **Format**, **Justification**, **Full**, or press **Ctrl+J**.

- **All**—This type of justification stretches lines of text between the left and right margins, regardless of their length. Whereas full justification adjusts the spacing between words, all justification adjusts the spacing between letters as well. This setting is used for letterhead, informal titles and headings, custom documents such as theater playbills, and special effects. To apply all justification, choose **Format**, **Justification**, **All**.

Before you choose which type of justification you want to use in your document, decide where you want the justification to take effect and then move the insertion point there. This might be at the top of the document, the top of a column, or the beginning of a paragraph. If you want to apply justification to a section of text, such as a multi-line title, select the text first.

Instead of using the menus, you can click the **Justification** button on the property bar and then choose the justification setting from the pop-up list. This method offers an advantage over the others in that you get a RealTime Preview of each justification setting when you hover over it.

You might be wondering how full justification (a smooth left and right margin) is accomplished. WordPerfect makes slight adjustments to the spacing between words so that each line extends from the left to the right margin. Adjustments to the spacing are slight, so you won't see huge gaps of space between words as you can with all justification.

Setting Tabs

Tabs may be one of the most misunderstood features in a word processor. Most of us press the Tab key without really thinking about it. We want to move over a bit, and Tab does that for us. What most people don't realize is that there is a lot more to the Tab feature than moving over a little. You can set specific tabs that simplify the process of typing text in columns. Four different types of tabs control how the text is placed at the tab setting. They are

- **Left Align**—Text flows from the right side of the tab stop. This is the "normal" tab.
- **Center**—Text is centered over the tab stop.
- **Right Align**—Text flows from the left side of the tab stop.
- **Decimal Align**—The numbers are aligned on their decimal points, which rest on the tab stop. You can change the alignment character to something other than a period (decimal point).

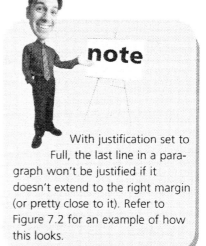

With justification set to Full, the last line in a paragraph won't be justified if it doesn't extend to the right margin (or pretty close to it). Refer to Figure 7.2 for an example of how this looks.

FIGURE 7.3
Using the ruler, you can set all types of tabs with just a few mouse clicks.

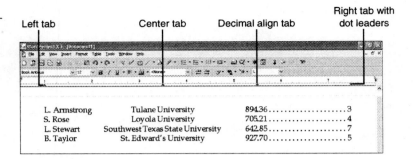

Turning on the Ruler

If you don't see the ruler at the top of the screen, turn it on by choosing **View**, **Ruler**. The default tab settings (every 1/2 inch) are shown with triangles in the tab area of the ruler (see Figure 7.4). The gray area identifies the margin area; the white area is the text area.

Clearing the Default Tabs

In most cases, you want to clear the default tabs before you create tabs at specific settings. This way, you don't have to move past the default tabs—you can go straight to the specific tabs that you set.

To clear all tabs

1. Right-click in the tab area of the ruler (refer to Figure 7.3) or right-click any tab marker to open the Tab QuickMenu (see Figure 7.5).
2. Click **Clear All Tabs** to delete the default tabs.

note You can add dot leaders to each of the four tab types. Dot leaders are useful when the space between columns is wide because they help the reader's eye travel across the gap. They are especially useful when preparing a table of contents.

FIGURE 7.4
Using the ruler, you can set all types of tabs with just a few mouse clicks.

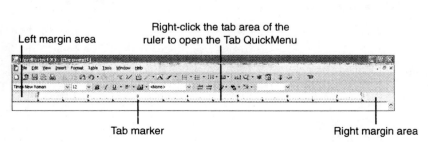

FIGURE 7.5
Using the Tab QuickMenu, you can clear the default tabs, set specific types of tabs, and return to the default settings.

Setting New Tabs

Setting new tabs is fast and easy. All you have to do is click on the ruler where you want a tab to be, and voilà!

To set a new tab

1. Click in the tab area of the ruler, in the place where you want to create a tab. (This inserts the default tab, which is a left-aligned tab.)
2. If you change your mind and you want to remove a tab, simply click and drag it off the ruler.

Changing the Tab Type

When you change the tab type, it stays selected until you select another tab type. So, if you change the tab type to Decimal, every time you click on the ruler, you will set a decimal tab.

To change the tab type

1. Right-click the tab marker to open the QuickMenu.
2. Choose a tab type from the QuickMenu.
3. Click on the ruler where you want to set the tab.

Editing Tab Settings

When you set a tab (or modify the default tab settings in any way), a margin icon appears in the left margin area (refer to Figure 7.5). Click the margin icon to display a tab bar, which shows the tab settings for the current paragraph. You can make changes to the tabs on the tab bar using the same methods that you use for the ruler. When you're finished, click anywhere in the document window to close the tab bar.

After you've typed the text, you might decide to move things around a bit. Good news! You don't have to delete a tab and then create a new one—you can just move it instead. Before you do, select the tabbed text. That way, your changes will be applied to all the tabbed text, not just to the tabbed text after the insertion point.

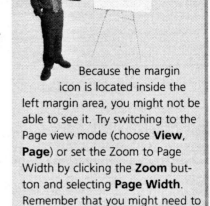

note

Because the margin icon is located inside the left margin area, you might not be able to see it. Try switching to the Page view mode (choose **View, Page**) or set the Zoom to Page Width by clicking the **Zoom** button and selecting **Page Width**. Remember that you might need to use the horizontal scrollbar to scroll over to the left.

To move a tab

1. Select the tabbed text.
2. Click and drag the tab marker (on the ruler or on the tab bar). When you do, a bubble appears, telling you where the tab will fall when you release the mouse button, and a guideline appears in the text so that you can see the effect on existing text (see Figure 7.6).
3. When you're satisfied with the tab position, release the mouse button to drop the tab.

When you're ready to return to default tab settings (so you can use regular tabs and indent later in the document), right-click in the document where you want to make the change and choose **Default Tab Settings**.

This is a good time to bring the Tab Set dialog box to your attention. Everything you can do from the ruler and more is available in this dialog box. Right-click the ruler, and then choose **Tab Set** to open the Tab Set dialog box (see Figure 7.7). Alternatively, choose **Format, Line, Tab Set**.

caution

When you're working with tabs, it's important that you select the text you want to work with first. You need to be sure that you are creating new tab settings exactly where you want them so that they don't reformat the wrong text. Otherwise, some of the text is formatted with the original tab settings, and the rest of the text is formatted with the new tab settings. Believe me, it isn't pretty. This is where Undo comes in handy.

FIGURE 7.6
Even if you've already typed the text, you can freely move the tabs around. The guideline shows you where the text will be as you click and drag the tab.

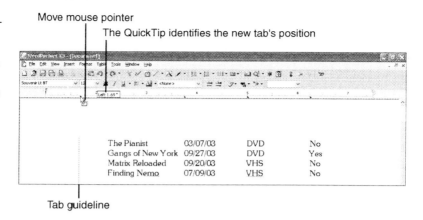

FIGURE 7.7
The Tab Set dialog box offers options that aren't available when you use the ruler.

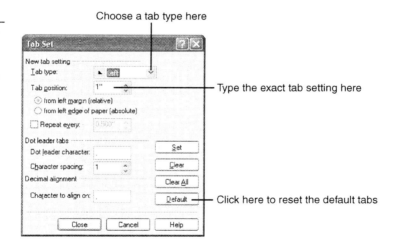

Indenting Text

Indentation is often used to set quotations apart from the rest of the text. It also is used to emphasize text or to place a paragraph in a subordinate position beneath another paragraph. When you create a bulleted or numbered list, WordPerfect inserts an Indent command after the bullet or number so that the text you type isn't aligned under the bullet or number, but rather under the first word of the text. For more information on creating bulleted or numbered lists, see Chapter 11, "Creating Lists and Outlines."

The four ways to indent text are as follows:

- **Indent** moves every line within a paragraph to the next tab setting (to the right). By default, this moves the text over 1/2 inch every time you choose Indent.
- **Double Indent** moves every paragraph line in from the left and right sides, to the next tab setting. By default, this indents the text by 1/2 inch on the left and 1/2 inch on the right.
- **Hanging Indent** leaves the first line at the left margin—all the other lines are indented (on the left side) by 1/2 inch.
- A **Back Tab** temporarily releases the left margin so that the first line of a paragraph starts at the tab setting inside the left margin; all other lines are aligned at the left margin.

> **caution**
> The Indent feature uses the tab settings to indent your text. Changing the default tab settings affects how text is indented. If you plan on indenting text and setting specific tabs in the same document, don't change the tabs at the top of the document. Change them just before you want to type the tabbed text. Then, after you've typed the text, restore the default tab settings.

To indent a new paragraph, choose **Format**, **Paragraph**, **Indent** (**F7**) and then type the text. Choose **Format**, **Paragraph**, **Double Indent** (**Shift+Ctrl+F7**) for a double indent or choose **Format**, **Paragraph**, **Hanging Indent** (**Ctrl+F7**) for a hanging indent (see Figure 7.8). As usual, if you've already typed the text, click in the paragraph before applying an indent style.

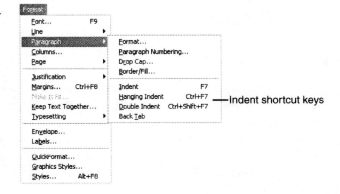

FIGURE 7.8
One of the Indent commands on the Paragraph menu, Back Tab, doesn't have a shortcut key assigned to it.

If QuickIndent is enabled, you can quickly indent paragraphs with the Tab key. Type the text first, and then press **Tab** at the beginning of the first *and* second lines. QuickIndent converts those tabs into an indent. You can also quickly create a hanging indent by pressing **Tab** at the beginning of any line *except* the first line in a paragraph.

To turn the QuickIndent feature on and off, choose **Tools**, **QuickCorrect**. Click the **Format-As-You-Go** tab, and then enable or disable the check box next to **QuickIndent** (in the list of Format-As-You-Go choices).

If you want the first line of every paragraph to be indented automatically (rather than pressing Tab each time), use the First Line Indent option.

To set a first-line indent

1. Choose **Format**, **Paragraph**, **Format** to open the Paragraph Format dialog box (see Figure 7.9).
2. Type the amount that you want the first line indented in the **First Line Indent** text box. (A tab indents the first line by 1/2 inch.)
3. Click **OK**. All new paragraphs from this point on will have the first line indented.
4. To remove a first-line indent, set the value back to 0 (zero) inches.

FIGURE 7.9
Type the value for the first-line indent in increments of inches. For example, 1/4 inch would be .25".

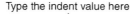
Type the indent value here

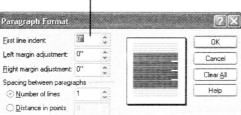

Adjusting the Spacing Between Lines and Paragraphs

As you might remember from Chapter 1, "Getting Started and Finding Help," the default line spacing setting is single-spacing. Some types of documents, such as manuscripts, grants, and formal reports, require a certain line-spacing setting for submission.

The accepted standard is to leave a blank line between paragraphs, so you just press Enter twice after you type a paragraph, right? That's not a problem—until you decide to change the line spacing to double. Now you've got the space of two lines between each paragraph. Furthermore, these extra lines leave space at the top of a page.

Making adjustments to the spacing between lines and paragraphs is another way to tailor your document to certain specifications and accepted standards.

Adjusting the Line Spacing

Let's say that you want to print out a document for someone else to review. You might consider changing to double- or triple-spacing so that person has room for writing comments. After you incorporate that person's changes, you just switch back to single-spacing.

To change line spacing

1. Click where you want the change to take effect (or select the text you want to change).
2. Choose **Format**, **Line**, **Spacing** to open the Line Spacing dialog box (see Figure 7.10).
3. Either type a value or click the spinner arrows to increase or decrease the value in the **Spacing** text box. Use 1 for single-spacing, 1.5 for one-and-a-half spacing, 2 for double-spacing, and so on.

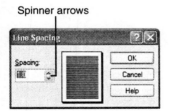

FIGURE 7.10
You can specify the number of blank lines you want between each line of text by typing the value or clicking the spinner arrows.

The new line-spacing setting takes effect at the beginning of the paragraph where the insertion point is resting, and it remains in effect throughout the rest of the document, or until you change the line spacing again.

Adjusting the Spacing Between Paragraphs

Rather than insert extra blank lines, you can adjust the spacing between paragraphs. This way, you always get the same amount of space between each paragraph (no matter what you do to the line spacing), and you don't have extra blank lines floating around.

To change the paragraph spacing setting

1. Click where you want the change to take effect.
2. Choose **Format**, **Paragraph**, **Format** to open the Paragraph Format dialog box (refer to Figure 7.9). In the **Spacing Between Paragraphs** section, you can enter the number of lines or the number of points that you want between each paragraph.
3. Either type the value or click the spinner arrows to increase or decrease the value.
4. Choose **OK** to close the dialog box.

> **note**
>
> Some documents might require more than one type of line spacing in them. For example, in a double-spaced document, you would typically switch to single-spacing for lists or quotations.

Keeping Text Together

As you create or revise a document, you never have to worry about running out of room. WordPerfect creates a new page for you as soon as you reach the bottom of the current page. It's so transparent that you probably don't even stop to think about it—that is, until you preview the document and realize that you have headings and paragraphs separated by a page break.

You can prevent this situation by identifying the text that should stay together when a page break is encountered. You can use three features to do this: Widow/Orphan Protection, Block Protect, and Conditional End of Page. Choose **Format**, **Keep Text Together** to display the Keep Text Together dialog box (see Figure 7.11).

FIGURE 7.11
The options in the Keep Text Together dialog box prevent important information from being separated by a page break.

Enabling Widow/Orphan Protection

Widow/Orphan Protection prevents a single line of a paragraph being left behind at the bottom of a page or getting pushed to the top of the next page. The first line of a paragraph that gets left behind at the bottom of a page is called an *orphan*. A *widow* is the last line of a paragraph that gets pushed to the top of a page.

To turn on Widow/Orphan Protection

1. Position the insertion point where you want Widow/Orphan Protection to start (usually at the top of the document).
2. Choose **Format**, **Keep Text Together** to open the Keep Text Together dialog box.
3. Enable the check box in the **Widow/Orphan** section.
4. Choose **OK** to close the dialog box.

Using Block Protect

Use the Block Protect feature when you want to keep a section of text together on the same page. As you edit the document, and the block moves near a page break, WordPerfect decides whether the block will fit on the current page. If it doesn't fit, the entire block gets moved to the top of the next page. Block Protect works well for keeping figures or tables and explanatory text together. You can also use it to protect numbered paragraphs, lists, and outlines.

To turn on Block Protect

1. Select the text (and figures or tables) that you want to keep together.
2. Choose **Format**, **Keep Text Together** to open the Keep Text Together dialog box.
3. Enable the **Keep Selected Text Together** check box.
4. Choose **OK** to close the dialog box.

caution
If you block protect large sections of text, you're likely to have big chunks of whitespace in the middle of your document.

Setting a Conditional End of Page

The Conditional End of Page feature keeps a certain number of lines together when a page break is encountered. You might use Conditional End of Page at the beginning of a heading so that you can specify how many lines of the following paragraph you want to keep with the heading.

To turn on Conditional End of Page

1. Position the insertion point at the beginning of the heading.
2. Choose **Format, Keep Text Together** to open the Keep Text Together dialog box.
3. Enable the **Number of Lines to Keep Together** check box.
4. In the text box, type the number of lines that you want to keep together. Count the heading line as one of the lines, and if there is a blank line between the heading and the paragraph, count that, too.
5. Choose **OK** to close the dialog box.

The Absolute Minimum

This chapter started a three-chapter series on formatting. The topics covered in this chapter focused on formatting lines and paragraphs.

- You learned how to center a line of text using the Center feature. You also learned how to align text against the right margin with the Flush Right command.
- The Justification feature was introduced, and you saw how to justify text so that both margins are smooth.
- You learned how to use tabs to format information in columns.
- You learned how to properly indent text for quotations and numbered lists.
- Adjusting the spacing between lines and paragraphs makes it easier to read long passages of text.
- You learned that it isn't "good form" to have headings separated from the text, or to have a single line at the top or the bottom of a page, or to have key pieces of information split between two pages. You saw how to use the WordPerfect features to keep text together.

In the next chapter, you will learn how to apply formatting to pages.

IN THIS CHAPTER

- Learn how to manually insert a page break to start on a new page.
- Switch to a different paper size or orientation.
- Learn how to subdivide a page into multiple sections.
- Discover how to include page numbers, headers, and footers in your documents.
- Use the Suppress and Delay Codes features to prevent certain page elements from printing.
- Add some punch with a plain or fancy border around a page.
- Use Make It Fit to shrink or expand a document into a certain number of pages.

WORKING WITH PAGES

In previous chapters, you learned how to format sections of selected text and paragraphs. This chapter deals with formatting that you apply to the entire page. Features such as headers and footers, page numbers, and borders are applied to a whole page, not just a section of a page.

In those situations in which you don't want these elements included on a page, you can use the Suppress and Delay Codes features. For example, you might want the title page included in the page count, but you don't want to print a page number at the bottom of the title page.

Inserting a Page Break

You've probably already noticed that WordPerfect creates a new page for you whenever you fill up the current one. It happens automatically, so you don't even have to think about it. However, there are situations when you want to create a new page even though you haven't filled up the current page. Title pages come to mind, and so do headings that you want to place at the beginning of a new page.

To create a new page, you insert a page break on the current page. This type of page break is known as a *hard page*. The new page that WordPerfect creates for you is called a *soft page*.

> **tip**
>
> In a long document, you might decide to precede a major section with a hard page break so that each section begins on a new page. If, during heavy revisions, these hard pages get moved around to the wrong places, use Find and Replace to quickly strip out all the hard page codes (or only the ones that you don't need anymore).

To insert a hard page break, press **Ctrl+Enter**. In Page view mode, you will see a gray space between the two pages (see Figure 8.1). In Draft view mode, a page break displays as a horizontal double line.

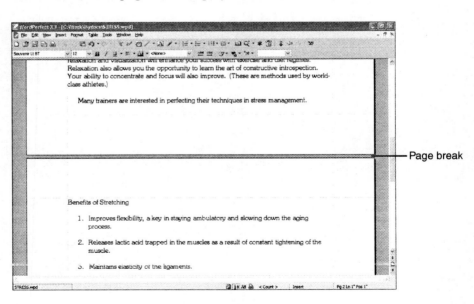

FIGURE 8.1
In Page view mode, a representation of the printed page is displayed, so you can see the space between pages.

When you insert a page break, a hard page code [HPg] is inserted in the document. To remove a page break, delete the [HPg] code using one of the following methods:

- Click at the end of the paragraph, just before a page break, and press **Delete**.
- In the Reveal Codes window, if the red cursor is to the left of a code, press **Delete**; if the red cursor is to the right of a code, press **Backspace**.
- You also can click and drag a code out of the Reveal Codes window to delete it.

Changing Paper Size and Orientation

By default, the paper size in the U.S. version of WordPerfect is 8 1/2 inches by 11 inches (other countries have different standards for paper size). Text is formatted in *portrait orientation*, which means that the paper is taller than it is wide. Think of a portrait photograph.

If you create only standard business documents, you might never switch to a different paper size. However, when you need to create an envelope, print on legal-size paper, or rotate a document to landscape orientation, you switch to a different paper size.

To change to a different paper size

1. Choose **Format**, **Page**, **Page Setup**, or choose **File**, **Page Setup**.
2. If necessary, click the **Page Setup** tab to display the paper sizes available for the current printer (see Figure 8.2).

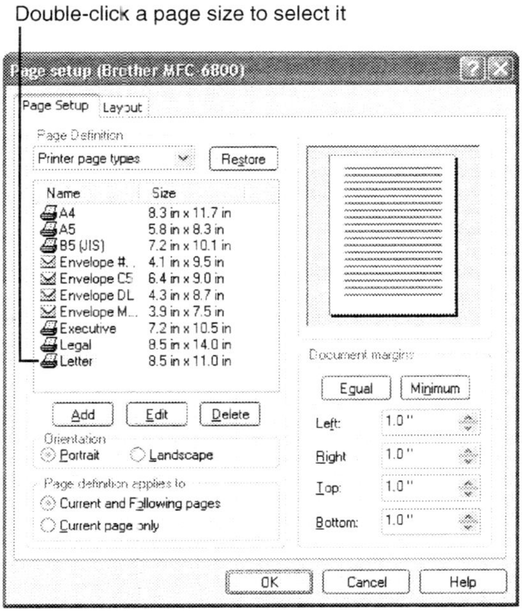

FIGURE 8.2
You can choose a different paper size or switch to a different orientation in the Page Setup dialog box.

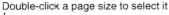
Double-click a page size to select it

3. Scroll down through the list of paper sizes and select a new paper size.
4. (Optional) If you want to rotate your text into a landscape orientation, click **Landscape**.
5. Select **Current Page Only** if you want to change the paper size only for the current page, or select **Current and Following Pages** to apply the change to the current page and the rest of the document.
6. Click **OK** when finished.

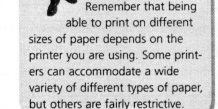

Remember that being able to print on different sizes of paper depends on the printer you are using. Some printers can accommodate a wide variety of different types of paper, but others are fairly restrictive.

Subdividing Pages

A single physical page can be subdivided into multiple logical pages. Let's say that you need to design some invitations to a reception, and you want to print four of them on an 8 1/2×11-inch piece of card stock. You would subdivide the page into four logical pages—each with a copy of the invitation. Another example might be a notice that you want to distribute to your child's classroom. I usually put two notices on a page so that I can quickly tuck the notice into their folders. In this case, you would divide the page in half, so you can place one notice on the top and one on the bottom.

The physical page maintains the original dimensions of the paper. Logical pages are pieces of the physical page, but they are still considered individual pages for purposes of page numbering. For example, if you subdivide a page into six logical pages and then turn on page numbering, the logical pages are numbered 1 through 6. The Labels feature uses the same concept to separate a sheet of paper into individual labels.

To subdivide a page

1. Choose **File**, **Page Setup** or **Format**, **Page**, **Page Setup**.
2. Click the **Layout** tab, and then take a look at the Divide page section (see Figure 8.3).

FIGURE 8.3
By default, the number of columns and rows is set to 1.

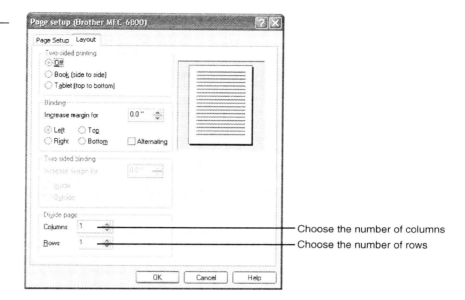

3. Choose the number of columns and rows by either typing in the number or clicking the spinner arrows. The sample page illustrates how the paper will be subdivided.
4. Before you click **OK**, click the **Page Setup** tab and look at the margin settings. WordPerfect uses the current margins for each logical page, so if you keep the default 1-inch margins, you will have a 1-inch border around each logical page that you won't be able to use. That's a lot of wasted space.
5. Click the **Minimum** button to quickly set the margins to the minimum allowed by your printer.
6. Click **OK**. Figure 8.4 shows the first logical page in a subdivided page. To move to the next page, press **Ctrl+Enter**.

> **tip**
> If you are creating invitations or announcements, it's common practice to center the text on the page. Because each section is a logical page, you format it just as if it were a full-size page. Click in the logical page that you want to center and then choose **Format**, **Page**, **Center**. Choose **Current Page** if you want to center only the current page, or choose **Current and Subsequent Pages** to center all the pages from this point forward.

FIGURE 8.4
Each logical page can be formatted as a separate page. In this example, a total of three logical pages are in one physical page.

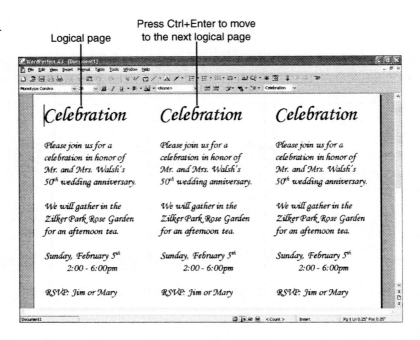

When you divide the current page, it affects all following pages in the document. To switch back to a single physical page, you will have to go back into the Page Setup dialog box and set the rows and columns back to 1. Be sure the insertion point is at the top of the page that you want to switch back to, or you might accidentally revert a subdivided page back to a single physical page. If this happens, each subdivided page becomes a physical page, so you won't lose your text; it just gets spread out. Choose **Undo** to get things back the way they were.

To go back to a single physical page

1. Choose **File**, **Page Setup**.
2. Click the **Layout** tab.
3. Choose **1** in the Columns text box and **1** in the Rows text box.
4. Click **OK**.

Adding Page Numbers

Page numbers should be used on virtually every document longer than 4–5 pages. Page numbers help us keep our places when we are reading, not to mention saving our reputations when we drop a stack of printouts on the office floor.

WordPerfect's page number feature has some depth to it. You can start by inserting page numbers at the bottom of every page and progress to creating customized page numbers using chapter and volume numbers. This book covers most of the page numbering features, but if you want more information on the complex uses for page numbering, you should refer to the WordPerfect Help topics.

Inserting Page Numbers in a Preset Position

The quickest way to add page numbers is to choose from the 10 different predefined locations where page numbers can be inserted. WordPerfect inserts the code for the page number and keeps the page numbers updated, no matter how many changes you make to the document.

To insert a page number

1. Move to the page where you want the numbering to start.
2. Choose **Format**, **Page**, **Numbering** to display the Select Page Numbering Format dialog box.
3. Open the **Position** drop-down list to open the list of positions that you can choose from (see Figure 8.5).

FIGURE 8.5
The quickest way to insert a page number is to choose one of the predefined page number positions.

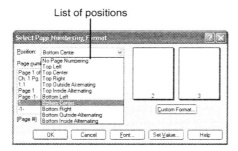

List of positions

4. Select a page number position from the list.
5. Click **OK** to insert a basic page number that starts on the current page and continues through the rest of the document. Figure 8.6 shows a document with simple page numbers at the bottom center of the page.

Page numbers are printed on the top or bottom line in the text area of the page, *not* in the margin space. WordPerfect inserts a blank line to separate the page number from the rest of the document text. This reduces the amount of text that would normally fit on the page by two lines. If you decrease your top or bottom margin (depending on where you put the page numbers) to approximately 2/3 inch, you can regain the lost space, and the page numbers will appear to print in the margin space.

note

If you don't want the page number to appear on the first page (or on any other page), see the section titled, "Using the Suppress Feature," later in this chapter.

FIGURE 8.6

The most common page-numbering scheme is to position the number at the bottom center of every page.

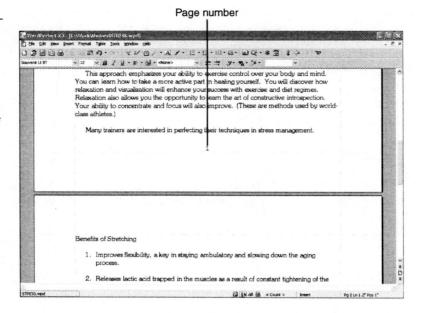

Page number

That's the quick way to insert a page number. If you want to get a little fancier, there are plenty of other page-numbering options to choose from:

- **Page numbering format list**—Choose from the list to select a different format for the page numbers, such as letter and Roman number styles.

- **Font**—Open the Page Numbering Font dialog box, where you can choose a font, font size, color, or attributes for the page number.

- **Custom Format**—Open the Custom Page Numbering dialog box. From here, you can create a combination page number style that can include the volume number, chapter number, or secondary page number. You can also create a customized "page x of y" page number style that includes a volume or chapter number.

- **Set Value**—Open the Values dialog box, where you can type the new number to use for any of the page numbering components. This is also where you can reset page numbering by setting the page number back to 1.

> **tip**
>
> A "page x of y" page number tells you the number of the current page (x) and the total number of pages in the document (y). To create a "page x of y" page number; select **Page 1 of 1** in the **Page numbering format** list box.

Frequently, different numbering styles are used for the introductory pages, the body of the document, and the closing sections. This is easily accomplished in WordPerfect. Select the format for the page numbers at the top of the document, again at the main body, and then again at the closing section. While you're switching to a different number format, you can restart the page numbering at the same time.

Inserting Page Numbers Manually

Although there is plenty of flexibility in the 10 predefined page number positions, you're not limited to them. You can insert a page number anywhere in the document. You might, for example, want to refer to the current chapter number within the text. Or you might want to insert a chapter or volume number directly into a title.

To insert a page number elsewhere in a document

1. Position the insertion point where you want the page number to appear.
2. Choose **Format**, **Page**, **Insert Page Number**. The Insert Page Number dialog box appears with options for inserting primary and secondary page numbers, chapter and volume numbers, and the total pages number (see Figure 8.7).

> **caution**
> WordPerfect uses the font set in the Document Initial Font dialog box for page numbers. This might or might not match the font that you selected in the document. There are two ways to synch the fonts. You can set the font that you want for the body text and the page number in the Document Initial Font dialog box (by choosing **File**, **Document**, **Default Font**). Or, choose a font in the Page Numbering Font dialog box that matches the one you've used in the document.

FIGURE 8.7
Use the Insert Page Number dialog box to insert a page number anywhere in a document.

Page number styles

Set a new page number

3. Choose the type of number that you want to insert.
4. (optional) Click **Value/Adjust** to open the Values dialog box, where you can change to a different page number method (numbers, letters, or Roman numerals) or set the page number (see Figure 8.8). Click **Apply** and then click **OK** when you're finished.

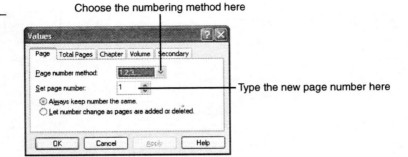

FIGURE 8.8
Choose a different numbering method in the Values dialog box.

5. Click **Insert** (in the Insert Page Number dialog box). The number is inserted at the insertion point.
6. Continue inserting numbers as needed: Click in the document window and reposition the insertion point; then click in the dialog box to make it active again. Choose another number type, and then click **Insert**.
7. Click **Close** when you're finished inserting page numbers.

Adding a Header or Footer

Headers are used for inserting information that you want printed at the top of every page; footers are for information that you want printed at the bottom of every page. Headers and footers can contain page numbers, titles, the filename, revision dates, the author's name, or any other information about the document.

Creating a Header or Footer

Generally, you need to create the header or footer on the page where you want it to start. On pages where you don't want the headers and footers to print (such as the title page, first page of a letter, and so on), you can suppress the header and footer by selecting it in the Suppress dialog box. You can also use Delay Codes to postpone the effect of a formatting code.

To insert a header or footer

1. Position the insertion point on the page where you want the header or footer to appear.
2. Choose **Insert**, **Header/Footer** to open the Headers/Footers dialog box (see Figure 8.9).

FIGURE 8.9
In the Headers/Footers dialog box, Header A is already selected.

3. Click the button for the header or footer you want to create.
4. Click **Create**. What happens next depends on which view mode you're using. Either way, the property bar now has some handy buttons you can use:

   - In Page view mode, the insertion point moves up to the top of the page, within the header guidelines (see Figure 8.10).
   - In Draft view mode, the insertion point moves to a separate header/footer-editing window. You won't be able to see the document text, only the text of the header as you type it.

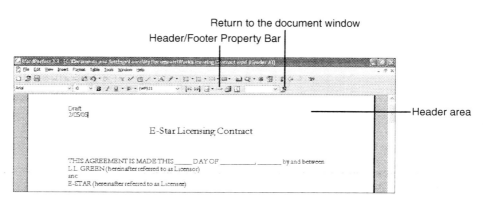

FIGURE 8.10
In Page view mode, you create and edit the header or footer onscreen, not in a separate window, as with Draft view mode.

5. Type the text of the header or footer. Using the menus, add the necessary graphics, tables, and other formatting elements. (Features that can't be used in a header or footer are grayed out on the menus.)

CHOOSING A HEADER/FOOTER FONT

Header and footer text in the same font size as the document text is distracting at best and downright ugly at worst. If you're using a 12-point font for the body text, step down at least 2 points, preferably 4 points, for the header or footer text.

Sans-serif fonts are smooth without the small "tick" marks on the letters. Serif fonts, like the font used in this book, have those "tick" marks. If you've selected a sans-serif font (such as Arial) for your headings and a serif font (such as Times New Roman) for your text, you might also consider using the sans-serif font for the header and footer text to further set it apart from the body text.

6. Click the **Close** button, or press **Ctrl+F4**, to switch back to the document window. If you are in Page view, you can click in the body of the document.

If you are working in Page view mode, you will see the header or footer text onscreen with the rest of the document text. In Draft view mode, you won't see header or footer text unless you edit the header or footer.

Working with Headers and Footers

For the most part, it's faster to create a new document by revising an existing document, especially if a lot of specific formatting is involved. If you're doing this, be sure that you edit the header or footer to reflect the changes in the document.

To edit a header or footer

1. Choose **Insert**, **Header/Footer**.
2. Select the appropriate header or footer from the Headers/Footers dialog box.
3. Click **Edit**.

> **caution**
> WordPerfect automatically inserts a blank line between the document text and the header or footer. Don't insert a blank line in the header or footer unless you want to increase the distance to two lines.

Because headers and footers are printed within the text area of a page, you should decrease the margins to allow more space for the body text. It's more attractive to pull the header or footer into the margin space. Be sure to change the margins in the DocumentStyle (choose **File**, **Document**, **Current Document Style**), or your changes won't affect the placement of the headers and footers. In fact, any formatting codes that you want to apply to headers and footers, as well as the body text, should be inserted in the DocumentStyle rather than in the document itself.

CHAPTER 8 WORKING WITH PAGES **145**

As you continue to work with headers and footers, take note of the header/footer buttons on the property bar:

- Click the **Header/Footer Prev** button to move to the previous header or footer.

- Click the **Header/Footer Next** button to move to the next header or footer.

- Click the **Page Numbering** button to insert page numbers. A drop-down list of options appears, so you can select the type of page number you want to insert.

> **caution**
> Be sure the insertion point is on a blank line when you click the Horizontal Line button; otherwise, the graphics line will land right on top of your text.

- Click the **Horizontal Line** button to insert a graphic line in the header or footer.

- Click the **Header/Footer Placement** button to open the Header or Footer Placement dialog box (see Figure 8.11). The default is to print the header or footer on every page.

FIGURE 8.11
Specify on which pages you want the header or footer to print in the Placement dialog box.

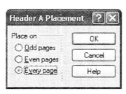

- Click the **Header/Footer Distance** button, and then type the distance that you want between the header or footer and the body text in the Distance dialog box (see Figure 8.12).

FIGURE 8.12
You can adjust the space between the header (or footer) and the text in the Distance dialog box.

> **TWO HEADERS ON A PAGE**
>
> In WordPerfect, you can create up to two headers and two footers on a page. It's nice to be able to create one header for odd pages and another header for even pages. Another way you might take advantage of this is to create two headers on the same page. One might contain something standard, such as the title of the document and a page number. The other would contain something that changes periodically in the document, such as a chapter name. To keep the two headers from overlapping, place the first header's text at the left margin and the second header's text flush against the right margin. Also, be sure you use short titles and chapter names so they don't run into each other in the middle of the page!

Suppressing and Delaying Formatting

There are distinct advantages to placing all the formatting codes at the top of your documents. For one, it's much harder to accidentally delete a code that is at the very top of a document (versus at the top of any page). Another advantage is that everything is all in one place, and you don't have to go hunting around for a code.

So, you put all the codes at the top of the document, and they take effect on the first page. Fabulous! Except for one thing. You don't want the header and footer to print on the title page. So, how do you keep your codes at the top of the document, and keep the header and footer from printing? By using Suppress and Delay Codes.

Using the Suppress Feature

The Suppress feature is designed to prevent headers, footers, watermarks, and page numbers from printing on a particular page. Suppress is frequently used to keep these items from printing on a title page. Simply place a Suppress code at the top of every page on which you don't want a header, footer, page number, or watermark to print and let WordPerfect take care of the rest!

To suppress a header, footer, page number, or watermark

1. Move to the page where you want to suppress the element.
2. Choose **Format**, **Page**, **Suppress**. The Suppress dialog box opens (see Figure 8.13).
3. Click the check box next to the elements that you want to suppress, or click the check box next to **All** to select all the elements at one time.
4. Click **OK**.

FIGURE 8.13

In the Suppress dialog box, choose the page elements you do not want to print on the current page.

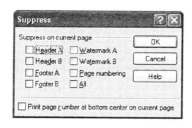

Inserting a Delay Code

The Delay Codes feature is used to postpone the effect of formatting changes for a specified number of pages. Delay Codes are used when you want to skip more than one page (such as skipping past the table of contents, preface, or other introductory material before printing headers, footers, or page numbers).

To create a Delay Code

1. Choose **Format**, **Page**, **Delay Codes**. The Delay Codes dialog box appears (see Figure 8.14).

FIGURE 8.14

Type the number of pages that you want to skip in the Delay Codes dialog box.

2. Type the number of pages in the **Number of Pages to Skip Before Applying Codes** text box (or click the spinner arrows to select the number).
3. Click **OK** to switch to the Define Delayed Codes editing window.
4. Use the menus or the buttons on the feature bar to insert the necessary formatting codes (see Figure 8.15).

FIGURE 8.15
You can postpone the action of many formatting codes by placing them in delay codes.

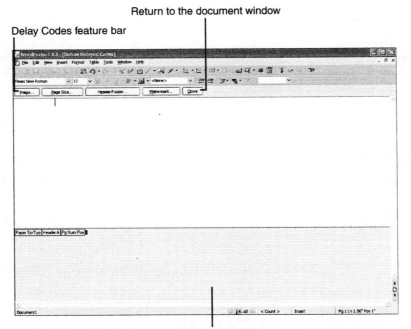

5. Click the **Close** button to return to the document window.

Even if the insertion point is in the middle of a page, WordPerfect places this Delay Code at the top of the page: [Delay: #]. The # represents the number of pages you want to skip. (WordPerfect calculates the number of pages to skip based on physical pages, not page numbers.) If your insertion point is on page 5 and you set a Delay Code to skip 3 pages, the code [Delay: 3] is inserted at the top of page 5. On the page where the formatting takes effect, a [Delay Codes] code that contains the actual codes is inserted at the top of that page. Move the red Reveal Codes cursor to the left of this code to expand the code and reveal the codes within.

The key to understanding the Delay Code feature is recognizing that you are actually inserting formatting codes into a code, not in the document. If you create Header B in a Delay Code, you can't edit that code from the document window; you can only create

> **tip**
> You might consider putting Delay Codes in the default document style (DocumentStyle) so that they are safe from accidental deletion. The DocumentStyle code is the very first code in a document. To edit the DocumentStyle, turn on Reveal Codes and double-click the [Open Style: DocumentStyle] code at the top of the document. Or choose **File, Document, Current Document Style**.

another Header B. The two headers are independent of each other. In fact, the header/footer that you create in a Delay Code will override the header/footer that you create in the document.

To adjust the formatting in a Delay Code, you must edit the Delay Code by turning on Reveal Codes and double-clicking the [Delay: #] code.

Adding Borders Around Pages

WordPerfect comes with a nice collection of decorative borders that you can place around a page. These ready-to-use designs are perfect for announcements, invitations, and a variety of presentation materials. Some of the designs can be used to create your own decorative paper.

There are two types of borders: line and fancy. The line borders are more formal, but they are also more versatile. There are 32 predefined line borders to choose from, and because you can edit these predefined borders to change the color and the line style, the possibilities are endless.

To add a border around the page

1. Move to the page where you want to add a border.
2. Choose **Format**, **Page**, **Border/Fill**. The Page Border/Fill dialog box opens (see Figure 8.16).

FIGURE 8.16

In the Page Border/Fill dialog box, you can choose the border that you want to place around the page.

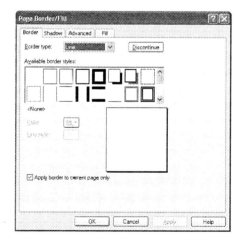

3. Scroll through the **Available Border Styles** list box to see all the predefined borders; then select a border. After you've chosen a border, you have the following options:

- You can change the color of the border. Click the **Color** button, and then click a color swatch on the palette (see Figure 8.17).

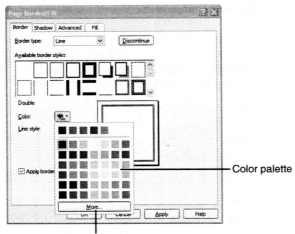

FIGURE 8.17
You can choose any color from this palette to add color to a page border.

- You can change the line style used in the border. Click the **Line Style** button, and then click a line style from the palette (see Figure 8.18).

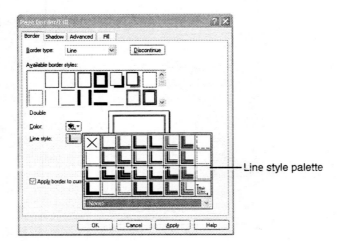

FIGURE 8.18
You can choose a line style from this palette for the page border.

CHAPTER 8 WORKING WITH PAGES

- By default, **Apply Border to Current Page Only** is selected. Disable this option if you want the border to be applied to the current page and all other pages in the document.
- To remove a page border, click in the page; choose **Format**, **Page**, **Border/Fill** to open the Page Border/Fill dialog box; and click the **Discontinue** button.

> **caution**
> When you create a border using the line styles, WordPerfect automatically allows space between the text and the border, which is positioned on the margins. A fancy border can overwrite the text, so you might have to make some adjustments to the margins.

The line borders are the "serious" borders. The fun borders are called "fancy" borders. There are 36 to choose from. Fancy borders are automatically applied to the current page and the following pages. You can remove a fancy border from the current and following pages by choosing **Discontinue** in the Page Border/Fill dialog box. To give you an example, suppose you create a 10-page document and want to apply the fancy border to the first three pages only. To accomplish this, you would click on page 1 and apply the border. Then, you would scroll down and click on page 4 so you can open the Page Border/Fill dialog box, and choose **Discontinue**.

To select a fancy page border

1. Choose **Format**, **Page**, **Border/Fill**.
2. Open the **Border Type** drop-down list and choose **Fancy**. The list of fancy borders appears in the Available Border Styles window (see Figure 8.19). A preview of the selected border shows you how a page will look with the border.

FIGURE 8.19
There are 36 different fancy borders to choose from in the Page Border/Fill dialog box.

Click here to switch between line and fancy borders

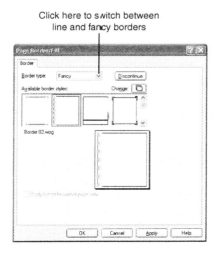

Using the Make It Fit Feature

It happens to the best of us. You've just finished a carefully thought-out memo, and you're ready to send it off. However, when you print it, you notice that the last two lines of the memo have spilled over to the second page. Ack! You really need to get it down to one page, so you sit down to play around with the margins and font size.

Stop! There is a feature that can do this for you, in just seconds. Make It Fit makes text fit in the number of pages that you specify—within reason, of course. You can't make one page of text stretch out into three pages, and you can't take three pages of text and expect to squeeze it into one page. The number of pages that you specify must be at least 50% of the current size.

You can use Make It Fit on selected text or on the entire document; so if you want to work on only a section of text, select it first.

To use Make it Fit on your document

1. Choose **Format**, **Make It Fit** to open the Make It Fit dialog box (see Figure 8.20). If you selected text, the Top and Bottom margin options won't be available.

FIGURE 8.20
Make It Fit adjusts margins, font size, and line spacing to resize a document so that it fits within a certain number of pages.

2. Take a look at the current number of pages, and then type the number of pages that you want to fill in the **Desired Number of Pages** text box.
3. Select the options that you want Make It Fit to use to reformat the text.
4. Click **Make It Fit**.

If you have hard page codes in the document, you will get a message to warn you that these codes might affect how well the document is formatted.

The Absolute Minimum

This is the second chapter in a three-chapter series on formatting. The topics in this chapter focus on formatting pages.

- You learned how to insert a page break so that you could start working on a new page.
- You saw that not every document is printed on an 8 1/2×11-inch piece of paper, and you learned how to switch to a different paper size and orientation.
- You saw how useful it is to subdivide a single page into multiple pages.
- Adding page numbers to a document can be done in just a few seconds with the Page Numbering feature.
- Adding headers and footers to a document allows you to display important information at the top and bottom of a page.
- You learned how to use the Suppress and Delay Codes features to prevent certain page elements from printing on a page.
- Borders are not essential formatting elements, but they are easy to work with, and they give simple documents a polished appearance.
- The Make It Fit feature is a great time-saver when you need to force a document into a certain number of pages.

In the next chapter, you will learn how to create styles to automate repetitive formatting tasks and to ensure formatting consistency across documents.

IN THIS CHAPTER

- Learn about the different types of styles and create your own styles on-the-fly with QuickStyles.
- Apply the styles that come with WordPerfect to your own documents.
- Create and edit your own styles to speed up your formatting tasks and to ensure a consistent appearance.
- Use QuickFormat to copy the formatting from one section of text to other sections.

USING STYLES FOR CONSISTENCY

This chapter teaches you how to use the formatting commands you learned in previous chapters to create *styles*. A style is a collection of commands that you can apply all at once, instead of working through the same series of steps, over and over again, to apply formatting.

Styles speed up the formatting process and make it possible to make editing changes on-the-fly. They also ensure a consistent appearance among documents. For example, you could use styles for book manuscripts, presentation materials, financial reports, legal briefs, medical reports, and more.

Understanding Styles

A style is basically a collection of formatting commands, such as font type, size, underlining, and so on, that you put together and save with a name. The next time you want to apply those commands to some text, you use the style instead. Obviously, applying a style is much faster than repeating a series of steps to generate the proper format.

But that isn't the only reason you want to use styles. The real benefit is when you start fine-tuning the format. Let's say that you decide not to italicize your headings. If you had italicized the headings by selecting the text and applying italic, you would have to go back to each heading and remove the italic code. Instead, you create a heading style so that all you have to do is remove the italic from the style and voilà! Every heading is automatically updated to reflect the new formatting in the style.

Think about this for a minute. You can format an entire project, such as a newsletter, and then go back and play around with the styles and have the changes reflected automatically, throughout the whole document. Furthermore, if you are trying to achieve some sort of consistency among the documents that you and your co-workers create, a set of standard styles is the way to go.

There are two types of styles in WordPerfect: open and paired.

Open Styles

An *open style* is turned on and left on. The settings in the style stay in effect through the end of the document, or until another corresponding open style is found. The DocumentStyle, which contains the settings for the entire document, is an open style. Another example might be an open style that you insert in the document to start a different method of page numbering. That style remains in effect until another page numbering open style is found.

Paired Styles

As opposed to an open style that continues until (and unless) a different style is inserted, a *paired style* is self-limiting. A paired style is really two styles used in tandem ("paired"): an on style and an off style, similar to the pair of bold codes that surround boldface text. The first code turns on bold; the second code turns it off. It's the same with paired styles. The first code turns on the style formatting; the second turns it off. Both paragraph (or heading) and character styles are paired styles.

A common example is a heading style that changes the font size, applies bold, and marks the text for a table of contents. The codes before the text increase the font size, turn on bold, and begin marking the text for the table of contents. The ending code switches back to the original font size, turns off bold, and ends the marking for the table of contents.

Using QuickStyle to Create Your Own Styles

What if I told you that all you need to create your own collection of styles is a formatted document or two? Seriously. You've already put in the time to set up everything—here's your chance to take advantage of it! All you have to do is click in some formatted text in your existing document and then use QuickStyle to combine all the formatting codes in your selection into a custom style, as explained below.

You could also type some "dummy" text in a blank document and format it the way you want. Then use the QuickStyle feature to save that formatting as a style.

> **tip**
> You can open the QuickStyle dialog box by opening the drop-down Styles list on the property bar and selecting **QuickStyle** (on the bottom of the list).

To use QuickStyle to create a style

1. Position the insertion point anywhere in the formatted text. For example, in Figure 9.1, the formatted text is a heading that uses a 14-point Arial italic font. You don't even have to select the text.

FIGURE 9.1
You can format text first, and then use QuickStyle to create a style based on the format you used.

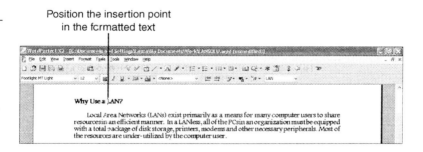

2. Choose **Format**, **Styles** (**Alt+F8**) to open the Styles dialog box.
3. Click **QuickStyle** to display the QuickStyle dialog box (see Figure 9.2).

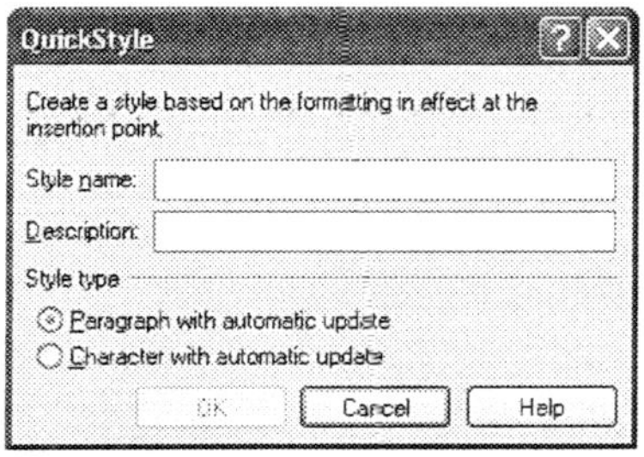

FIGURE 9.2
In the QuickStyle dialog box, you name the style and select the type of style you want to create.

4. Type a name for the style in the **Style Name** text box. The name can be up to 20 characters long.

5. (Optional) Type a longer description in the **Description** text box. This can be useful later if you want to use the style but can't remember what it does by the name alone.

6. Choose **Paragraph with Automatic Update** if you want the style to apply to an entire paragraph, or **Character with Automatic Update** if you want to format only selected text.

7. Click **OK** to add the style to your current document and to return to the Styles dialog box. Your new style appears in the **Available Styles** list (see Figure 9.3).

8. Choose **Close** to close the Styles dialog box.

tip

When you select a style, WordPerfect displays the effect of the style in the **Preview** box and also shows the description if you provided one.

FIGURE 9.3
The newly created style appears in the list of Available Styles.

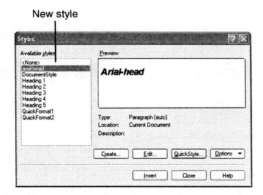

Using WordPerfect's Existing Heading Styles

WordPerfect has a few predefined heading styles that you can use in your documents. If you're in a hurry, or you don't care to learn how to create your own heading styles, you can use WordPerfect's heading styles to format your text.

To apply one of WordPerfect's heading styles

1. Select the text that you want to format.

2. Click the **Styles** drop-down list on the property bar (see Figure 9.4).

FIGURE 9.4
The fastest way to select a style is to choose one from the Styles list on the property bar.

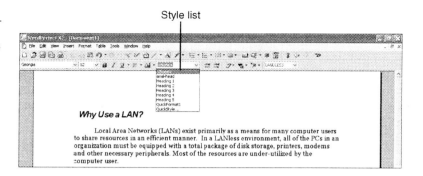

3. Click the style you want to use. WordPerfect applies the style to the text.

Notice that if you hover over a style name, the RealTime Preview feature shows you how the heading will look with that style applied. To select a style from the Styles dialog box

1. Choose **Format**, **Styles** (**Alt+F8**). WordPerfect displays the Styles dialog box.
2. In the **Available Styles** list, click the style you want to use. WordPerfect displays an approximation of the effect of the style in the **Preview** box (see Figure 9.5).

FIGURE 9.5
The Styles dialog box enables you to preview the effect of a style before you insert it.

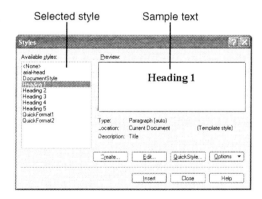

3. Click **Insert** to apply the style to the selected text.

Building Your Own Styles

The heading styles are convenient, but they have limited use, so you will probably want to start creating your own styles right away. You've already seen how the QuickStyle feature makes it easy to create styles from text that you have already formatted.

You can also create a style from scratch with the Styles Editor. The next time you start a new project, take a few minutes and create the styles that you will need. Then you can apply the styles as you generate the content.

To build your own style

1. Choose **Format**, **Styles** (**Alt+F8**) to open the Styles dialog box.
2. Choose **Create** to open the Styles Editor dialog box (see Figure 9.6).

FIGURE 9.6
The Styles Editor allows you to create styles from scratch.

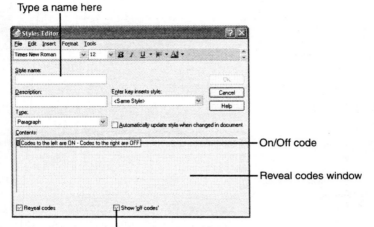

3. Type a style name in the **Style Name** text box.
4. (Optional) Type a description (for example, centered, 14-point Arial text) in the **Description** text box.
5. In the **Type** drop-down menu, choose **Paragraph** if you want the style to apply to an entire paragraph, **Character** if you want to format only selected text, or **Document** to create an open style that you can apply anywhere in a document and have the rest of the text formatted with it.
6. Use the menus and the property bar in the Styles Editor to insert formatting codes just as you would in a document. The menus in the Style Editor do not contain all of WordPerfect's formatting commands and features; only the commands and features that can be used in a style are available.

> **caution**
> Although WordPerfect X3 is compatible with Microsoft Word in most respects, Word cannot use text in a style. If you create a WordPerfect style that contains text, the text won't display when your document is converted into Word. If the document is edited in Word, the text might not reappear when the document is reopened in WordPerfect.

7. When you're finished, click **OK** to save your style in the current document.
8. Choose **Close** to close the Styles dialog box.

If necessary, place a check mark next to the **Show 'Off Codes'** option. In the Reveal Codes window, you should see a code that says Codes on the left are ON - Codes on the right are OFF. This is actually one of the more powerful aspects of the Style feature. You can position a set of codes that should be in effect *before* the selected text and another set of codes to be in effect *after* the selected text. You can also include text before or after this code if you want to include text in the style. For example, a heading style might have a font code to select a different font for the heading before the text and another font code to switch back to the body text font after the heading text.

By default, styles you create from scratch are saved only in the current document. To make those styles available in all new documents, be sure to do the following before creating a style: Choose **Format**, **Styles**, then click **Options**, **Settings**. Choose **Save New Styles to Default Template**, and click **OK**.

Editing Styles

Using the same techniques you learned in the previous section on creating your own styles, you can edit your styles and make adjustments to them. You can also edit the DocumentStyle, which contains the formatting codes for all new documents. This is how you can customize the default settings to suit your needs.

Revising Your Styles

After you create a style and apply it to some text, you can make changes to that style, and those changes will automatically be reflected in any text to which the style has been applied. You will think someone just waved a magic wand over your document because it's almost instantaneous.

To edit a style

1. Choose **Format**, **Styles** (**Alt+F8**) to open the Styles dialog box.
2. Select the style that you want to edit in the **Available Styles** list.
3. Click **Edit** to open the Styles Editor dialog box (refer to Figure 9.5) and display the contents of the style.
4. Either use the menus to insert new codes, or double-click the existing codes to edit them.
5. Click **OK** when you're finished with your changes.
6. Click **Close** to close the Styles dialog box and update the document.

Customizing the Default Settings

As mentioned in Chapter 1, WordPerfect has a set of default format settings. The margins are 1 inch on all four sides, documents are single-spaced, there are tabs every 1/2 inch, and so on. These settings are stored in the default template. Because of these defaults, you can start creating documents as soon as the software is installed.

After you've worked in WordPerfect for a while, you might develop a set of formatting standards that you use in your documents. Instead of making these selections every time you create a document, you can edit the default settings to meet your needs.

> **tip**
> If you want to create a new style that is similar to another style, you can save some time by editing one of your existing styles rather than creating a new style from scratch. When you edit your style, give it a new name and then make the changes.

The three ways to edit the default settings for the current document are as follows:

- Choose **File**, **Document**, **Current Document Style**.
- Choose **Format**, **Styles**. Select **DocumentStyle** in the **Available Styles** list; then choose **Edit**.
- Turn on Reveal Codes (choose **View**, **Reveal Codes**; **Alt+F3**). In the Reveal Codes window, double-click the **Open Style: DocumentStyle** code at the beginning of the document.

WordPerfect displays the Styles Editor dialog box with the default language code in the Reveal Codes window (see Figure 9.7). Make the necessary changes. The selections that you make here will be reflected in the document as soon as you switch back to it.

FIGURE 9.7
Edit the Document Style to customize the default settings.

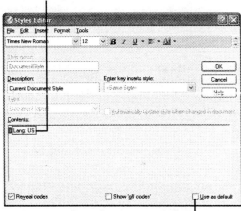

Default language code

Click here to save the changes to the default template

If you want your new settings to affect all new documents, you will have to save the changes to the default template. Place a check mark in the **Use as Default** check box. You will be prompted to apply this new style to all new documents. Click **Yes** to save your changes, or **No** to abandon the changes.

Changes to the default template do *not* change the styles in documents that you have already created. Such changes apply only to new documents that you create after updating the default template.

Using QuickFormat

WordPerfect's QuickFormat feature enables you to create a temporary style that you can then apply to other parts of the document. It's perfect for those situations in which you need to do some repetitive formatting, but you don't really need to create a style.

1. Begin by choosing the formatting you want to apply to another section of text—either a heading or any contiguous characters. The formatting you choose at this point will be copied to other sections of the document.
2. Position the insertion point anywhere in the formatted text.
3. Choose **Format**, **QuickFormat**, or click the **QuickFormat** button on the toolbar. WordPerfect displays the QuickFormat dialog box (see Figure 9.8).

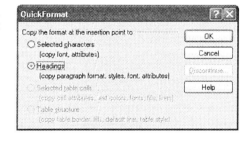

FIGURE 9.8
The QuickFormat dialog box enables you to capture a formatting style and apply it to selected text or headings.

4. Click **Headings** or **Selected Characters**, depending on whether you want to apply the style to a heading you've created (or text that you wish to use as a heading) or to any other text that you select.
5. Click **OK**. A new mouse pointer appears; this one is shaped like a paint roller (see Figure 9.9).

FIGURE 9.9
The mouse pointer changes to indicate that you will apply a heading style when you click the mouse.

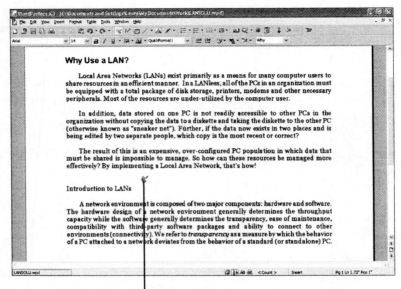

The QuickFormat paint roller pointer

6. If you chose **Headings**, click anywhere in the paragraph that you want to format; the formatting will be applied to the entire paragraph. If you chose **Selected characters**, click and drag the mouse pointer across the text that you want to format; the formatting will be applied to the selected text.

7. Continue through the document, clicking each heading or selecting sections of text to apply the QuickFormat style.

8. To turn off QuickFormat, choose **Format**, **QuickFormat**; or click the **QuickFormat** button on the toolbar.

THE ABSOLUTE MINIMUM

This is the last chapter in a three-chapter series on formatting. This chapter covered the use of styles.

- Right off the bat, you used the QuickStyle feature to create styles based on text you had already formatted.
- WordPerfect includes heading styles that you can use right away to apply to headings and titles in your documents.
- You learned how to build your own styles in the Styles Editor.
- The DocumentStyle code can be revised to customize the default settings for all new documents.
- The QuickFormat feature creates a temporary style that you can use to repeat formatting in a document.

In the next chapter, you will learn how to use one of the most versatile features in WordPerfect—the Table feature. From a simple list with several columns to forms to a mini-spreadsheet, you will use the Table feature often.

PART III

Organizing Information

Creating and Formatting Tables 169

Creating Lists and Outlines 199

IN THIS CHAPTER

- Learn how to create and edit tables to help you organize information.
- Discover how to add fancy table lines, borders, or shading.
- Learn to use tables for basic spreadsheet-like calculations.
- Learn how to convert existing text into a table, or table text to regular text.

CREATING AND FORMATTING TABLES

So, you're not even sure what a table is, let alone why you might want to use one? That's a fairly typical response, but after you learn how easy and useful WordPerfect tables can be, you will wonder how you ever got along without them.

Any time you need to organize information in rows and columns, for a team roster or an inventory list, you will want to use a table. In fact, with very little effort, you can use tables to create simple lists, invoices, schedules, calendars, programs, dialogue scripts, and more. And even if you're not quite ready to venture off into the world of spreadsheets, you can use WordPerfect to perform spreadsheet-like calculations.

Creating Tables

The basic steps for creating a table are simple. Begin by trying to determine how your information needs to be organized. How many columns of information will you need (for example, name, address, phone number, and email)? Then if you can, estimate the number of rows you need (for example, the number of people on your team roster—see Figure 10.1).

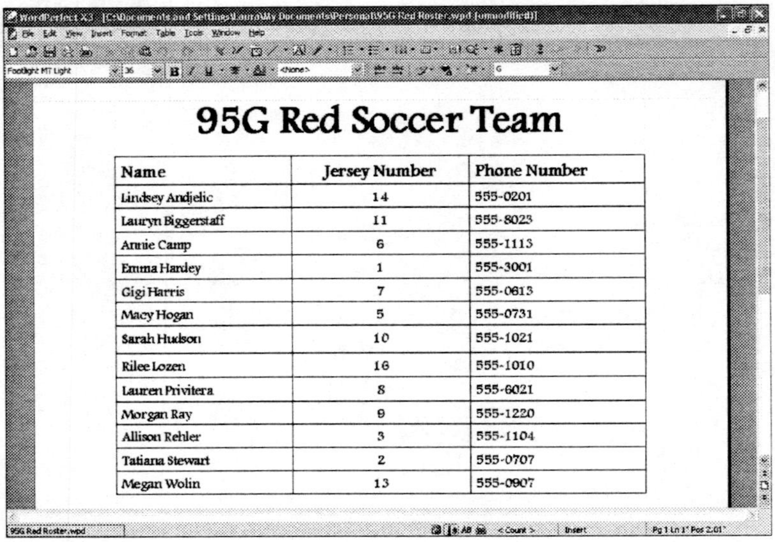

FIGURE 10.1
WordPerfect tables can be used for all sorts of tasks, such as team rosters, calendars, invoices, and much more.

For now, let's just create a simple table, and then I'll explain what you've done:

1. Choose **Table**, **Create** (or press **F12**).
2. In the Create Table dialog box, leave the number of columns at 3, and change the number of rows to **4** (see Figure 10.2).

FIGURE 10.2
Use the Create Table dialog box to choose the number or rows and columns you want in your table.

3. Click **Create** to create the table shown in Figure 10.3.

FIGURE 10.3
Tables quickly and easily help organize information into rows and columns.

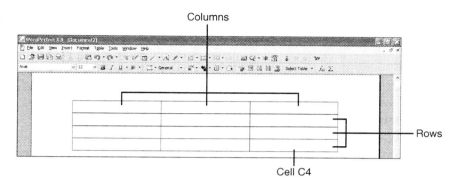

Tables look and function a lot like spreadsheets. In fact, the terminology is the same: Information is placed in *cells*, which are the intersection of *rows* and *columns*. For example, in the table shown in Figure 10.3, the last cell (row 4, column C) is named cell C4.

That was pretty easy, wasn't it? Well, believe it or not, there is an even easier way to create a table. First, make sure the insertion point is *not* in a table. Now, click the **Table QuickCreate** button on the toolbar and, holding down the mouse button, drag the mouse down and to the right until you obtain a grid that matches the number of rows and columns you want (see Figure 10.4). Release the mouse button, and there you have it!

> **tip**
>
> One of the great strengths of the Table feature is that you can select commands from a QuickMenu for virtually every task. It's fast—all you do is right-click in a table and choose a command, and it's easy—you don't have to look through the "big" Table menu to locate a command

FIGURE 10.4
Dragging the mouse on the Table QuickCreate button is a quick and easy way to create the exact size table you want.

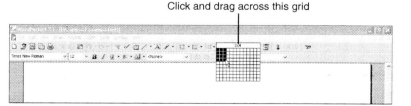

Working with Tables

One of the biggest advantages of using a table is the ease with which you can work with information within a table. Think about each table cell as a miniature document with its own margins and formatting. You can enter and edit text in a cell just as you do in a document.

Typing in Tables

A cell can contain more than one line of text. As you enter text, WordPerfect wraps the words within the cell, adding lines to the row to accommodate what you type (see Figure 10.5).

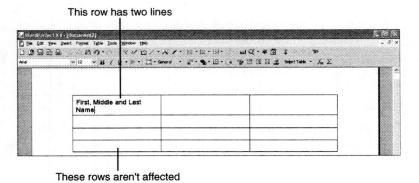

FIGURE 10.5
Notice that lines are automatically added to the row to accommodate the text.

To move around in a table

1. Click anywhere in a table to move the insertion point.
2. Press the **Tab** key to move to the next cell to the right or, when you reach the end of a row, Tab moves you to the first cell of the next row.
3. Press **Shift+Tab** to move back to the previous cell.

Adjusting the Column Widths

When you create a WordPerfect table, certain default settings apply:

- The rows and columns are evenly spaced.
- There's no special formatting of the contents of the cells.
- Single lines separate the cells of the table.
- There's no special border around the table.
- The tables are full-justified (the tables themselves extend from margin to margin).

The real beauty of WordPerfect tables is that you can easily make all kinds of adjustments to these default settings. When you make changes to the shape, size, and number of table cells, columns, and rows, you are editing the layout of the table, or the table structure.

Okay, so you don't necessarily want evenly spaced columns or rows. After all, you don't need the same amount of space for a phone number as you do for a name, right?

Let me show you how to adjust the column widths. (We'll talk about how to change some of the other features later in this chapter.)

To change column widths

1. Position the mouse pointer over a line separating the two columns you want to change. The mouse pointer changes to a thick vertical bar with left and right arrows.

2. Click and drag the **column separator line** to the right or to the left, thus widening one column and narrowing the other. A QuickTip bubble tells you how wide the column(s) will be when you release the mouse button (see Figure 10.6).

FIGURE 10.6
Use the mouse to drag table column lines and change the width of table columns.

3. When you get the column widths that you want, release the mouse button.

You can repeat this process with other columns until your table looks just the way you want it.

Sometimes you just want to be sure that the column is wide enough to display the information on one line. To adjust a column width to match the cell contents, choose **Size Column to Fit** from the **Table** menu. You can also right-click anywhere in a table and choose **Size Column to Fit** from the Table QuickMenu.

tip

Don't forget to use the Undo button if you make a mistake either creating or modifying a table. Just click the **Undo** button or press **Ctrl+Z**.

Adding Rows and Columns

A common problem in using tables is that you're never sure just how many rows or columns you're going to need. One easy way to add rows at the bottom of the table is to press the Tab key in the last column of the last row. Rows and columns also can be added anywhere in a table.

To add rows or columns to a table

1. Position the insertion point where you want to add a new column or row.
2. Choose **Table**, **Insert**. WordPerfect displays the Insert Columns/Rows dialog box (see Figure 10.7).

FIGURE 10.7
The Insert Columns/Rows dialog box enables you to change the number of rows or columns in your table.

3. Either type the number of rows or columns you want to insert, or click the spinner arrows to select the number.
4. By default, WordPerfect inserts columns or rows *before* the current cursor position. If you want them to appear *after* the current cursor position, choose **After**.
5. Click **OK** to insert the rows or columns.

Deleting Rows or Columns

Occasionally, you overshoot the mark and end up with more rows or columns than you need. Rather than leave them empty, delete them from the table.

To delete rows or columns

1. Click in the first row or select the column that you want to delete.
2. Choose **Table**, **Delete** to open the Delete Structure/Contents dialog box (see Figure 10.8).

FIGURE 10.8
Use the Delete Structure/Contents dialog box to remove unneeded table rows or columns.

3. Specify the number of rows or columns you want to delete and click **OK**.

Remember, when you delete rows or columns, the contents are also erased. Click the **Undo** button or choose **Edit**, **Undo** (**Ctrl+Z**) if you accidentally delete important data.

> **tip**
> The absolute easiest way to insert or delete rows is to use the keyboard. Position the insertion point where you want to add or delete a row, and press **Alt+Insert** to add a row or **Alt+Delete** to delete a row. If you don't like taking your hands off the keyboard, these two shortcuts are real timesavers!

Joining and Splitting Cells

Another useful way to modify the layout of your table is to join cells or to split them. For example, you might want to make the entire top row of your team list a single cell to use as a title row. To do this, you need to join all the cells in the top row.

Or you might decide that you need two separate pieces of information in place of one single cell. In this case, you need to split a single cell into two cells.

To join cells

1. Click in the first cell you want to join (for example, cell A1).
2. Click and drag the mouse to the last cell in the group you want to join (for example, D1).

3. Choose **Table**, **Join**, **Cell**. WordPerfect automatically joins the selected cells, combining any information that was in those cells in to the new cell.

From now on, WordPerfect will treat the joined cells as a single cell. If you want to revert to the original cell division, you can split the cells.

Also, there are times when you need to create additional cells in a row or column. This is particularly useful if you're trying to create a special form.

To split a cell

1. Position the insertion point in the cell you want to split.
2. Choose **Table**, **Split**, **Cell**.
3. In the Split Cell dialog box, specify how many columns (horizontal cells) or rows (vertical cells) you want.
4. Click **OK**.

Figure 10.9 shows an example of a form in which several cells have been joined, whereas others have been split.

FIGURE 10.9

You can join or split cells in a table to create useful table layouts, such as in a form.

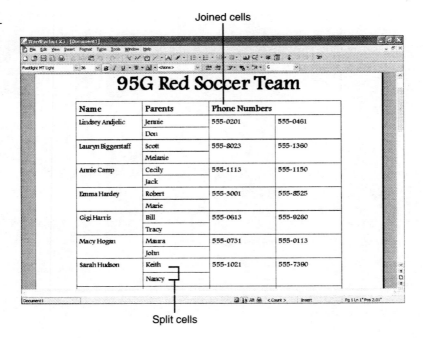

Formatting Tables, Columns, and Cells

We've just talked about features that help you create the layout, or structure, of a table. But you also want your text to look good, and that's why it's important to understand how text attributes and text alignment are applied to table cells. Basically, things are done the same way you would do them in a document. Keep in mind that each cell functions independently of the others and can be formatted separately.

Formatting the Entire Table

When you want to apply a broad brush and format elements of the entire table, you use the Table tab of the Table Format dialog box.

To format a table

1. Position the insertion point in the table. If you don't, you won't be able to open the Table Format dialog box.

2. Choose **Table**, **Format** (**Ctrl+F12**). Or, my personal favorite, right-click in the table and choose **Format**. WordPerfect displays the Properties for Table Format dialog box. (We'll just call it the Table Format dialog box.)

3. Click the **Table** tab to make changes to the entire table (see Figure 10.10).

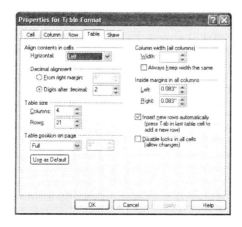

FIGURE 10.10
Use the Table tab of the Properties for Table Format dialog box to make changes to the entire WordPerfect table.

Each time you choose a text formatting option, you have to consider whether that attribute should apply to the entire table, to a column, or to a cell or group of cells. Changes you make to a specific cell or group of cells have precedence, or priority, over changes you make to columns. Changes made to cells or to columns have precedence over changes made to the entire table.

Keep this in mind, especially as you format columns. Any alterations to a cell that you might have made (and forgotten about) will not change when you specify something different with column or table formatting.

> **tip**
>
> As you format your table, it's often useful to move from the general to the specific. For example, format your entire table first, then your columns, and then your cells. This helps avoid precedence conflicts.

In the Table tab of the Table Format dialog box, you can see what the current format settings are and make changes to the table format, position, or size. For example

- **Align contents**—Normally, all cell contents are left aligned. Click the drop-down menu to make text centered, flush right, or decimal aligned.
- **Table size**—Although you can easily add or delete rows or columns, you can also change here the number of rows or columns in your table.
- **Table position**—WordPerfect tables stretch from margin to margin. You can also center or right- or left-align a table instead.

Formatting Text in Columns

When you need to format all the cells in a column, or a selected group of columns, you use the controls on the Column tab of the Table Format dialog box.

To format a column or selected columns

1. Click in the column you want to format.
2. Choose **Table, Format (Ctrl+F12)**.
3. In the Table Format dialog box, click the **Column** tab. WordPerfect displays the dialog box controls for formatting columns (see Figure 10.11).

FIGURE 10.11

To format columns, use the Column tab in the Table Format dialog box.

One of the most commonly needed column formats is the horizontal alignment of text. In the Align Contents in Cells area of the Table Format dialog box, you can click the **Horizontal** drop-down menu to choose Left, Right, Center, Full, or All alignment.

Formatting Rows

Working with rows is different from working with cells or columns because you're not really applying formatting to cell contents within a row. Instead, you're only changing row structure and function.

It might seem logical to click the Row tab to format all the cells in a row. Not so! You must first select all the cells in the row, then access the Table Format dialog box, and choose cell format options.

> **caution**
> Don't forget that if you have already formatted an individual cell, column formatting will not change that cell's format. To correct this, position the insertion point in the individual cell, access the Table Format dialog box, and on the **Cell** tab, click **Use Same Alignment as Column**.

As you've probably noted, WordPerfect automatically determines the amount of vertical space in a row based on the amount of text in its cells. The cell requiring the most vertical space sets the height for the entire row.

You can easily and quickly change a row's height by dragging the bottom line of the row up or down. WordPerfect displays a QuickTip showing the size the row will become when you release the mouse button (see Figure 10.12).

FIGURE 10.12
You can easily change the height of a WordPerfect table row by dragging the horizontal line below the row.

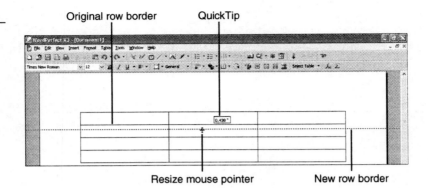

Sometimes you need to set a specific row height—for example, if you want to create a calendar in which all rows are the same height, regardless of the number of events on any given day.

To set a fixed row height

1. Select the row or rows you want to format.
2. Open the Table Format dialog box (press **Ctrl+F12** or choose **Format** from the **QuickMenu** or from the **Table** menu).
3. Click the **Row** tab. WordPerfect displays options for formatting a row (see Figure 10.13).

> **tip**
>
> If the cell row seems too high, check to see whether you have an extra hard return in any of the cells in that row. Choose **View**, **Reveal Codes** (**Alt+F3**) to turn on Reveal Codes. Locate and delete the hard return, and the row will return to its normal height.

FIGURE 10.13
To alter the structure of a row, click the Row tab in the Table Format dialog box.

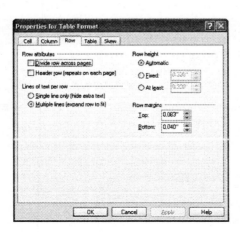

4. Click **Fixed** and, in the text box, type the height of the row (for example, 1.0" for a calendar row).
5. Click **OK** to apply the change and return to the table.

In addition, WordPerfect X3 has an "At Least" option that lets you specify a minimum row height. This option is a happy medium between the "Automatic" setting and the "Fixed" setting. It prevents WordPerfect from automatically shrinking the row height based solely on the amount of text—allowing you to insert plenty of whitespace above or below the text—while at the same time ensuring that the row will expand to accommodate new text as it is added.

Once in a while, you will have table cells with a lot of text in them, or you will have extremely long tables, with many rows. On the Row tab of the Table Format dialog box (refer to Figure 10.13), two options can help you deal with those situations:

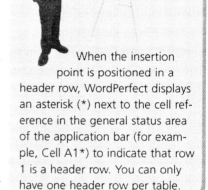

note

When the insertion point is positioned in a header row, WordPerfect displays an asterisk (*) next to the cell reference in the general status area of the application bar (for example, Cell A1*) to indicate that row 1 is a header row. You can only have one header row per table.

- **Divide Row Across Pages**—If you have cells with an unusually large amount of text, WordPerfect forces the entire cell to wrap to the next page. That can leave a lot of blank space. If instead you want to break the cell at the page break, just click **Divide Row Across Pages**.

- **Header Row**—If you create a table several pages long, you might want certain information (such as column headings) to repeat at the top of each page. Such rows are called *header rows*. To create a header row, first position the insertion point in the row you want to designate as a header row; open the Table Format dialog box, click the **Row** tab, and click the **Header Row** check box.

Formatting Cells

Within cells, you format text as you normally do in a document. Simply select the text and add whatever attributes you want. However, you can also format a cell so that any text you add to it automatically looks like everything else in the cell.

Formatting Text Attributes

For example, if you want all the text in a cell to be bold, first select the cell (move the mouse pointer to the edge of the cell, and click when the pointer turns to an arrow; see Figure 10.14); then click the **Bold** button on the toolbar or press **Ctrl+B**.

FIGURE 10.14
You can apply text attributes to cells using the same methods you use for text outside a table.

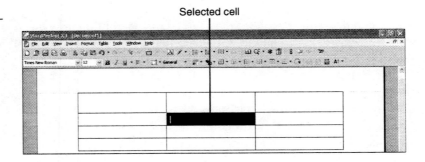

Formatting Cell Attributes

In the preceding section, you learned how to change table cell text attributes, such as bold, font size, and so on. To change other format options for a single cell, position the insertion point in the cell you want to change; then choose **Table**, **Format** (**Ctrl+F12**). WordPerfect displays the controls for formatting cells (see Figure 10.15).

FIGURE 10.15
To format specific cells in a table, use the Cell tab in the Table Format dialog box.

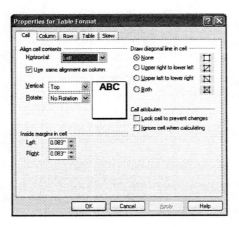

To change the format of a group of cells, simply select the cells you want to change and open the Table Format dialog box. The changes you choose from the Cell tab then apply to each of the selected cells.

WordPerfect offers several useful options for formatting cells, such as those found in the Align cell contents area:

- **Horizontal**—Click the drop-down menu to choose Left, Right, Center, Full, All, or Decimal Align alignment for all text in the selected cells.
- **Use Same Alignment as Column**—If you previously formatted a cell, and now want to make it the same as all other cells in the column, enable this option.

- **Vertical**—Normally, WordPerfect aligns all text in a cell at the top of the cell. Instead, you can choose **Bottom** or **Center** to align text vertically at the bottom or center of the cell.
- **Rotate**—The default selection for text is No Rotation. You can rotate the text within a cell by choosing 90 Degrees, 180 Degrees, or 270 Degrees from the Rotate menu.

If you create tables or forms for someone else's use, you might find it useful to lock certain cells. Locking a cell prevents any changes to the cell, either to the structure or the contents. To lock a cell, click the **Lock Cell to Prevent Changes** check box.

You can do some fairly complex calculations in tables. In fact, users have told me of their relief when they discovered that they could build spreadsheets in WordPerfect without having to learn another program. In most cases, a table with calculations will have column headings and other cells that contain text mixed in with the cells that contain values. To avoid throwing off your calculations, tell WordPerfect to ignore that cell when calculating the values. To ignore a cell, click the **Ignore Cell When Calculating** check box.

Finally, you can include two-part information in a cell. Choose one of the options in the **Draw Diagonal Line in Cell** section to add diagonal lines to cells. This might be useful if you need to track in a single cell the number of potential attendees and the actual number of people who attended, or whenever you want to track two pieces of information in a cell (see Figure 10.16).

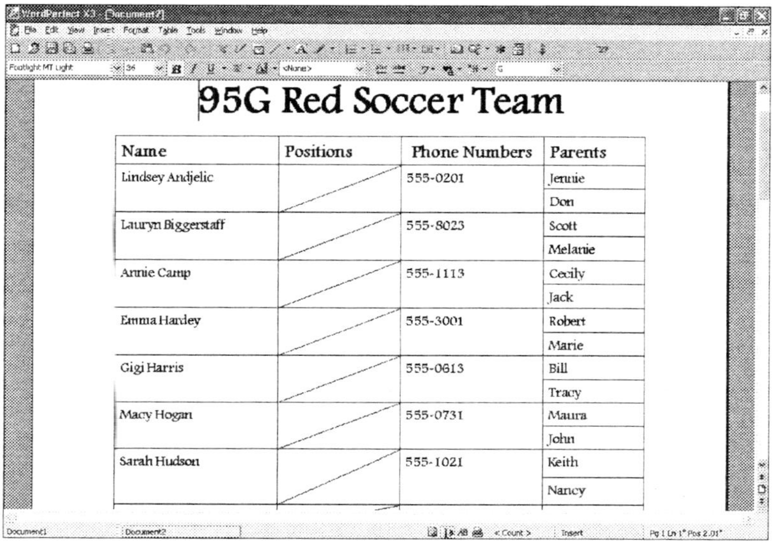

FIGURE 10.16
In this example, you are keeping track of two positions for each player.

Changing Lines, Fills, and Borders

Although the layout and content of your table are most important, with WordPerfect you can also make your tables pleasingly attractive. It's easy to change the lines around table cells so that you can highlight important cells. You can also quickly switch to a different border to make the table more attractive. Finally, a fill can be added to emphasize important information.

Using SpeedFormat

By default, single lines separate WordPerfect table cells and create a border around the table, but no other special formatting is assigned. To help you quickly spruce up your table with special formatting, WordPerfect provides several predefined styles.

To use SpeedFormat to apply a table formatting style

1. Position the insertion point anywhere within the table.
2. Choose **Table**, **SpeedFormat**. WordPerfect displays the Table SpeedFormat dialog box (see Figure 10.17).

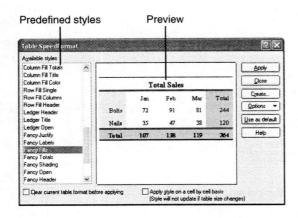

FIGURE 10.17
When you select a SpeedFormat style such as Fancy Fills, you apply a predefined set of formats, lines, and fills to your table.

3. Select a style in the **Available Styles** list box. WordPerfect shows you what it looks like in the preview box. For example, if you select the **Fancy Fills** style, WordPerfect formats your table with a centered title bar and with shading and line changes to set off the data (refer to Figure 10.17).

Not all designs match the function of the table you are creating. For example, the Single Bold Title style actually changes the structure of your table. If you don't like the format you select, you can simply select other styles until you find the one that works best for your table. Or, use Undo to reverse your changes and start from scratch.

> **tip**
>
> Although you can change the design and format of a table at any time, SpeedFormat usually works best if applied before making other format changes. Therefore, if you know what kind of look you want, use SpeedFormat immediately after creating your table.

Changing the Lines

SpeedFormat might just be overkill, especially if all you want to do is change the line style for a few lines.

To change individual cell lines

1. Select the cells you want to change. For example, if you want to change the line beneath the cells in the first row, select all the cells in the first row.
2. Choose **Table**, **Borders/Fill** (**Shift+F12**). WordPerfect displays the Properties for Table Borders/Fill dialog box (see Figure 10.18). For simplicity, I'll refer to it as the Table Borders/Fill dialog box from now on.

FIGURE 10.18
Use the Table Borders/Fill dialog box to change lines and fills in WordPerfect table cells.

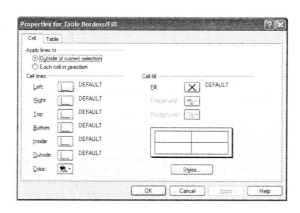

3. Determine which side of the cell(s) you want to change, and then click the corresponding palette button to select a line style (see Figure 10.19). For example, you might click the **Bottom** button and choose **Double Heavy** from the palette.

FIGURE 10.19
You can select a line style from the line style palette or click the palette's drop-down menu for a more complete list of line styles.

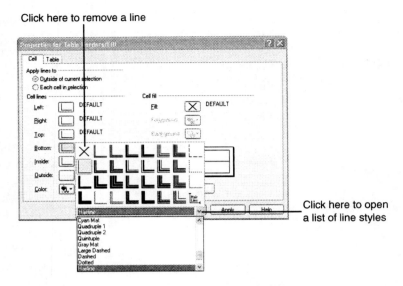

4. WordPerfect displays an example of what you have selected (see Figure 10.20). If you like what you see, click **OK** (or click **Apply** if you want to stay in the dialog box and make other changes).

FIGURE 10.20
The preview box in the Table Borders/Fill dialog box lets you see the effect of your choice before applying it to your table.

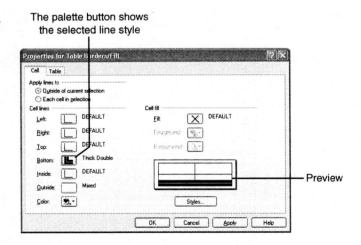

You might not want any lines at all. For example, you might want to organize your information but not have it look like a table. With all the lines removed, your text looks formatted into columns. The bonus is that tables are much easier to work in than columns.

One disadvantage of removing table lines is that you won't be able to see where the cells begin and end. Table guidelines show you how the table is laid out, but they don't print. It's the perfect solution! Choose **View**, **Guidelines** and enable/disable the check box next to **Tables** to turn them on/off. (Note: Table gridlines do the same thing, but if you *are* using borders in your table, those borders won't display if gridlines are turned on—although they will print. Also, gridlines will display only when at least one border is turned on.)

To remove all the table lines

1. Click the **Table** tab while in the Table Borders/Fill dialog box.
2. Choose <**None**> as the default Line style. Alternatively, you can choose **Table**, **SpeedFormat** and select the **No Lines No Border** style.

> **caution**
> If you make changes to your table lines first and then apply a SpeedFormat or change the default table line, you might not get the result you want because the original changes take precedence. In some cases, it is easier to start over than to sort it all out. Choose **Table**, **SpeedFormat**; click **Clear Current Table Format Before Applying**; and then select the <**None**> style.

Changing the Fill Pattern

Fills are nothing more than color or shaded cell backgrounds. A fill color can be applied as a solid color or in a pattern with foreground and background colors. The idea is that you can have some fun with this if you want.

To add fill patterns to a cell

1. Click in the cell where you want a fill. If you want to add a fill to more than one cell—for example, the entire first row of cells—select all the cells you want to change.
2. Choose **Table, Borders/Fill** (**Shift+F12**). WordPerfect displays the Table Borders/Fill dialog box (refer to Figure 10.18).
3. Click the **Fill** palette button (see Figure 10.21) and select a fill pattern.

FIGURE 10.21
You can select a fill style from the fill style palette or click the palette's drop-down menu for a more complete list of fill styles.

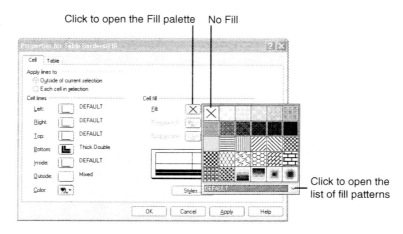

4. Click **OK** to apply the fill pattern.

As you begin to experiment with these options, here are a few things to keep in mind:

- If you choose a solid pattern, you can choose a color from the Foreground palette. Changing the background color has no effect on solid colors.
- If you choose a pattern, you can choose a color from both the Foreground and Background palettes. Pattern lines use the foreground color.
- If you choose a gradient shading pattern, you get to choose a start color and an end color. WordPerfect blends the background from one color to the other.

caution

If you have table gridlines turned on, the fill pattern won't show up onscreen; you must turn off gridlines to see it. However, turning table guidelines on or off won't make a difference.

Choosing a Table Border

By default, a WordPerfect table has no border, so you can quickly improve the appearance of a table by applying one of the border styles.

To add a border style

1. From the **Table** menu or from the **QuickMenu**, choose **Borders/Fill**. Or, press **Shift+F12**.
2. In the Table Borders/Fill dialog box, click the **Table** tab to display table-related lines and fill options (see Figure 10.22).
3. In the **Table Border** area, choose a border style by clicking the **Border** button. Note the resulting effect in the preview box.
4. Click **Apply** to apply the change and remain in the dialog box, or click **OK** to apply the change and return to your table.

tip

If you plan to include text in a filled cell, it's best to use a light shade of gray, 10% or less, or a light color such as yellow. Otherwise, text won't show up very well.

CHAPTER 10 CREATING AND FORMATTING TABLES

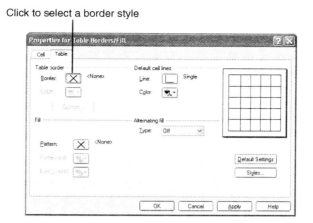

FIGURE 10.22
You can use the Table tab of the Table Borders/Fill dialog box to apply a table border.

Using WordPerfect Tables for Calculations

WordPerfect isn't a full-blown spreadsheet program, but for many different types of calculations, WordPerfect is definitely up to the task. For example, you might want to calculate a total of reservations for your team's final banquet. WordPerfect can do that and much more. In fact, users can construct small spreadsheets in WordPerfect and turn to Quattro Pro only for larger, more complex spreadsheets.

Using QuickSum

Suppose you have a team list, with a column indicating the number of persons attending the team banquet (see Figure 10.23).

FIGURE 10.23
The QuickSum feature lets you add up a column of numbers, such as in this list of team dinner reservations.

Name	Phone Number	# of Tickets
Lindsey Andjelic	555-0201	27
Lauryn Biggerstaff	555-8023	13
Annie Camp	555-1113	15
Emma Hardey	555-3001	29
Gigi Harris	555-0613	33
Macy Hogan	555-0731	45
Sarah Hudson	555-1021	23
Rilee Lozen	555-1010	31
Lauren Privitera	555-6021	39
Morgan Ray	555-1220	40
Allison Rehler	555-1104	55
Tatiana Stewart	555-0707	24
Megan Wolin	555-0907	31
Total # of Tickets Sold		405

A blue triangle indicates a cell with a formula

To create a formula that calculates the total

1. Position the insertion point in the cell where you want the total to appear.
2. Choose **Table**, **QuickSum** (or press **Ctrl+=**). WordPerfect inserts a formula that adds up all the cells above the formula in a column or all the cells to the left of the formula in a row. Notice the blue triangle in the lower-right corner—this indicates a cell with a formula.

If you edit numbers in cells that are included in a QuickSum, the total is automatically recalculated as you work. In a large table, the recalculating process can slow down the operation of your system. In this situation, you might prefer to turn off the automatic recalculate and calculate manually when you are finished editing.

A QuickSum formula in a column adds all the numbers in cells directly above it; a QuickSum at the end of a row adds all the numbers to the left of it. If a cell is empty, QuickSum doesn't calculate any cell above the empty one, so make sure you have numbers in all the cells, even if some of the numbers are zero.

To turn off the automatic recalculate

1. Choose **Table**, **Calculate**. WordPerfect displays the Calculate dialog box (see Figure 10.24).
2. Choose **Off** in the Automatic calculation section.

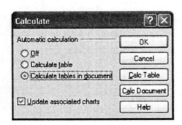

FIGURE 10.24
Use the Calculate dialog box to update calculations in your table or to turn on automatic calculation (recommended).

To manually recalculate a table

1. Choose **Table**, **Calculate** to open the Calculate dialog box.
2. Click the **Calc Table** button. Alternatively, you can right-click the table and choose **Calculate** from the table QuickMenu.

Inserting Formulas

QuickSum is a great feature, especially when you are frequently totaling up numbers in a column. But wait—there's more! You can create spreadsheet-like formulas in a WordPerfect table that perform a variety of calculations on the figures.

The same math addition and subtraction operators (+, -) that you learned in elementary school are used to build formulas in WordPerfect tables. An asterisk (*) is used as a multiplication symbol instead of ×, and the slash (/) is used as a division symbol instead of a dash (-). So, if you want to multiply two cells and divide by a third, your formula might look like this: C5*F14/A2.

When you create a formula in a cell, the result of the formula is displayed in the cell, not the formula itself. If you select a cell with a formula, the formula is displayed in the input line where you can edit it. You cannot edit the result of a formula—you can only edit the formula itself. Let's say that you have a simple invoice in which you want to multiply the number of items sold by the cost of each unit.

To insert a formula

1. Choose **Table**, **Formula Toolbar**. WordPerfect displays the Formula toolbar (see Figure 10.25).

FIGURE 10.25

The Formula toolbar helps you create and edit spreadsheet formulas.

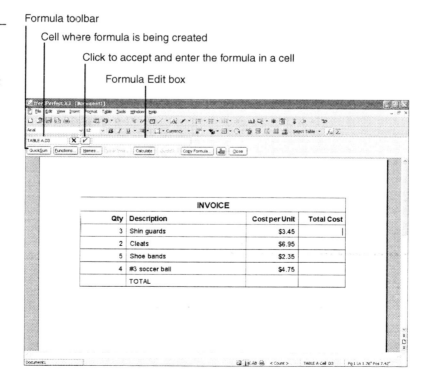

2. Position the insertion point in the cell where you want the formula (for example, in column D of the third row).

3. Click in the **Formula Edit** box (to the right of the blue check mark button) to begin the formula edit process.

4. You can type the cell references and math symbols by hand, but you can also just click on the cells you want to include and add the math operators. For example, you could type **A3*C3**, or you could click in cell **A3**, type the **asterisk**, and then click in **C3**. The result is the same.

5. Press **Enter**, or click the blue check mark button to place the formula in the target cell (for example, D3).

It's easy to get mixed up, so if it doesn't work right the first time, just click **Undo** and try again. You will get the hang of it in no time.

You could repeat the preceding steps for each row of the invoice, but an easier way is to copy the formula. WordPerfect automatically adjusts the formula for each row:

1. Position the insertion point in the cell with the formula.

2. On the Formula toolbar, click **Copy Formula**. WordPerfect displays the Copy Formula dialog box (see Figure 10.26).

3. Click the **Down** radio button, and then indicate how many times to copy the formula (for example, 3).

4. Click **OK**, and WordPerfect copies the formula down (in our example, to the next three cells).

Notice that you can also copy a formula directly to a specific cell. Simply type the cell address in the **To Cell** text box in the Copy Formula dialog box.

> **tip**
>
> You probably noticed the $ signs in Figure 10.25. What you might not realize is that you don't have to type them. Instead, you can save yourself time and trouble by letting WordPerfect automatically format your numbers for you.
>
> Choose **Table, Numeric Format**. WordPerfect shows you a dialog box that lets you change the numbering style for cells, columns, or the entire table. You can format numbers for currency, percentage, fixed decimal places, and more. Notice that there are different tabs for cell, column, and table, so make sure you click the right tab for the area of the table that you want to work on.

FIGURE 10.26
Use the Copy Formula dialog box to copy formulas instead of re-creating them.

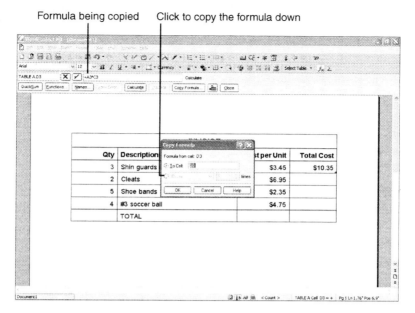

Inserting Functions

Okay, now things are getting technical. What's a function? It's nothing more than a word that describes a mathematical process. For example, SUM is a function that adds, or sums, all the values in a given group of cells.

Suppose, for example, that you now want to add all the extended prices on your invoice. You could use the QuickSum feature, but you can also use the SUM function. The SUM function is more flexible because you are actually building the formula and indicating which cells to sum instead of letting QuickSum figure it out.

To insert a function in a formula

1. Position the insertion point at the bottom of the list of numbers.
2. Click in the **Formula Edit** box on the Formula toolbar.
3. Type **SUM(D3:D6)**. This simply means, "sum all the numbers in cells D3 through D6."
4. Click the blue check mark button, or press **Enter**. WordPerfect puts the function formula in the proper cell and makes the calculation (see Figure 10.27).

FIGURE 10.27
Functions, such as SUM, are simply shortcuts that enable you to make spreadsheet-type calculations.

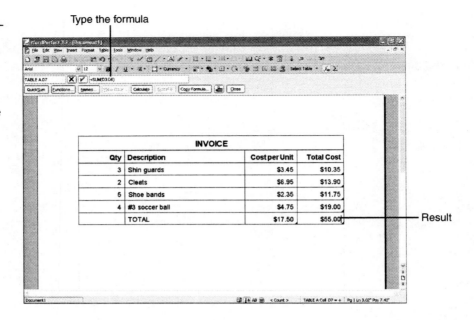

WordPerfect's table formulas are based on spreadsheet technology. Although WordPerfect tables are not suited for heavy-duty spreadsheet applications such as Quattro Pro, they're just fine for the day-to-day calculations we have to make. Many of us can avoid spreadsheet programs altogether just by using WordPerfect tables.

WordPerfect has more than 500 built-in functions. For more information on the functions and how to insert them into a formula, search for "table functions" in the Help Index.

> **tip**
> If you point to a cell that contains a formula, a QuickTip will appear with the formula inside. This is very handy when you are double-checking your formulas because all you have to do is point to a cell and hesitate for a second. The QuickTip appears, you verify the formula, and you're ready to move to the next formula.

Converting Text to a Table, or a Table to Text

"Now you tell me about tables," you say. You already painstakingly created some rows and columns of data, but would rather see this information in a table. Or, perhaps you want to convert a table list to a simple text list. Fortunately, WordPerfect provides a simple method for creating a table from text formatted in tabular columns (columns with tabs between them). In fact, this capability might be one of the easiest, yet most practical uses for tables.

Converting Tabular Columns to Tables

Suppose you have a list of company employees that includes names, offices, and telephone numbers. Single tabs separate the three columns of data, as follows:

    Lin, Ting-Yi   VH299 7-6543

    Rohde, Kathy   VH287 7-1408

    Samuels, Jodi   VH246 7-4965

To convert data in tabular columns to a table

1. Select all the text to the end of the last line of data.
2. Choose **Table**, **Convert**. WordPerfect displays the Convert: Text to Table dialog box (see Figure 10.28).

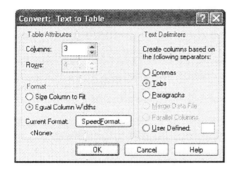

FIGURE 10.28
When you convert text to a table, the Tabs option is selected by default.

3. Take a look at the options and make any necessary selections; then click **OK**. WordPerfect converts your tabular columns of data into a table (see Figure 10.29).

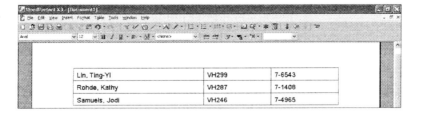

FIGURE 10.29
After converting data from tabular columns into a table, you might need to adjust the column width.

Converting Tables to Other Formats

At some point, you might want to use your table data in another format. For example, you need to export the information to a format that can be used in a non-WordPerfect database.

To convert table data to another format

1. Position the insertion point in the table and choose **Table**, **Convert**. WordPerfect displays the Convert: Table to Text dialog box, shown in Figure 10.30.
2. Select one of the following options to separate the cells:

   - You can separate the data from each cell in a row with commas, hard returns, tabs, or with any other character you specify. Note that rows of data themselves are separated by hard returns.
   - You can change the data into a WordPerfect merge file format, where each cell is separated by an ENDFIELD code, and each row is separated by an ENDRECORD code. See Chapter 14, "Using the Merge Feature," for more information on merge data files and merge field codes.

> **caution**
> Although converting text to tables is easy, the key to a successful conversion is making sure that a single tab separates the text columns. If, for example, you use more than one tab to separate some of the entries, WordPerfect adds extra cells in the table for the extra tabs. The result can be messy. If this is the case, use **Undo** to restore the text columns. Remove the extra tabs and try again.

FIGURE 10.30
The Convert: Table to Text dialog box enables you to convert table data into other formats.

The Absolute Minimum

In this chapter, you learned how to work with one of the most versatile features in WordPerfect—tables. From start to finish, you learned how to create a table, how to edit cell contents, how to format the table, and how to include calculations on values.

- You saw how easy it is to create tables, using the dialog box or by clicking and dragging across the Table palette.
- You learned how quick it is to move around in a table by clicking the mouse or by pressing Tab and Shift+Tab.
- It's a simple process to adjust column widths, to add/delete rows and columns, and to join or split rows/columns, as you fine-tune the table structure.
- You now understand how to format table elements, taking the order of precedence into account.
- Borders, lines, and fill can all be altered to fit the situation and to emphasize important parts of the table.
- Formulas can be inserted to calculate values just as you would in a spreadsheet program. Quite a few spreadsheet calculations can be performed in WordPerfect tables using the built-in functions.
- It's easy to convert an existing table into text or to convert tabbed columns into a table, so if you already have content that you want in a table, you won't have to retype anything.

In the next chapter, you learn how to organize information into lists and outlines.

IN THIS CHAPTER

- Learn how to create lists with bullets or numbers.
- Explore how to change bullet and number styles.
- Discover how useful outlines can be and how easy they are to create and edit.
- Learn how to collapse or expand outlines, and how to change outline styles.

CREATING LISTS AND OUTLINES

WordPerfect is great for creating and editing paragraphs of text, but it's also well-suited to creating structured lists and outlines that make it easy for the reader to quickly grasp the important items or ideas in your document. To illustrate, I could go on and on about various types of lists, including descriptions about each type. On the other hand, I could simply create a bulleted list, which I suspect you will find quicker and easier to understand. Lists or outlines are perfect for

- To-do lists
- Agendas for an upcoming meeting
- Notes for a speech you have to give
- Summary notes for a class you've attended
- Executive summaries for more extensive reports
- Summary items for overhead transparencies

Working with Lists

You could just use the "brute force" method to create lists or outlines like those shown in Figure 11.1 (type a number, type the text, type the next number, and so on). Or, you could take a few minutes to learn how this powerful WordPerfect feature can automate your list making and, over the course of the next several months, save yourself literally hours of time and trouble. Figure 11.1 shows the three different types of lists that can be created in WordPerfect—numbered lists, bulleted lists, and outlines.

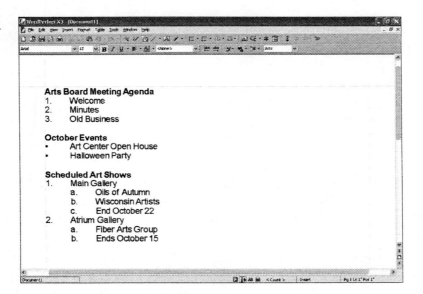

FIGURE 11.1
WordPerfect helps automate the process of creating numbered or bulleted lists and outlines.

Creating Bulleted Lists

A *bulleted list* uses bullets, or symbols, to delineate the different levels in a list. The default bullet is a medium-sized solid black bullet, but you can switch to a different type of bullet, or you can use one of the symbols from the WP character sets.

To create a bulleted list

1. Choose **Insert**, **Outline/Bullets & Numbering**. WordPerfect opens the Bullets & Numbering dialog box.
2. Click the **Bullets** tab to display a list of predefined bullet list styles (see Figure 11.2).

FIGURE 11.2

The Bullets tab of the Bullets & Numbering dialog box offers several bullet styles for your list.

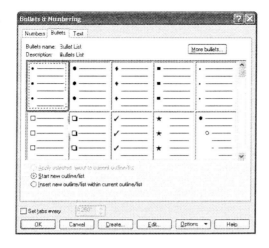

3. Click the bullet style you want to use and click **OK**. WordPerfect inserts the chosen bullet style, which includes the bullet character and an indented paragraph.
4. Type the text of the first bullet.
5. Press **Enter**. WordPerfect inserts a new bullet (see Figure 11.3).

FIGURE 11.3

When you use a bullet style, pressing Enter automatically adds a new bulleted line.

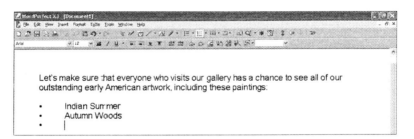

6. Repeat steps 4 and 5 until you finish the list, and then press **Enter** one last time.
7. Press **Backspace** to erase the last bullet and to turn off the bullets. You can also press **Ctrl+H**, or click the **Bullet** button on the toolbar if you prefer.

 You can also start a bulleted list by clicking the **Bullet** button on the toolbar, which places the currently selected bullet style in your document. If you don't like the current bullet style, select the list; then click the **drop-down arrow** on the **Bullet** button to see a palette of available bullet styles. Hover the mouse pointer over a bullet style to see the effect in WordPerfect's RealTime Preview, or click **More** to go to the Bullets & Numbering dialog box (refer to Figure 11.2). To turn off the bullet style, simply click the **Bullet** button again.

Creating Numbered Lists

For some reason, when using a word processing program, most of us forget how good computers are with numbers. A computer "thinks" in zeros and ones, so calculating numbers is what computers do best. This comes in handy when WordPerfect automatically updates your numbered lists as you revise the document.

To create a numbered list

1. Choose **Insert**, **Outline/Bullets & Numbering**.
2. Click the **Numbers** tab to choose a number style (see Figure 11.4). Use the scrollbar to see all the styles.
3. If you simply click **OK** without choosing a different style, WordPerfect uses the default style that includes a number, followed by a period and an indent code.
4. Type some text, and when you press **Enter**, WordPerfect automatically increments the number for you.
5. Press **Backspace** to turn off the numbered list.

You can quickly start a numbered list by clicking the **Numbering** button on the toolbar. Choose different styles by clicking the drop-down arrow on the Numbering button.

> **tip**
>
> Another quick and simple way to start a bulleted list is to type an asterisk (*) and then press **Tab**. WordPerfect's QuickBullets feature automatically starts a bulleted list, which you then continue by adding bullets, or turn off the bullet feature as you do with any bulleted list. For more information on this feature, see "Customizing Format-As-You-Go" in Chapter 6, "Using the Writing Tools."

> **tip**
>
> In the Bullets & Numbering dialog box, click one of the samples to display the name and description under the dialog box tabs. This is especially helpful when you are looking for a style that someone else has recommended.

FIGURE 11.4
WordPerfect provides several predefined numbered list and outline styles.

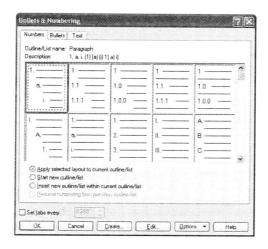

Editing Lists

It stands to reason that as soon as you complete a list of items, something will come up, and you will need to edit those items. You will need to know how to add or delete list items and how to add blank lines.

Here are a few of the more useful and important ways of modifying a bulleted or numbered list:

- **Add an extra blank line between list items**—As you create the list, press **Enter** a second time before typing the list item. If you've already typed an item, place the insertion point on the line, press **Home** to move to the beginning of the line (after the number), and then press **Enter** to add a new blank line.

- **Add a new list item**—Position the insertion point at the end of an existing list item; then press **Enter**. WordPerfect automatically inserts a new bullet or number. If you are working in a numbered list, notice how WordPerfect automatically inserts the correct number. Also, notice that if you add or delete a numbered item, WordPerfect adjusts all the numbers following the inserted item.

- **Remove a line**—Simply delete all the text on the line, and press **Backspace** to delete the bullet or number. Press **Backspace** again to remove the blank space between the list items.

- **Turn off bullets or numbers**—When you're finished with the list, click the Number or Bullet button on the toolbar to turn off the automatic bulleted or numbered list.

Changing the Bullet or Numbering Style

WordPerfect makes it easy to change your mind or to exercise artistic freedom. Bulleted and numbered lists are no exception. You can change the bullet or number style even after you have created the list.

To change the bullet or numbering style for a list

1. Position the insertion point at the top of the list.
2. Open the Bullets & Numbering dialog box by choosing **Insert**, **Outline/Bullets & Numbering**.
3. Click the **Numbers** or **Bullets** tab, depending on the style you want to change to (refer to Figures 11.4 or 11.2, respectively). You can change any list from one style type to another. For example, you can change a numbered list to a bulleted list, and vice versa.
4. Click the style you want. The three options at the bottom of the tab—Apply Selected Layout to Current Outline/List, Start New Outline/List, and Insert New Outline/List Within Current Outline/List—control how the styles are applied (see Figure 11.5).

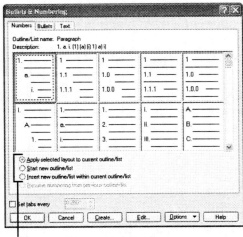

FIGURE 11.5
When you select a different bullet or numbering style, you have additional options for how to apply that style.

Select one of these three options

Only two of the options are likely to be generally useful to you. These are

- **Apply Selected Layout to Current Outline/List**—This option simply changes the style for the entire list.
- **Start New Outline/List**—This option starts a new style at the insertion point. If you are in the middle of a list, the new style applies to all the remaining items in the list. If you are at the end of a list, it simply starts a new list, beginning at number 1 if you are using numbers (see Figure 11.6).

FIGURE 11.6

You can use numbering/outline options to create new lists or to change the style of all or part of an existing list.

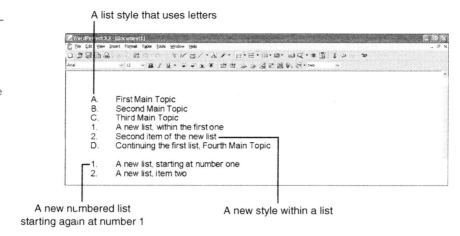

Working with Outlines

Outlines are a lot like lists, but they add another dimension of detail. For example, in a list, every item has the same relative importance (1, 2, 3, and so on). Outline items, on the other hand, are arranged in different levels of importance (1, 1a, 1b, 2, and so on). Consider the two lists shown in Figure 11.7.

FIGURE 11.7

Outlines look a lot like lists, but outline sublevels provide more flexibility in organizing information.

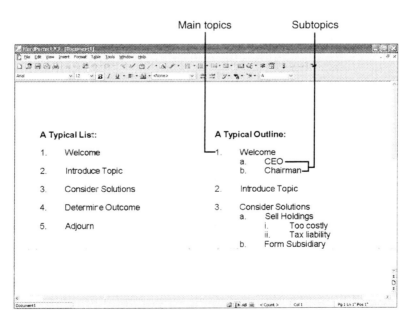

In Figure 11.7, the second list's sublevels provide additional details about the major topics in the list.

WordPerfect's outlines are easy to work with, and the little bit of time required to learn about them is more than justified by the time and effort they can save you. Consider this: Outline items are automatically renumbered as you add, delete, or rearrange them. It's very cool.

Creating Outlines

WordPerfect offers several outline styles, but the default is called Paragraph Numbering. Let's first step through the basics to show you just how easy it is to create a multilevel outline. We can return to the details after that.

To create an outline

1. Choose **Insert**, **Outline/Bullets & Numbering**. WordPerfect displays the Bullets & Numbering dialog box.
2. Click the **Numbers** tab. The Paragraph style is selected by default (refer to Figure 11.4).
3. Click **OK**. WordPerfect places a number, followed by a period and an indent.
4. Type the content of the first outline item (refer to the outline in Figure 11.7 for sample text you can type).
5. To insert the next number, press **Enter**. If you want to move the number down another line before you type, press **Enter** again.
6. To create the next level, press **Tab**. WordPerfect moves to the next tab stop and, in this case, changes the number to a letter.
7. Type the content of the first subtopic.
8. Press **Enter**. WordPerfect inserts the next number or letter at the same level as the preceding paragraph.
9. Type the second subtopic and press **Enter**.
10. Before typing, press **Shift+Tab** to move back to the left and switch to the previous outline level.
11. Continue typing and inserting numbers until you finish the outline. Here is a quick reference of keystrokes:
    - Press **Enter** to add a new numbered line.
    - Press **Tab** to move to the next level.
    - Press **Shift+Tab** to return to a previous level.
12. Press **Enter** one last time, and then press **Backspace** to delete the extra outline number and to turn off outlining.

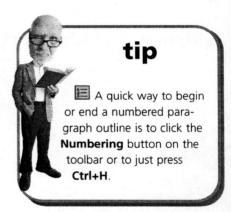

tip

A quick way to begin or end a numbered paragraph outline is to click the **Numbering** button on the toolbar or to just press **Ctrl+H**.

Using the Outline Property Bar

Whenever the insertion point is located within a list or outline, the Outline property bar appears (see Figure 11.8).

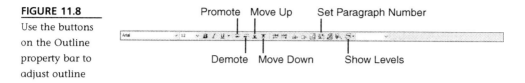

FIGURE 11.8
Use the buttons on the Outline property bar to adjust outline items.

Several of these buttons add functionality that most of us will rarely use. Some, however, might just be useful shortcuts:

- **Promote**—Changes an outline item to a higher level (for example, a main topic rather than a subtopic).
- **Demote**— Changes an outline item to a lower level (for example, a subtopic rather than a main topic).
- **Move Up**— Moves an outline item up in the outline.
- **Move Down**—Moves an outline item down in the outline.
- **Show Family**—Displays the family (subtopics) of the selected outline item.
- **Hide Family**—Hides the family (subtopics) of the selected outline item.
- **Set Paragraph Number**— This is useful for starting a new outline (at number one) when another outline already exists in the document.
- **Show Levels**— Expands or collapses an outline.

Editing an Outline

The nifty thing about outlines is how easy it is to add, move, or delete outline items. WordPerfect automatically numbers and renumbers everything, so you don't have to worry about it. You can insert items in the middle of an outline, rearrange outline items, and promote/demote outline items, all in just a few quick steps.

Inserting Items in an Existing Outline

Let's say that you've decided to follow the advice of your high school English teacher and create all the main topics of your outline, and then go back and add subtopics, and even sub-subtopics. When you go back to add the subtopics, you will be adding items to an existing outline.

To add an outline item to an existing outline

1. Position the insertion point at the end of the line preceding where you want to add a new line.
2. Press **Enter**. WordPerfect adds a new number at the same level of the preceding line (see Figure 11.9).

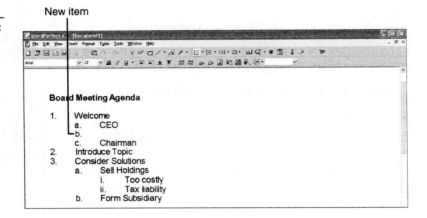

FIGURE 11.9
When you insert a line in the middle of an outline, WordPerfect automatically numbers the new line and renumbers all the following lines.

3. If you want to change the outline level of the new item, press **Tab** to move to the right and **Shift+Tab** to move to the left.
4. Type the text of the outline item.

Rearranging Outline Items

It's also easy to rearrange the items in an outline. For example, you decide that item five really belongs after item two, so you need to cut item five (and everything that falls beneath it) and move it under item two. One easy method is to move an item using the Outline property bar. The other is to move an item by cutting and pasting.

To move an item using the Outline property bar

1. Position the insertion point on the item to be moved.

2. Click the **Move Up** button or the **Move Down** button on the Outline property bar.

To move an item along with its related subtopics, or to move several outline items at once, you simply select and then cut or copy the outline items. However, positioning the insertion point can be tricky. Instead, follow these easy steps:

1. Position the mouse pointer in the left margin area next to the item to be moved. The pointer turns into an arrow that points up and to the right (see Figure 11.10).

FIGURE 11.10
Click in the left margin next to the outline items you want to select.

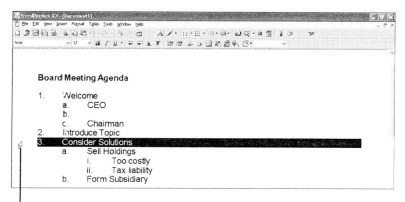

New mouse pointer shape

2. To select just one outline item, double-click in the margin area. WordPerfect selects the entire outline item (refer to Figure 11.10).

3. To select several outline items, click and drag the mouse downward. You might have to drag the mouse to the far right of the last line to select everything in that last line (see Figure 11.11).

FIGURE 11.11
Drag the mouse from the left of the first outline item to the end of the last outline item to select multiple outline items.

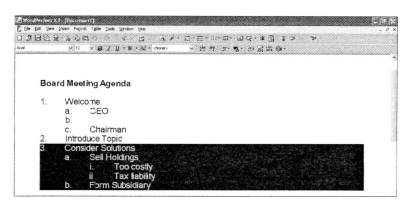

4. With the items selected, use your favorite method to cut or copy.

5. Next, move the insertion point to the line *after* the item where you want to paste the outline items.

6. Press the **Home** key *twice*. Pressing Home only once moves the insertion point to the beginning of the text in the line, but after the number. Pressing Home twice moves it to the absolute beginning of the line, before the number.

7. Use your favorite method to paste the outline items.

Note that when you cut outline items, WordPerfect renumbers everything following it, and when you paste them back, WordPerfect once again automatically adjusts the outline numbers.

Promoting/Demoting Outline Items

Finally, you can also adjust outline levels by *promoting* or *demoting* outline items. For example, if you decide that a certain subtopic deserves the same importance as a main topic, you can *promote* it. In other words, you can change the numbering from "a" to "1." Conversely, if you decide to reduce the importance of an item, you can demote it in the outline.

To promote or demote an outline item

1. Position the insertion point on the item you want to promote or demote.
2. Press **Home** *once* to move the insertion point to the beginning of the line, but following the outline number.

3. Press **Shift+Tab** to promote the item (move it to the left). You can also click the **Promote** button on the Outline property bar.

4. Press **Tab** to demote the item (move it to the right), or click the **Demote** button on the Outline property bar.

Collapsing and Expanding Outlines

WordPerfect makes it easy to develop two or more different outlines from the same original outline. Let me give you an example. You might need to prepare an agenda for those attending a meeting that shows only the main outline items. However, you need a second, more detailed agenda, so you can make sure that everything goes according to schedule. All you have to do is create the full agenda or outline and then hide the sublevels you don't want others to see. This is called *collapsing* an outline. You could then print the collapsed copy of your agenda for the participants and an expanded copy of the agenda for your use.

To collapse an outline, showing only the main topics

1. Position the insertion point somewhere in the outline so that the Outline property bar appears (refer to Figure 11.8).

2. Click the **Show Levels** button. WordPerfect displays a list of levels, One through Nine, and <None> (see Figure 11.12).

FIGURE 11.12
The Show Levels button enables you to collapse or expand your outline.

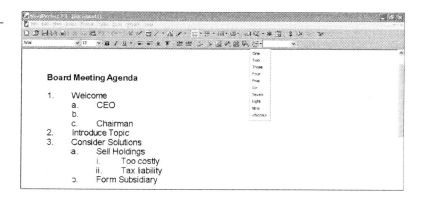

3. Click the number of levels you want to display; for example, **One**. WordPerfect collapses the outline to display only the first-level outline items (see Figure 11.13).

FIGURE 11.13
A collapsed outline shows only the major topics. The subtopics are still there. You just expand the outline to see them again.

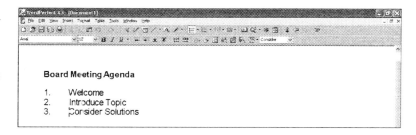

4. To display all levels again, repeat steps 1–3, choosing **Nine**.

Changing the Outline Style

The default outline style in WordPerfect is Paragraph (1, a, i, and so on). You probably remember this as the traditional outline style you learned in high school. There are other outline styles as well. Fortunately, WordPerfect makes it easy to change outline styles.

To change to a different outline style

1. Select the part of the outline that you want to change.
2. Choose **Insert**, **Outline/Bullets & Numbering**. WordPerfect displays the Bullets & Numbering dialog box (refer to Figure 11.4).

> **caution**
> If you select <None>, WordPerfect hides the entire outline and turns off the Outline property bar. To get your outline back, you have to choose **View**, **Toolbars**; select the **Outline Tools** toolbar; and then click the **Show Levels** button and choose the number of levels you want to display.

3. Choose the outline style you want, and click **OK**. WordPerfect automatically changes the outline style (see Figure 11.14).

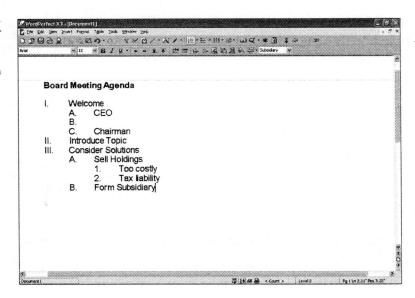

FIGURE 11.14
The structure of an outline does not change when you apply a different outline style.

THE ABSOLUTE MINIMUM

In this chapter, you discovered some easy and practical ways to organize information other than in plain paragraphs. Whether you're creating a simple to-do list or a complex outline for a speech you have to give, WordPerfect lists and outlines are just the ticket.

- You discovered how easy it is to create and edit bulleted lists.
- Numbered lists are also useful because you can add, remove, or move items, and WordPerfect automatically renumbers your list.
- You saw how you could switch to a different bullet or number style after you create a list.
- Outlines give you the added dimension of subtopics, and again, WordPerfect automatically keeps track of the proper outline numbering.
- You learned how to edit outline items and how to collapse and expand your outlines.
- Changing to a different outline style won't affect the structure of the outline.

In the next chapter—Chapter 12, "Working with Graphics"—you get to play with graphic images, lines, and other visual elements that spice up and enhance the content of your documents.

Adding Visuals

Working with Graphics 215

Sharing Data 243

IN THIS CHAPTER

- Learn how to insert horizontal and vertical graphic lines.
- Find out how to import graphics into WordPerfect.
- Learn how to create and use text boxes.
- Add borders and fills to graphics and text boxes, and learn how to wrap text around them.
- Learn how to add a watermark to your pages.
- Explore creating and layering your own drawings (shapes).

WORKING WITH GRAPHICS

Words are great. They're the stuff of *Grapes of Wrath*, *To Kill a Mockingbird*, and *The Catcher in the Rye*. Just think what the authors of those famous works could have done with a word processing program such as WordPerfect! Although you and I are pretty good with words, we could use a little help in making our words communicate more effectively. That's where graphics come in.

Graphic elements range from simple lines or shapes that we create ourselves, to clip art created by artists who are much better at art than we are. WordPerfect makes it so easy to insert and manipulate graphics that you don't have to be an artist to create documents with a polished and professional appearance.

Working with Graphic Lines

Although they might not seem like it, lines in WordPerfect are a simple form of graphics. In fact, some of the things you learn about graphic lines will help you as you work with more complex things such as shapes or clip art. So, graphic lines are a good place to start the discussion.

Inserting Standard Lines

There are two basic types of lines in WordPerfect: horizontal and vertical. The most commonly used type is the horizontal line, which helps the reader visually separate sections of your document.

For example, when you create a memo, you often separate the heading information (TO:, FROM:, RE:) from the body of the text with a line that extends from one margin to the other. The default horizontal graphic line is a thin line that stretches from the left to the right margin (see Figure 12.1).

To create the default horizontal line

1. Position the insertion point on the line where you want to create the graphic line.
2. Choose **Insert**, **Line**, **Horizontal Line** (**Ctrl+F11**).

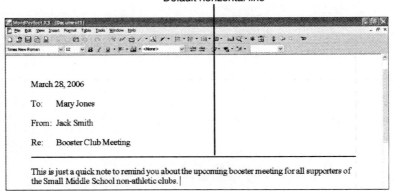

FIGURE 12.1
The default horizontal line extends from the left margin to the right margin.

WordPerfect places a perfectly measured horizontal line in your document (refer to Figure 12.1). No muss, no fuss! "But," you ask, "why can't I just type a bunch of underlines?" Graphic lines have distinct advantages over lines created with characters. First, if you change your margins, the line might end up being too long and will wrap to the next line, or it might be too short, not reaching all the way to the right margin. Second, if you change your font, the width of the underline characters changes and again your line might be too long or too short. Graphic lines, on the other hand, fit neatly from margin to margin, regardless of the margin settings or the text font.

The other graphic line type, vertical lines, has a different purpose. Often, they are used with newspaper-style columns and help the reader follow the flow of the text (see Figure 12.2).

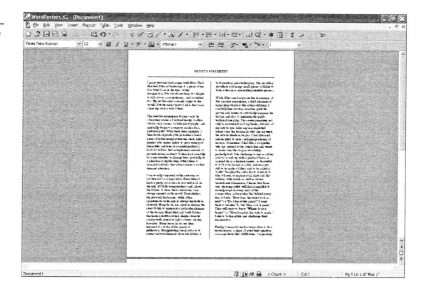

FIGURE 12.2
Vertical lines are often used to separate columns of text.

To insert a vertical line, position the insertion point at the left margin and simply choose **Insert, Line, Vertical Line**. WordPerfect inserts a vertical line at the left margin that extends from the top to bottom margins (see Figure 12.3). Note, however, that because the default vertical line is nearly on top of the text, you will probably want to move the line over a little.

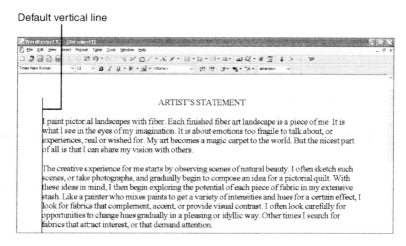

FIGURE 12.3
The default vertical line practically stands on top of the text, so you might need to adjust its location.

Customizing Graphic Lines

Fortunately, you can customize your lines to meet your needs. One way is simply to drag the lines to another location. The other is to create a line as long and as thick as you want, located exactly where you want it. Suppose that you want to move the vertical line you just created a bit to the left, into the left margin.

To move a graphic line

1. Position the mouse pointer over the graphic line until the pointer leans to the right.
2. Click the mouse, and small black boxes appear at each end of the line and also in the middle (see Figure 12.4). These boxes are called *sizing handles* and can be used to manipulate a graphic image.

FIGURE 12.4
Sizing handles are used to change the shape of a graphic element.

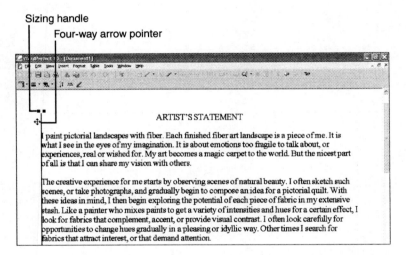

3. Position the mouse pointer over the selected graphic until it turns into a four-way arrow, which is the move pointer (refer to Figure 12.4).
4. Click and hold down the mouse button while you drag the line to its new location.
5. When the line is where you want it, release the mouse button. If you don't get it quite right, repeat steps 3 and 4 until you do (see Figure 12.5).

FIGURE 12.5
The vertical line has been moved away from the text into the left margin.

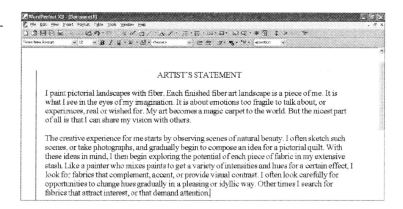

It doesn't make any difference whether you're moving a horizontal or a vertical line; the steps to move it are the same. You select the line by clicking on it; then move the line by dragging it to a new location.

Most of us prefer simply to drag graphic elements to position them and use sizing handles to resize them. However, sometimes you need more precise control of a line: the length, width, thickness, color, or the position on the page. Suppose that you want to create a three-inch signature line at the end of a legal agreement.

To create a custom line

1. Position the insertion point where you want to insert the line.
2. Choose **Insert**, **Line**, **Custom Line**. WordPerfect displays the Create Graphics Line dialog box (see Figure 12.6).

FIGURE 12.6
Using the Create Graphics Line dialog box, you can create a custom line of any length, thickness, color, or location.

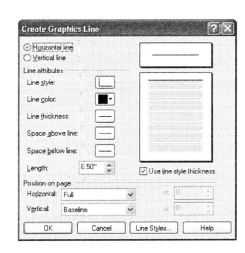

3. Change the line options as desired. For example,

- **Vertical line/Horizontal line**—Choose the type of line you want to create. This selection determines some of the other options available to you.
- **Line attributes**—Choose the style (single, double, dashed, and so on), color, thickness, spacing, and length.
- **Position on page**—If you set a horizontal line's horizontal position to Left, whatever size line you create will begin at the left margin. To place a vertical line between columns, choose the horizontal position **Align with Columns**. Choose **Set** from either the **Vertical** or **Horizontal** dropdown lists, then indicate a starting point from the left edge of the page in the At text box. If necessary, specify the length of the line in the Length text box.

4. The preview box shows you what your line will look like. When you're satisfied, click **OK**. WordPerfect inserts the line into your document (see Figure 12.7).

FIGURE 12.7
You can use horizontal, vertical, or custom lines all in the same document.

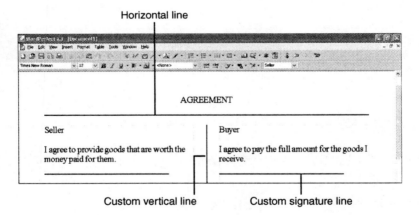

Inserting Graphic Images

Graphic lines are simple and are rather practical graphic elements. However, I'll bet that you really want to know about putting pictures in your document. You've probably heard about clip art, but that is just one of the many graphic elements you can add to a WordPerfect document. Some of the things you can add include

- WordPerfect's own clip art images
- Pictures you take with a digital camera
- Images you scan yourself
- Graphic images from the Internet
- Background graphics called watermarks
- Graphic shapes such as stars, boxes, or arrows

Working with graphics is fun! But try not to get too carried away. At the very least, you might find yourself spending a lot of time trying to get things just right. At the worst, you will focus so much on the graphical elements that you neglect to write good text.

Inserting Clip Art

The easiest place to start is with WordPerfect's own clip art images—predesigned artwork that comes with the WordPerfect program. The steps to insert and manipulate these graphic images also apply to most other graphic elements, including graphic lines, which you just learned about.

To insert a clip art image in your document

1. Position the insertion point at the location where you want to insert the graphic image.

2. Choose **Insert**, **Graphics**, **Clipart**, or click the **Clipart** button on the toolbar. WordPerfect displays the Scrapbook dialog box (see Figure 12.8), which contains thumbnail images of the clip art on your system, along with photos, video, and audio clips.

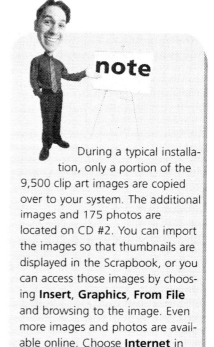

note

During a typical installation, only a portion of the 9,500 clip art images are copied over to your system. The additional images and 175 photos are located on CD #2. You can import the images so that thumbnails are displayed in the Scrapbook, or you can access those images by choosing **Insert**, **Graphics**, **From File** and browsing to the image. Even more images and photos are available online. Choose **Internet** in the Scrapbook and follow the prompts.

FIGURE 12.8
Depending on your version of WordPerfect, the WordPerfect Scrapbook provides access to up to 9,500 clip art images (on CD), as well as photos, audio, and video clips.

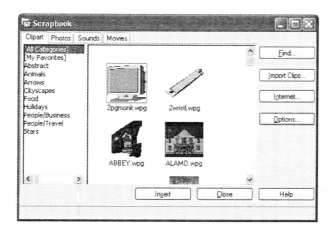

3. Scroll through the list of images and select the one you want.
4. Click **Insert** to place the image in your document. Or, if you prefer, you can double-click an image to insert it into the document.
5. Click **Close** to clear the Scrapbook dialog box.

Notice how the image pushes aside the text that surrounds it, in the shape of a rectangle (see Figure 12.9). You will also note that a special Graphics property bar appears to help you manipulate and modify the image. And don't forget that nearly anything that's available on the property bars is also available on the QuickMenu. If you get into the habit of right-clicking graphics so you can select from the QuickMenu, you'll save yourself oodles of time.

FIGURE 12.9
Graphic images are placed in graphics boxes that you can manipulate with the sizing handles and several options on the Graphics property bar, or the QuickMenu.

The rectangle that surrounds the image is called a *graphics box*, and when selected it is surrounded by eight black boxes called *sizing handles* (refer to Figure 12.9). If you click elsewhere in the document, you deselect the graphic box and the handles disappear. When you click an image, you select the object and the sizing handles reappear.

Note that if you accidentally insert the wrong image, you can delete it. Just select the image and press **Delete**.

Moving and Sizing an Image

Before we talk about other types of images, you probably want to know how to make the clip art behave the way you want it to. It might be too large or too small, and almost certainly it won't be positioned exactly where you want it.

To move an image

1. Click *once* on the image to select it; the sizing handles appear. Remember that double-clicking takes you to the graphics editor.
2. Position the mouse pointer over the image until it turns to the four-sided move pointer.
3. Click and drag the image to the new location.
4. Release the mouse button.

Part of the problem in placing the graphic might be that the image is too large or too small. You can change the size of a graphic image this way:

1. Select the image, and then move the mouse pointer to one of the corner sizing handles until the pointer turns into a two-way arrow. This is called a *resizing pointer* (see Figure 12.10).

> **caution**
>
> Be careful not to double-click a clip art image after you've inserted it into your document. Doing so actually transfers you to the Corel Presentations graphics program where you can edit the clip art image itself. Menus and toolbars change drastically. If this does happen, simply click outside the image area to return to WordPerfect and your document.

FIGURE 12.10

To resize a graphic image, drag the corner sizing handles.

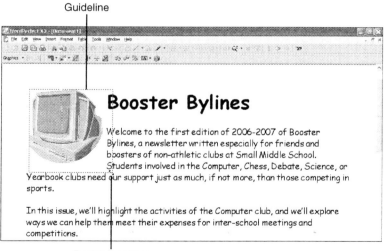

2. Click and drag the sizing handle toward the center of the image to make it smaller or away from the center to make it larger. As you click and drag, you'll notice a dotted outline around the image. This guideline shows you how the image will look when you release the sizing handle.

3. Release the mouse button. You might need to further adjust the location of the image as described previously.

Dragging the corner sizing handles keeps the image proportional. If you want to distort an image, drag the top, bottom, or side sizing handles. You can produce some interesting images using this method, such as short, fat giraffes or long, skinny pigs. For example, in Figure 12.11, the image on the left has the original proportions. The image in the middle is taller as a result of clicking and dragging the bottom center sizing handle downward to increase the length. The image on the right is wider after clicking and dragging a side sizing handle outward to increase the width.

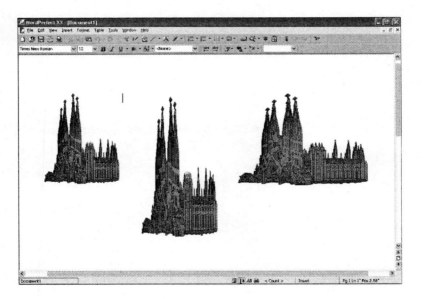

FIGURE 12.11
You can alter the proportions of an image by clicking and dragging the top, bottom, or side sizing handles.

Importing Graphics

WordPerfect's clip art is extensive and useful. But often the precise image you need just can't be found in WordPerfect's clip art library. Fortunately, you can import almost any type of graphic, from almost any source. The Internet has a vast collection of free clip art that you can download and use in your documents. You can also convert graphics created in other applications to WordPerfect format. Finally, if you have a printed copy of an image, it can be scanned and inserted into a document.

Inserting Other Graphic Types

Whether you use a graphic image created in another graphics program, a scanned graphic, or an image from the Internet, the procedure for inserting it is the same.

WordPerfect capably converts to the WordPerfect format a variety of graphics, such as the GIF, JPG, TIFF, or PCX graphics format. For a complete list of the formats that you can convert in WordPerfect, search for "graphic file import formats" in the Search tab of the Help Topics dialog box.

To convert a graphic from another format, all you have to do is insert the image, and WordPerfect takes care of the rest. If, for some reason, WordPerfect doesn't recognize a graphic format, it tells you, and you will have to find another format for the image you want.

To insert a graphic image from a non-WordPerfect file

1. Position the insertion point approximately where you want to place the graphic image.
2. Choose **Insert**, **Graphics**, **From File**. WordPerfect displays the Insert Image dialog box. It looks a lot like the File Open dialog box, and you use it the same way to locate and insert a graphic image that you've saved to your disk. You might have to browse to locate the file you want.
3. Select the file you want to use, and click **Insert**. WordPerfect converts the file to a WordPerfect format and inserts it into your document (see Figure 12.12).

FIGURE 12.12
You can insert nearly any kind of graphic image, including scanned images or graphics from the Internet.

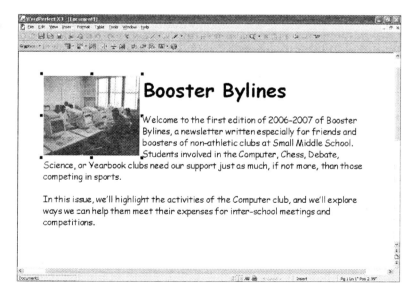

4. At this point, you can move and size the image just like you did the clip art image.

Using Images from a Scanner

Any image, black-and-white or color, can be scanned and inserted into a document. The quality of the scanned image is directly related to the quality of the scanner. If you aren't satisfied with the scanned image, you might consider paying a print shop to scan the image for you.

To scan an image directly into your WordPerfect document

1. Position the insertion point where you want the image.
2. Choose **Insert**, **Graphics**, **Acquire Image**. Depending on the scanner you have, a scanning software program appears. Each scanning program is different, but you should consider these options, if available:
   - Choose the type of scan that matches the image: color, grayscale, or black and white.
   - Crop (trim) the scan to just that part of the overall image you want.
   - If you can, specify the size of the resulting image. For example, the original might be only 1/2" by 1/2", but if you scan it at 2" by 2", the result will be much cleaner and you won't have to stretch the image. Likewise, you can make a much larger image smaller so that it doesn't take up so much space on your hard drive.
   - Apply settings such as color balance or brightness and contrast.
3. When you're ready, scan the image. The scanning program either sends the result to a file on your system or inserts it directly into your WordPerfect document.
4. If the image isn't inserted directly into WordPerfect, choose **Insert**, **Graphics**, **From File** and browse to the scanned image so that you can insert it yourself (see Figure 12.13).
5. Size and move the image just as you would any graphic.

note

Graphics come in two basic flavors: vector and bitmap. WordPerfect's own clip art images (.wpg) are *vector* graphics, which are created by using mathematical calculations. When you stretch such an image, the lines remain smooth because WordPerfect knows how to recalculate to fill in the lines. On the other hand, *bitmap* graphics (.jpg, .gif, .tiff, .bmp, .pcx)—such as those you find on the Internet or that come from scanned images—are made up of individual blocks of color called *pixels*, which aren't quite so easy to manipulate. In particular, bitmap images do not enlarge as cleanly as vector art does. Very small bitmap images tend to have "jaggies" (jagged edges) when you stretch them to make them larger.

FIGURE 12.13
Some applications allow you to scan directly into WordPerfect, whereas others save the file to disk.

Using Images from the Internet

You can even use images you obtain from the Internet. But first, a word of caution—just because you *can* use Internet images doesn't necessarily make it *legal*. Copyright laws apply to Internet graphics just as they apply to print graphics. Depending on how and where your document will be used, you might need to seek permission to use Internet images in your documents.

To download an Internet image and use it in a WordPerfect document

1. Locate an image using your Internet browser; then right-click the image you want to download.
2. In Netscape choose **Save Image As**, or in Internet Explorer choose **Save Picture As**.
3. Provide a name and local destination (for example, c:\My Pictures\happyface.jpg). Don't change the filename extension for the image—for example, .gif or .jpg.
4. Click **Save** to save the image.
5. Switch to WordPerfect and choose **Insert**, **Graphics**, **From File**.
6. Browse to the location where you saved the image, select the image, and click **Insert**.

WordPerfect converts the image from the Internet format (.gif or .jpg) and places it in the document. See Figure 12.14 for an example of an Internet image, at both normal and enlarged sizes. You then can move or size the image.

FIGURE 12.14
Small bitmap images downloaded from the Internet might have jagged edges if you try to enlarge them.

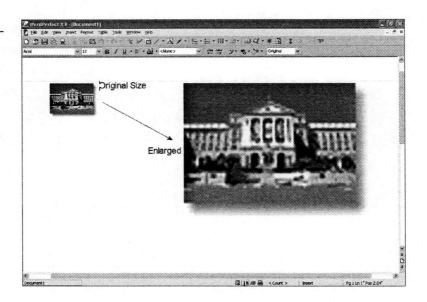

Creating Text Boxes

A text box is just what you would expect: a box that you can type text into. Text boxes in a graphics chapter? You might be wondering how text boxes fit in a chapter on graphics. Well, the box that contains the text is a graphics box, so you treat text boxes just like graphic images.

What's nifty about text boxes is that you can create some text, such as a sign or a label, and then move it on top of other text or graphic images. See "Layering Graphics" at the end of this chapter for more information.

To create a text box

1. Position the insertion point approximately where you want the text box to begin.
2. Choose **Insert**, **Text Box**. WordPerfect places an empty text box at the right of the screen (see Figure 12.15).
3. Type the text you want. You can change the font style, size, color, or other attributes, and you can include hard returns, just as you would with regular text.
4. When you're finished editing the text content of the box, you might want to size the text box to match the contents. Note that when you size a text box, the text reformats to fit the new contours of the box.
5. To move the box, move the mouse pointer to the edge of the text box. When it changes to a move pointer (refer to Figure 12.15), click and drag the box. Drop the box into a new position.

If you want to make some changes to the text after the text box is deselected, you need to move the insertion point inside the box first. If the first click simply places sizing handles around the box, you'll need to click the box a second time to activate a thick border around the box. At this point, the insertion point is inside the box and you can edit the text. Note that if you click in the middle of the text box, you can skip the sizing handles and go straight to the thick border.

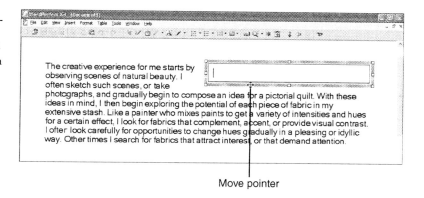

FIGURE 12.15
Text boxes let you put text in a box that you can place anywhere on the document, even in the margins.

Move pointer

Setting Border, Wrap, and Fill Options

Graphics boxes—whether they contain clip art, scanned images, or text—are like containers you place into your text. The way your document's text flows around these graphics boxes is called *wrap*. A box can also have a visible border, and it can be filled with a pattern or color.

Wrapping Text Around Graphics Boxes

You can make your text wrap around graphics boxes in several ways. By default, WordPerfect text moves aside to make room for graphics boxes, but you can change the settings to have the text appear in front of, or behind, the box (see Figure 12.16).

To change how text wraps around a box, right-click the graphics box and choose **Wrap** from the context menu. WordPerfect displays the Wrap Text dialog box (see Figure 12.17). You can also click the **Wrap** button on the Graphics property bar to display a drop-down list of options, but to see the Graphics property bar, you must have first selected the graphics image or text box (click on the edge of a text box to select it). Some of the more useful options from the Wrap Text dialog box are illustrated in Figure 12.16.

> **note**
> With the Contour option selected, text wraps around the image in the box, not the box itself (refer to Figure 12.16). This eliminates the extra whitespace between the graphic and the text. Note that if you add a border of any kind to a contoured graphics box, the wrap option reverts back to Square.

FIGURE 12.16
Wrapping text means making room around a graphics box for the text that surrounds it. You can also place graphic images in front of or behind the text.

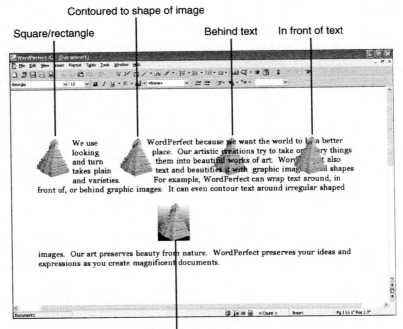

FIGURE 12.17
The Wrap Text dialog box shows you various ways to wrap text around graphics boxes.

Adding Borders to Graphics Boxes

If you really want to set off your graphics, you can put a border around them. By default, text boxes have a single line border and graphic boxes have none. You can switch to a different line border, or a decorative border, in just a few steps.

To change the border around a graphics box

1. Click the graphics box that needs a border. Remember, you have to click the edge of a text box to select it.

2. Click the **Border Style** button on the Graphics property bar. WordPerfect displays a palette of border styles (see Figure 12.18).

FIGURE 12.18

Select graphics box border styles from the Graphics property bar. Click the box with the X in it to remove a border.

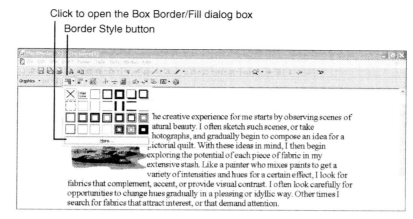

3. Hover the mouse pointer over the border you want to activate in RealTime Preview, which shows you how the border will look if you apply it to the graphic.
4. Select a border style from the palette. WordPerfect adds it to your graphics box (see Figure 12.19).

FIGURE 12.19

Graphics boxes stand out more clearly with an appropriate border, such as this drop-shadow border.

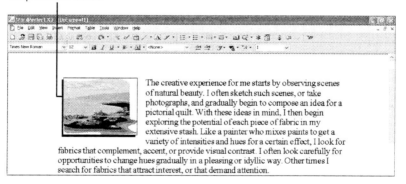

If you're feeling particularly adventurous, you can click the **More** button on the Border Style palette to display the Box Border/Fill dialog box, where you can change line or shadow colors and styles, and more. Figure 12.19 shows a drop-shadow border on the left and bottom sides of the graphic box.

Adding Fills to Graphics Boxes

For effect, you can also provide a background pattern or shading to your graphics box, whether or not you use a border. Let me give you some examples. You might want to add a shaded background behind a clip art image or to text in a text box. If you have access to a color printer, you can use colors; otherwise, the shading is done in shades of gray.

To select a fill pattern and color

1. Click the graphics box to select it.

2. Click the **Box Fill** button on the Graphics property bar. WordPerfect displays a palette of fill patterns (see Figure 12.20).

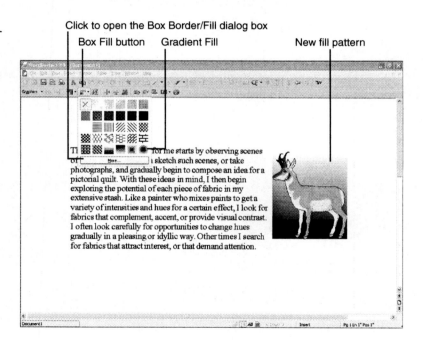

FIGURE 12.20
Gradient shading is just one of many fill patterns you can apply to graphics boxes.

3. Hover the mouse pointer over the pattern you want—for example, one of the gradient shadings on the bottom row of the palette. WordPerfect previews the effect in the document before you select it (refer to Figure 12.19).

4. Click the fill pattern you want to use. WordPerfect applies it to the graphics box.

Unfortunately, all the patterns on the palette are shades of gray. If you want to add color, click **More** on the Box Fill button. WordPerfect displays the Box Border/Fill dialog box, with the Fill tab selected (see Figure 12.21). Click the color buttons (in this case, Foreground and Background) and select the colors that you want to use.

(Depending on the graphic box you are editing, you may see Start Color and End Color options.) Click **OK** when you're finished.

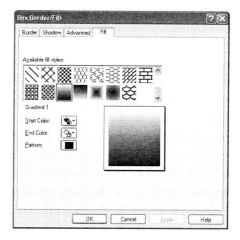

FIGURE 12.21
The Box Border/Fill dialog box helps you add color to fill patterns.

Adding Watermarks

If you hold a quality piece of bond paper up to the light, you will see a pattern, usually the name of the company that manufactured it. This is called a *watermark*. In WordPerfect, watermarks are much more versatile and can serve a useful purpose. They're simply lightly shaded versions of graphics or text images that seem to lie behind the body of text. Figure 12.22 shows you what a typical watermark might look like.

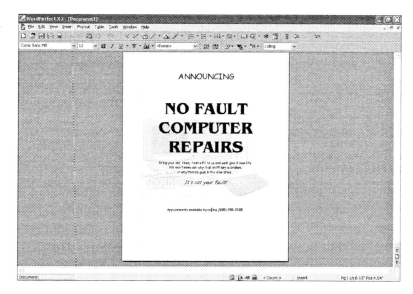

FIGURE 12.22
A watermark image is text or a graphic image, displayed at 25% brightness.

234 ABSOLUTE BEGINNER'S GUIDE TO **WORDPERFECT X3**

To create a watermark

1. Position the cursor at the beginning of the document.
2. Choose **Insert**, **Watermark**. WordPerfect displays the Watermark dialog box (see Figure 12.23).
3. If this is a new watermark, and the first one you've created in this document, choose **Watermark A** and click **Create**. Otherwise, choose another option, such as editing an existing watermark, or creating a second watermark (Watermark B). WordPerfect displays a blank, full page where you create or edit the watermark graphic (see Figure 12.24).

note

Watermarks function like headers in that they appear on every page, beginning at the page where you insert the watermark code and continuing until you turn off the watermark.

FIGURE 12.23
You can use the Watermark dialog box to create or edit background watermark graphics.

FIGURE 12.24
Watermarks are created in a separate watermark editing screen.

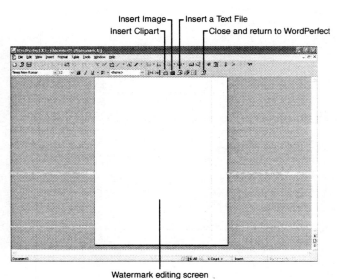

Insert Image — Insert a Text File
Insert Clipart — Close and return to WordPerfect

Watermark editing screen

4. You can use graphics from any source that you would use in the document itself. For example, you can choose **Insert**, **Graphics**, **Clipart** (or **From File**).
5. Insert the image to place it on the Watermark screen (see Figure 12.25).

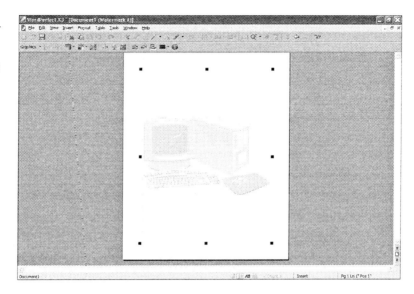

FIGURE 12.25
You manipulate a watermark graphics box just like any other graphics box.

Note that the graphics box, complete with sizing handles, fills the entire page. You can size and position the graphic image just as you do any other graphic image, using the mouse and the sizing handles.

The image itself is shaded lightly so as not to interfere with the text that will appear on top of it. Normally, you won't want to make this any darker; in fact, you might want to make it even lighter. To change the brightness or contrast of the watermark image, either click the **Image Tools** button on the Graphics property bar, or right-click the image and then choose **Image Tools**. WordPerfect displays an Image Tools dialog box in which you can choose from palettes of brightness and contrast (see Figure 12.26).

When you're satisfied with the look of the watermark, either choose **File**, **Close** if the watermark graphic is selected, or click the **Close** button on the Watermark property bar. WordPerfect switches back to the document window, where you can see how the watermark looks behind the text (refer to Figure 12.22).

FIGURE 12.26
You can use the Image Tools dialog box to change the brightness or contrast of a graphic image.

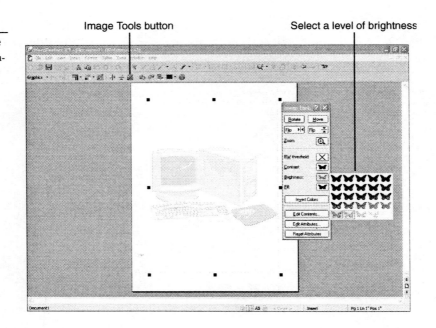

Inserting Shapes

Are you ready to become your own artist? Okay, maybe not, but at least you can create your own graphic shapes—such as boxes, circles, stars, arrows, or even smiley faces—and insert them into your documents.

There are several ways to access the graphic shape tools, but perhaps the easiest is to click the drop-down menu on the **Draw Combined Shapes** button on the toolbar. WordPerfect then displays a palette of choices (see Figure 12.27), which include several line styles, closed objects, and callout styles. By default, this button shows a diagonal line, but after you insert a shape, the picture on the button changes to the shape you inserted in your document.

FIGURE 12.27
Commonly used graphic shape types are included on the Draw Combined Shapes button on the toolbar.

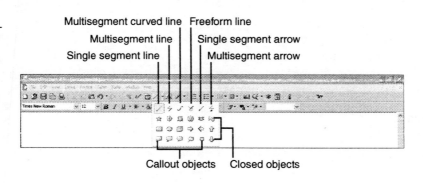

You can also get to shapes by choosing **Insert**, **Shapes** and selecting from the Draw Object Shapes dialog box, which gives you a more extensive selection of predefined shapes. Simply select one of the shape categories, and then select from the palette that appears (see Figure 12.28). For now, let's focus on the Draw Combined Shapes button. What you learn here will work with all the other shapes as well.

FIGURE 12.28
A more extensive arrangement of predefined shapes is available from the Draw Object Shapes dialog box.

WordPerfect's graphic shape types fall into three basic categories (refer to Figure 12.27 for examples). Although each has similar characteristics, you create, edit, and manipulate each slightly differently:

- **Lines**—Each of the line types has a beginning and end, and you can add arrow heads or tails to them.
- **Closed shapes**—These include boxes, circles, action buttons, and specialty shapes.
- **Callout shapes**—These are similar to closed shapes, but you can type text in them to make it easier to create callouts, which are like speech or thought bubbles found in cartoons.

Adding Line Shapes

Suppose you want to draw a line that connects a graphic image to some text in your document. You can use the line shape to quickly draw a horizontal or vertical line in your documents.

To draw a line shape

1. Click the drop-down menu on the **Draw Combined Shapes** button and click the line style you want to use from the palette (refer to Figure 12.27). WordPerfect displays the icon for that style on the button, and the button appears to be selected.
2. Move the mouse pointer to the text area and note that it becomes a crosshair pointer.

3. Position the pointer where you want the line to begin.
4. Click and drag to the opposite end of the line.
5. To complete a line, either release the mouse button or double-click where you want the line to end.

- If you're creating a single-segment line, follow steps 1 through 4 above, then release the mouse button to add the line on top of your text.
- If you're creating a multi-segment line, click once to start the line, click again to change directions, and double-click to complete the line.
- Freeform drawing works just like drawing with a pencil. Click and drag to draw, and release the mouse button to complete the line.

After you complete your line shape, note that WordPerfect places the shape in a graphics box, complete with sizing handles (see Figure 12.29). The shape also covers any text or other objects that lie beneath it. You can adjust the size of the box or move the box as needed.

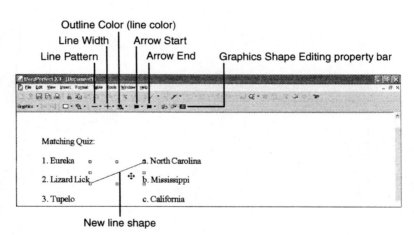

FIGURE 12.29
Use graphic shapes, such as lines, to add clarity to your document.

With the shape selected, WordPerfect adds the graphics line editing tools to the Graphics property bar (refer to Figure 12.29). These tools enable you to add arrow heads or tails; add shadows; or change line width, pattern, or colors.

Adding Closed Object Shapes

The line ends of closed object shapes come together, as in a circle, so the inside area is closed. These objects have thin single lines and are filled with an aquamarine-like green color. (Doesn't *everyone* like ocean colors?)

Let's use a five-point star as an example for creating a closed object shape:

1. Click the drop-down palette on the Draw Combined Shapes button to display the list of available shapes (refer to Figure 12.27).
2. Click a closed object, such as the five-point star. WordPerfect displays the star on the button, and the pointer turns into crosshairs.
3. Position the mouse pointer at one corner of the area you intend to fill with the shape (for example, the upper-left corner).
4. Click and drag the crosshair pointer to the opposite corner (for example, the lower-right corner). Continue holding down the mouse button while you move the pointer, until you have exactly the right size and proportions. If you accidentally release the mouse button, click **Undo** and try again.
5. Release the mouse button to place the object on the document (see Figure 12.3C).

FIGURE 12.30

Closed objects and callout shapes are filled with color. Note the glyph, which is used to change the style of a graphic shape.

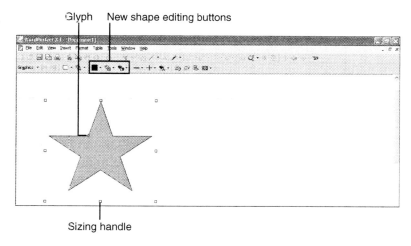

If the object has one or more *glyphs*—small pink-colored diamond handles—you can manipulate the shape or the perspective of the shape. For example, on the five-point star, you can drag the glyph toward the center of the object to create a skinny starfish look, or drag it away from the center to create a sheriff's fat star look. Whenever you see such a glyph, experiment with it to see what happens when you drag it.

With the closed object shape selected, WordPerfect modifies the graphics shape editing tools on the property bar (refer to Figure 12.29). The buttons on this toolbar are the same as those used for lines, except that the Fill Style, Foreground Color, and Background Color buttons replace the Arrow Start and End buttons.

When a closed shape is selected and the Fill palette is displayed, hovering the pointer over the colors will give a RealTime Preview of how the shape will look with that fill applied.

Adding Callout Shapes

You might not even know that the "speech bubble" you often see in cartoons is also called a *callout*. Callouts are similar to closed object shapes and are created in the same way. However, WordPerfect also creates a text box inside the closed shape, where you can type text to go along with the callout. Figure 12.31 shows a callout with text and a white fill background.

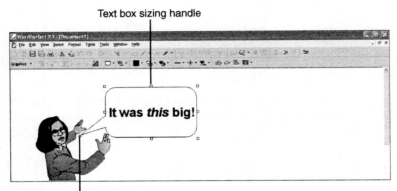

FIGURE 12.31
A callout is a closed object shape with a text box.

To fill in the callout text, simply type text in the box just as you would in any text box. Be sure you select the text box first, and then click again to select the text. By default, such text is centered both horizontally and vertically, but you can change the text just as you would any other text in your document.

You might want to resize the box or change its fill color. You can also drag the glyph at the end of the callout pointer to make it point where you want.

Layering Graphics

You might have already noticed that after you draw several images and move them around, a graphic image ends up covering another one. This can be an advantage. For example, you could layer

note

Callouts are a little different from other shapes in how you select and delete them. To select and delete a callout, you must click the pointer, not the text in the callout, to select it. If you click the text, you'll end up deleting the text, not the callout.

a text box and an arrow on top of a scanned photo. Other images or filled shapes, however, are opaque and might cover up something you want the reader to see.

Think of your document as a flat table, and each time you create a graphic image, you lay it down on the table. Sometimes, however, you want to change the order of the objects you have laid down.

For example, you created an arrow and then later decided to add a box that you want to appear behind it. Because it was created first, the arrow is at the bottom of the pile. Fortunately, it's simple to change the order of a graphic element.

To change the order of an object

1. Select the item by clicking it.
2. Click the **Graphics** button on the Graphics property bar to display a menu of options.
3. Choose the option you need that will send the object all the way to the back, send it back just one level, bring it all the way to the front, or bring it forward just one level.

You can also click the **Object(s) Forward One** and **Object(s) Back One** buttons on the Graphics property bar.

By changing the order of objects and layering them on top of each other, you can creatively present ideas and concepts that would never be possible with words alone (see Figure 12.32).

FIGURE 12.32
You can layer graphics objects and change their order to more clearly illustrate your document.

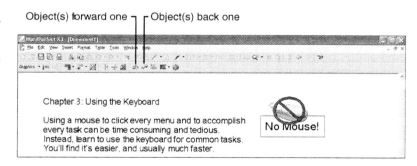

The Absolute Minimum

In this chapter, you learned that a well-chosen picture could be worth a thousand words. Graphic elements come in various forms and are easy to add to a WordPerfect document.

- Right away you discovered how easy it is to add graphic lines that don't get messed up when you change fonts or margins.
- You used clip art and other images to spice up your document, and you learned how easy it is to resize graphic images and move them exactly where you want them.
- Graphic images can come from many sources: WordPerfect's own clip art scrapbook, your scanner, or even the Internet.
- Text boxes are just another type of graphics box that you can position anywhere on the page, even on top of other text or graphic images.
- You found that watermarks are cool-looking background graphics that add class to your documents.
- Now you know how to create your own graphic shapes, such as lines, arrows, boxes, and even callouts, to better illustrate what you're trying to say.

In the next chapter, you will learn how to incorporate data from other sources into your WordPerfect documents.

IN THIS CHAPTER

- Learn how to use copy and paste to copy data from another program into WordPerfect.
- Use the Clipbook utility to maintain a library of clips that can be pasted into a document.
- Set up links between a WordPerfect document and data in other programs.
- Learn how to work with files in other formats.
- Learn some tricks for using data in unsupported formats.
- Publish WordPerfect documents to PDF and XML formats.

Sharing Data

You can bring information from other applications into WordPerfect using simple copy-and-paste techniques. The Windows Clipboard acts as a go-between, transferring the information between applications. If you have the Windows operating system on your computer, you have the Clipboard, so you're ready to go.

Because you can attach files to email messages, it's a common practice to communicate with people all over the world who use many different types of applications. You must be able to open and edit a file even if it wasn't created in WordPerfect. And you will need to save that file back to the native format so that the recipient can continue working with it. That's where the capability to convert files from other formats and save files to other formats comes in. WordPerfect has the most comprehensive set of conversion filters available on the market today. Period.

Copying Data from Other Programs

WordPerfect can do many things, but it can't do everything. You will occasionally have to switch to another application for a project. You can have the best of both worlds because you can pull that information into a WordPerfect document. You can do a simple copy and paste, or you can set up a link so that if the information is updated, the changes are automatically reflected in the document. Either way, it's simple to set up in WordPerfect.

Using the same techniques you learned in the "Moving and Copying Text" section in Chapter 4, "Revising Documents," you can copy information from another program and paste it into WordPerfect. The Windows Clipboard acts as a go-between, temporarily holding the cut or copied information until you can paste it into a WordPerfect document.

To move or copy information between programs

1. Open the source program (for example, Quattro Pro).
2. Select the information you want to move or copy.

3. Click the **Cut** or **Copy** button to cut or copy the selection.
4. Switch to the target program (for example, WordPerfect).

5. Click the **Paste** button to paste the selection.

When you paste information from another program into WordPerfect, the pasted information can include styles and other formatting from the source program. Text from Microsoft Word, for example, comes in with all the codes necessary to retain the original formatting of the text. In some cases, you don't want to bring in that formatting because it will conflict with the formatting that is already in place. In this situation, you want to use the Paste Special command to paste the text without the formatting.

To paste text without the formatting

1. Choose **Edit**, **Paste Special**.
2. Click **Unformatted Text** in the list box.

That's the quickest way to get information into WordPerfect, and believe me, you will use the techniques over and over again. You can copy and paste information from Web pages into WordPerfect and review it offline or share it with a colleague. You can copy and paste address information from your Outlook address book—and so on and so forth.

Using Corel's Clipbook

The Clipbook is a Clipboard program that improves on the Windows Clipboard. You can copy multiple sections of text and graphics objects to a clipboard, which you can then insert into any Windows application. Furthermore, you can create customized collections of clips and save them in clipboards for special projects.

For example, you can create clipboards of boilerplate sections of text that can be used to generate "form" documents in just a few keystrokes. I have been using Clipbook to save replies to frequently asked questions on the Corel newsgroups. You might want to use it to store items unique to certain projects that you work on.

On a network, Clipbook gives system administrators centralized control over standard paragraphs, letterhead logos, and more, rather than using QuickWord or QuickCorrect entries, which must be updated individually.

Loading the Clipbook Program

The first time you start Clipbook, you will have to use the Start menu. Click **Start**, **(All) Programs**, **WordPerfect Office X3**, **Utilities**, **Clipbook**.

I promptly created a shortcut on my desktop so that I don't have to scroll through the Programs menu each time. If you want to do the same, use the above steps to open the **Utilities** menu. Right-click **Clipbook**, and then choose **Send To**, **Desktop (Create Shortcut)**. A shortcut for the Clipbook program now appears on your desktop. It looks like a clipboard on a blue background, and there will be a tiny curved shortcut arrow in the lower-left corner.

When you select Corel Clipbook from the Programs menu, you might not see a program window on the screen, so you might think you've done something wrong. Take a look at the taskbar—you should see a nice little Clipbook icon in the system tray (next to the time). You can double-click the icon to open Clipbook.

The Clipbook window displays the cut or copied item, along with information about the clip, such as the source, the size, and when the clip was created (see Figure 13.1).

The name of the clipboard is displayed underneath the menu bar. When you first start using Clipbook, the default clipboard is called Clipboard 1. As you continue to build your clipboards, you can designate another clipboard as the default. Whichever clipboard is currently the default is the one where the clips that you cut or copy will be placed.

FIGURE 13.1
Each clipboard can hold up to 36 different clips, labeled 0—9 and A—Z.

List of clips in Clipboard 1

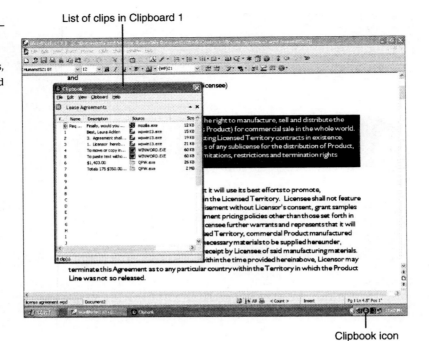

Clipbook icon

Using the Clipbook

When the Clipbook program is loaded, pressing the shortcut keys for cutting (**Ctrl+X**) or copying (**Ctrl+C**) opens the Clipbook window, where you can select a key under which the cut or copied item is stored.

To paste items from the Clipbook into any Windows application, simply press **Ctrl+V**, and then double-click the letter or number of the item to be pasted. You can also right-click any letter or number in the Key column of the Clipbook, and then choose Cut, Copy, or Paste to move the information.

If you prefer, you can use the mouse to move information to and from the Clipbook. To paste the information in the document and remove it from the Clipbook (cut and drop), click the **Key** letter or number and drag the item to your document. If you want to leave a copy in the Clipbook (copy and drop), hold down the **Ctrl** key, click the

Each clipboard is saved in a folder, so you can set up clipboards on a network drive so that the contents can be shared with other users. In the Clipbook dialog box, choose **Clipboard, Network** to display the menu items. The help topics have more information on networking clipboards.

Key letter or number, and drag the item to your document. When the mouse pointer moves into the WordPerfect document, the insertion point appears so that you can see where the text will be inserted when you release the mouse.

To see more information about a clip—for example, to see what kind of clip it is—right-click the Clipbook **Key** and choose **Properties**. You can assign a title and description in the Clip Properties dialog box (see Figure 13.2).

When you press Ctrl+C or Ctrl+X to copy or cut selected text, you activate the Clipbook. You can bypass the Clipbook by right-clicking the selection and choosing Cut or Copy, or by clicking the Cut or Copy buttons on the toolbar. This saves the selection to the Windows clipboard. You'll need to use the right-click menu or the toolbar buttons to paste the text too. Otherwise, you'll get the Clipbook when you press Ctrl+V. This is a nice workaround when you just need to cut or copy something quickly, without going through the Clipbook.

FIGURE 13.2
A title and description can be created for each clip in a clipboard.

When you are ready to create another clipboard, open the Clipbook dialog box (if it isn't already open) and choose **Clipboard**, **Create**. Type a new name and a description if you like. Choose **OK**. A new clipboard appears in the Clipbook window. You can select which clipboards to display in the Clipbook. Choose **Clipboards**, **Manage**, and then place a check mark next to the clipboard(s) that you want to display.

Using OLE to Link and Embed Data from Other Programs

Copying and pasting is one way to share data from one Windows application to another, but with *Object Linking and Embedding (OLE)*, you can do more. You can *link* data between two programs so that if the data changes in the originating program, it is automatically updated in WordPerfect. Linking is very important if you use data that requires constant updating, such as spreadsheets or databases. If you create a link to data, any changes to the data in the original application are automatically reflected in WordPerfect.

When you embed information from another program, WordPerfect inserts the information and remembers where the data came from. Embedded information can be edited from within WordPerfect—all you have to do is double-click it. WordPerfect creates an editing window with all the menus and toolbars from the original program.

The main difference between linking and embedding is that linked information maintains an active connection between the data in the WordPerfect document and the data in the original application. When you embed something in a WordPerfect document, you forego a link to the original data, but you do maintain a connection to the application. In either case, all you have to do to edit the data is double-click it. WordPerfect opens the original application and integrates it into the document window so that you can revise the data without ever leaving WordPerfect.

Using OLE to Create a Link to Existing Data

You can insert OLE objects in WordPerfect documents and take advantage of existing information created in other applications.

To create an OLE link

1. Choose **Insert**, **Object** to open the Insert Object dialog box (see Figure 13.3).

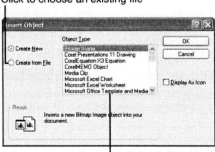

FIGURE 13.3
Use the Insert Object dialog box to select which type of OLE object you want to insert.

Click to choose an existing file

List of OLE-capable programs on your system

2. Click **Create from File**. The dialog box changes, and you now have a File text box and a Link check box (see Figure 13.4).
3. Click the **Browse** button to locate the file you want to insert.
4. By default, WordPerfect inserts the file as an embedded object. However, if you put a check mark in the **Link** check box, WordPerfect inserts the object as a linked object.
5. Click **OK** to insert the object into your document.

FIGURE 13.4
Use the Browse button if you don't remember the exact name and location of the object file.

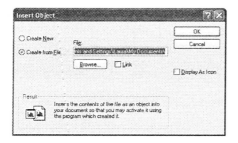

If you drag and drop the information from another program to WordPerfect, WordPerfect automatically establishes an OLE link. The procedure is similar to dragging and dropping text between WordPerfect documents. Not all programs will support this, so if it doesn't work for you, use the previous steps instead.

To create an OLE link with drag and drop

1. Locate the area in the WordPerfect document where you want to paste the data.
2. Switch to the source program and select the information.
3. If you want to leave a copy of the information in the application, hold down the **Ctrl** key and drag the selected information to the WordPerfect button on the taskbar. If you want to remove the information in the other application, click and drag without the Ctrl key.
4. When the WordPerfect window opens, drop the information into the WordPerfect document.

Creating a New OLE Object

You might decide to create a new object that you can insert into a document. Luckily, you don't even have to switch to another application; you can create it from within WordPerfect. For example, you can create a Quattro Pro notebook or a Presentation slide inside a WordPerfect document.

To create a new OLE object

1. Choose **Insert**, **Object** to display the Insert Object dialog box.
2. Select the object type from the list. Only the OLE-capable programs, also called *OLE servers*, that are installed on your system appear on the list (refer to Figure 13.3).

Some OLE server applications do not support in-place editing. Instead, they open a completely separate application window where you create or edit the object. You must exit the application to return to WordPerfect. Be sure you save your changes in the application before you return to WordPerfect.

3. Click **OK**. The OLE server application starts and takes control of WordPerfect's menus and toolbars. It also opens an editing window in which you can use all the application's procedures to create the object (see Figure 13.5). This is called *in-place editing*.

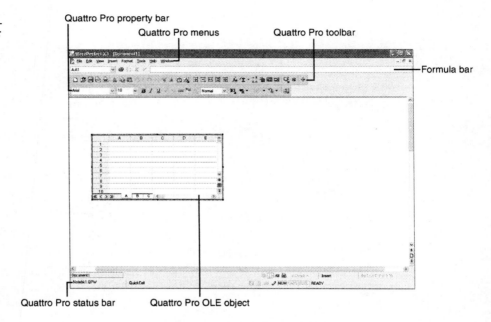

FIGURE 13.5
You can create or edit, in place, OLE objects such as a Quattro Pro notebook.

4. Close the OLE editing window by clicking in the document. When you close the OLE window, WordPerfect takes control of the menus and toolbars again.

Opening (or Importing) Files from Other Programs

When you open a file that isn't in WordPerfect format, the file is automatically converted before it is opened. You may or may not see a message box that indicates a file is being converted—it depends on how fast the conversion process is. The more memory your machine has, the less likely you are to see this message.

WordPerfect supports the conversion of many modern formats, including the following:

- Ami Pro 1.2, 1.2a, 1.2b, 2.0, 3.0
- ANSI/ASCII (Windows and DOS)

- HTML (Hypertext Markup Language)
- Microsoft Word 4.0, 5.0, 5.5 for DOS
- Microsoft Word 1.0, 1.1, 1.1a, 1.2, 1.2a, 2.0, 2.0a, 2.0b, 2.0c, 5.0, 6.0/7.0 for Windows
- Microsoft Word 97/2000, Microsoft Word 2002/2003
- Rich Text Format (RTF), RTF Japanese
- SGML
- UNICODE text
- WordPerfect Macintosh 2.0, 2.1, 3.0, 3.1/3.5
- WordPerfect 4.2, 5.0, 5.1/5.2, 6 through X3
- WordStar 2000 1.0, 2.0, 3.0
- WordStar 3.3, 3.31, 3.4, 4.0, 5.0, 5.5, 7.0
- XML (Extensible Markup Language; UTF-8, UTF-16 Big Endian and Little Endian)

A complete list of conversion filters appears in the Help topics. In the Help Index, type **import**, select the **file formats** subtopic under the Importing topic, and then click **Display**.

Saving (or Exporting) to Other File Formats

Even though many of your friends use Microsoft Word, you stubbornly refuse to give up WordPerfect. And you don't have to! WordPerfect Office X3 has the cleanest, most accurate set of conversion filters for Microsoft Word available anywhere. In fact, WordPerfect Office X3 does an even better job of converting Word files than previous versions. You can save your documents in Word format, and no one will even know the difference.

To save a document in a different format

1. Choose **File**, **Save As**. WordPerfect opens the Save As dialog box.
2. Type the name of the file you want to use, unless you intend to use the same name.
3. Click the **File Type** drop-down menu and select the file format you want to convert to (see Figure 13.6).
4. Click **Save**. WordPerfect converts the document into the selected format and assigns the proper extension. For example, if you save a document in Microsoft Word 97/2000/2002/2003 format, WordPerfect automatically assigns a .doc extension.

If you continue to work on the document and save it again, WordPerfect prompts you with the Save Format dialog box (see Figure 13.7). Unless you want to change back to the WordPerfect format, select the conversion format (for example, Microsoft Word 97/2000/2002/2003) and click **OK**.

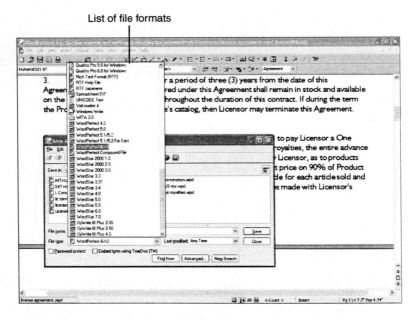

FIGURE 13.6
Select a file format from the File Type drop-down list to save the file in that format.

FIGURE 13.7
When you save a non-WP document, WordPerfect asks which format you want to save it to.

Installing Additional Conversion Filters

If you try to open a file and WordPerfect tells you the format of the document is not supported, don't despair. A regular WordPerfect installation installs only a limited number of conversion filters. You can easily copy the other conversion filters over from the WordPerfect Office X3 CD. You will be amazed at how many formats WordPerfect converts—a lot more than any other word processing program.

To install the additional conversion filters

1. Choose **Start**, **Control Panel**, **Add or Remove Programs**.
2. Scroll down and select the **WordPerfect Office X3** entry.
3. Click the **Change** button to start the Installation Wizard.
4. Choose **Change Which Program Features Are Installed** and click **Next**.

5. If necessary, click the **plus sign** (+) next to WordPerfect Office X3 to open the list of different components.
6. Click the **plus sign** (+) next to **Filters** to open the list of different conversion files. (You might have to scroll down to find the **Filters** option.)
7. Click the drop-down list button next to the category you are interested in and choose **This Feature Will Be Installed on Local Hard Drive**. Or, click the drop-down list arrow next to **Filters** and choose **This Feature Will Be Installed on Local Hard Drive** to install all the conversion filters at once.
8. Choose **Next**, and then **Begin**.
9. Click **Finish** to close the installation wizard. The new filters have been installed, and they are ready for use.

Using Data from Unsupported Formats

Creative minds working together are a great thing, but incompatible file formats are not. At some point, you're going to run into a file that WordPerfect can't open. When you try to open such a file, WordPerfect displays an error box (see Figure 13.8). There are a few methods for dealing with this problem:

- If you have access to the program used to create the file, open the document in that program and see whether you can save it to an intermediate format that WordPerfect understands; for example, Rich Text Format (.rtf) or Text (.txt). You might lose formatting in the translation, but at least you will preserve the content.

FIGURE 13.8
This error box is displayed when you try to open a file in an unsupported format.

- If you know the source of the document (for example, Microsoft Word 6.0), be sure you have the necessary conversion filters installed.
- If you think you know which program was used to create the file, but not the exact version, try selecting different versions of the program.
- When all else fails, you can usually open the file as an ASCII file. Try the CR/LF to SRt option first because it converts the hard returns at the end of ASCII lines to soft returns, which preserves the paragraph structure. You will lose all document formatting with this option. ASCII imports also usually require extensive editing to clean up the resulting conversion.

Publishing Documents to PDF

PDF is short for Portable Document Format, a file format developed by Adobe Systems. PDF captures formatting information from a variety of applications, making it possible to send formatted documents and have them appear on the recipient's system exactly as they appear on the originating system. PDF format is the accepted standard for electronic file distribution.

PDF has been supported in WordPerfect products since WordPerfect Office 2000. The built-in PDF functionality in WordPerfect X3 includes Adobe Acrobat 5.0 compatibility, which supports symbols and improved page numbering. If you had to purchase Adobe Acrobat separately, it would cost between $200 and $300.

tip

Adobe Acrobat Reader allows you to review, print, and share PDF files. You can install Adobe Acrobat Reader from the WordPerfect Office X3 CD #2 for the Standard and Professional versions, CD #1 for the Productivity Pack. Insert the CD and close the door to start the Setup program. Choose **Adobe Reader** setup, and then follow the instructions.

To publish a document to PDF

1. Choose **File**, **Publish to**, **PDF**. The Publish to PDF dialog box appears.
2. If necessary, click the **General** tab to display the options shown in Figure 13.9.

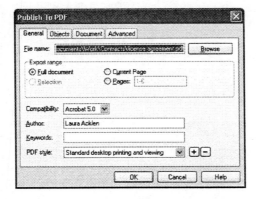

FIGURE 13.9
The General tab of the Publish to PDF dialog box has options for naming the new PDF file and selecting a compatibility setting.

3. Type a name for the file in the **File name** text box.
4. Verify the **Compatibility** setting. This should be set to the version of Adobe Acrobat that the intended recipient has on her system.
5. By default, WordPerfect publishes the entire document. Choose one of the following if you want to publish a smaller section:

- **Current Page**—Publishes the page where the insertion point is positioned.
- **Selection**—Publishes a selected area of the document.
- **Pages**—Types the page numbers for the pages that you want saved to PDF.

6. Choose **OK**. You'll see a status indicator that shows you the progress of the document. When this message box disappears, the process is complete.

There are other options under the Objects, Document, and Advanced tabs that you can explore when you're ready to publish more complex documents.

> **tip**
>
> One of the most exciting new features in WordPerfect X3 is the capability to import PDF files. Yes, you read that correctly: You can actually import a PDF file and then edit it in WordPerfect X3. Just open the file like you would any other, and WordPerfect will take care of the rest. See the help topics for more information, or consider picking up a copy of *Que's Special Edition Using WordPerfect Office X3* for more detailed information.

Publishing Documents to XML

You might be asking yourself, "What's the big deal about XML?" Let me try to explain it in simple terms. XML is becoming a standard format for many different types of devices, so XML gives you more options for file sharing and multiple device support.

Maybe an example would help: You create a document, and you need to be able to publish it on the Web and the corporate intranet and then download it to your boss's PDA. It sounds like something only a programmer would do, but these types of features are becoming more and more common as the popularity of these technologies increases.

The XML editor in WordPerfect X3 allows you to author, edit, and publish SGML or XML documents. The XML Editor Help has been rewritten to make the utility easier to use, especially for XML beginners. Still, this is a fairly technical feature, so don't feel bad if it doesn't make much sense right now.

To publish a file in XML

1. Choose **File**, **Publish to**, **XML**. The Publish to XML dialog box appears (see Figure 13.10).
2. Type a name for the file in the **XML File Name** text box.
3. In the Graphic Output Options section, select either **GIF** or **JPEG** and customize those settings.
4. Choose **Publish**. You might see a status indicator that shows you the progress of a document. When this message box disappears, the process is complete. Or, it might go by so fast that you don't even see it.

FIGURE 13.10
The Publish to XML dialog box has options for naming the new XML file and selecting graphic output options.

THE ABSOLUTE MINIMUM

This chapter explained how to incorporate information from other sources into WordPerfect.

- You learned how to use the Copy and Paste features to copy data from another program into WordPerfect.
- You learned how to use the Clipbook utility to save multiple clips for pasting.
- OLE allows you to create links to data so that any changes made to the data are automatically reflected in WordPerfect.
- You learned how WordPerfect easily converts files from other formats.
- You saw how WordPerfect can save a file in another format.
- Additional conversion filters can be installed from the Corel WordPerfect Office X3 CD.
- If the data is in an unsupported format, there are still a couple of things you can try, such as saving the file in another format that WordPerfect can understand.
- Whether your documents are headed for use in an older version of WordPerfect, another word processing application, or publishing to the Web in PDF or XML format, you have very powerful tools for creating shared documents.

In the next chapter of the book, you will learn how to use WordPerfect's merge tools to make your job easier and faster.

PART V

Automating Your Work

Using the Merge Feature 259

Using the Address Book 279

Working with Templates 297

Creating and Playing Macros 313

Using WordPerfect's Legal Tools 327

IN THIS CHAPTER

- Learn how to create a data file and enter information to be used in a merge.
- Create form files from scratch or from an existing document, and then merge the data file with the form file.
- Create envelopes and labels with information from the data file.
- Build a fill-in-the-blank form that prompts the user for information.

USING THE MERGE FEATURE

Most people think of anything using the Merge feature as a *mail merge*, but you can realistically pull together *any* type of information to produce *any* type of document. You might hear about using the Merge feature to produce personalized letters, envelopes, and labels, but it's also a very powerful tool for organizing key pieces of information.

Fill-in-the-blank forms are used in every type of business. A merge document can be set up to accept input so that you can fill in the form electronically. One advantage of this method is that an electronic form can be submitted via email, which speeds up the processing.

Working with Data Files

A *merge* is a combination of information from two different sources. Typically, you have a *form* file, which is the document, and a *data* file, which contains the information that you want to insert. The form file is just a regular document with merge codes in it. The merge codes act as markers for the information from the data file.

A data file is organized into records, which contain fields for every piece of information. Using the mail merge example, the data file is a list of names and addresses, and the form file is the letter. Each person, client, or event has a *record* that is divided into *fields*, such as name, company, address, and phone.

It's easier to build a data file first, so you can use the field names that you create, in the form document. Field names are used to identify the merge field codes that you create. For example, a typical data file might contain these fields: Name, Company, Address, City, State, Zip, Phone, Fax, and Email. Field names are optional, though—you can use Field1, Field2, Field3, and so on, if you prefer.

The main thing to keep in mind when you're creating the data file is that more fields mean more flexibility. For example, if you have three separate fields (instead of one field) for the city, state, and ZIP Code, you can sort the list by ZIP Code. The same goes for the name—if you use one field for first name and one field for last name, you can arrange the records by the last name, and you can break out the first name for a personalized salutation. Each field can be acted on individually.

Creating a Data File

It's easy to create a data file from scratch, but before you do, be sure you don't already have the information stored somewhere else. You can transfer information from other sources into a merge data file in several ways. You might have a little cleanup to do, but at least you aren't entering the information all over again. If you already have a file to work with, you can skip to the next section, "Importing Data into Merge Data Files," which contains information on importing data for use as merge data.

Follow these steps to create a data file from scratch:

1. Choose **Tools**, **Merge** (**Shift+F9**) to display the Merge dialog box (see Figure 14.1).
2. Click **Data Source** to open the list of data sources that can be used in a merge.
3. Click **Create Data File** at the bottom of the list of data sources to display the Create Data File dialog box (see Figure 14.2). This is where you create the field names.

FIGURE 14.1
Use the Merge dialog box to set up a data file and a form document, and then merge the two.

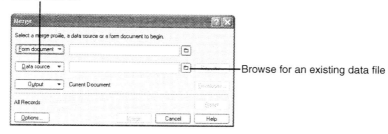

Create a data file

Browse for an existing data file

FIGURE 14.2
In the Create Data File dialog box, you can create and edit the field names for the data file.

4. Type the first field name in the **Name a Field** text box. A field name can be up to 40 characters long, and it can contain spaces.

5. Press **Enter** or click **Add** to insert the field name in the **Fields Used in Merge** list box.

6. Repeat steps 3 and 4 until you've entered all the field names. If you misspell a field name or change your mind, select the field, and then choose **Delete**. The order of the field names is important because this is the order in which you will type the information. If you need to rearrange the field names, select a name and click **Move Up** or **Move Down**. Figure 14.3 shows a typical list of field names.

7. Be sure to place a check mark in the **Format Records in a Table** check box to format the merge data in a table. I highly recommend that you do this because tables are so much easier to work with.

8. Click **OK** when you're finished. The Quick Data Entry dialog box appears (see Figure 14.4). You can use this dialog box to enter and edit records in the data file.

FIGURE 14.3
Here is a list of field names that you might use for a merge data file.

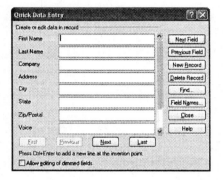

FIGURE 14.4
Most people prefer using the Quick Data Entry dialog box for creating and editing records in the data file.

Formatting a data file in a table has many advantages. In a table, each field has its own column, and each row is one record. Data files that aren't formatted as tables contain special codes, called merge codes, which separate the fields and records. You must be especially careful when editing this type of data file so that you don't accidentally delete one of the merge codes. The one disadvantage of formatting the records in a table is that if you have a lot of fields, you will get a table with a lot of columns, so it's harder to navigate around, and you won't be able to see all the information on one screen. To see all the columns, try changing the page format to landscape (**Format**, **Page**, **Page Setup**, and choose **Landscape** orientation).

Figure 14.5 shows two data files—the top is in table format and the bottom is not.

> **tip**
> You can move back and forth between records by clicking the **Previous** and **Next** buttons at the bottom of the Quick Data Entry dialog box. Click the **First** button to move to the first record; click the **Last** button to move to the last record.

FIGURE 14.5
Creating and maintaining merge data is much easier if the data is in a table.

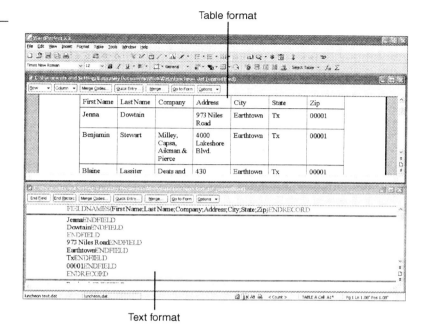

When you are ready to enter data into a merge data file, the Quick Data Entry dialog box is definitely the way to go. It simplifies the process of getting the information into the right fields and makes it easy for you to move back and forth between the records. As you enter the data, remember not to use extra spaces or punctuation. All the formatting, punctuation, and placement of the information is done in the form file.

1. Type the data for the first field. Don't include extra spaces or punctuation marks when you enter the data; for example, don't type a comma after the city. All formatting and punctuation marks should be in the form document.

2. Press **Enter** or **Tab** (or choose **Next Field**) to move down to the next field. Press **Shift+Tab** or choose **Previous Field** to move back up a field. You can also click in any field to move the insertion point.

3. Continue entering the information in each field. When you press **Enter** in the last field, a new record is created. You also can choose **New Record** from any field to create a blank record.

4. Click **Close** when you're finished entering data.

5. Click **Yes** to save the data file to disk. The Save File dialog box appears.

6. Type a name for the data file in the **File Name** text box, and then click **Save**.

7. Choose **Cancel** to clear the Merge dialog box.

When the Merge dialog box closes, you can see the data that you've entered so far. Figure 14.6 shows the data in table format. Notice that the Merge feature bar has been added to the top of the screen. The generic property bar has also morphed into the table property bar with a lot of buttons for working with tables.

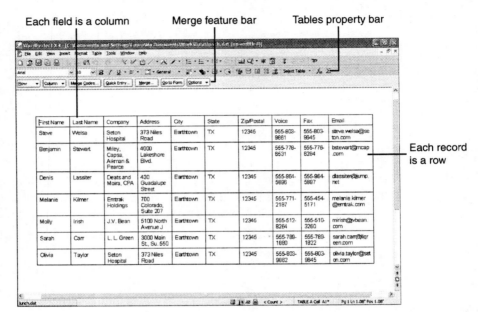

FIGURE 14.6
Formatting the records in a table has many advantages. Not only is it easier to read the information in table format, but also you can easily manipulate the data with the buttons on the table property bar.

After you've finished entering the information, you can always go back and edit it later. You can add and edit records directly (in the table), or you can click the **Quick Entry** button on the Merge feature bar to open the Quick Data Entry dialog box.

If you need to edit the field names, you can either edit the information in the first row of the table (the field name row), or you can do so from the Quick Data Entry dialog box (refer to Figure 14.4). Click the **Field Names** button to open the Edit Field Names dialog box, where you can add, rename, and delete field names.

Importing Data into Merge Data Files

You can use files from other applications as data files, and in some cases, you won't need to convert them before the merge. In addition to files from other word processing programs, WordPerfect supports the import of data files created in spreadsheet and database programs. Imported data files often contain numbers to identify the fields, rather than names. If field names were used in the source application, they are recognized and used by WordPerfect (see Figure 14.7).

FIGURE 14.7
This text data file has a field name record, so the fields can be identified by name rather than by number.

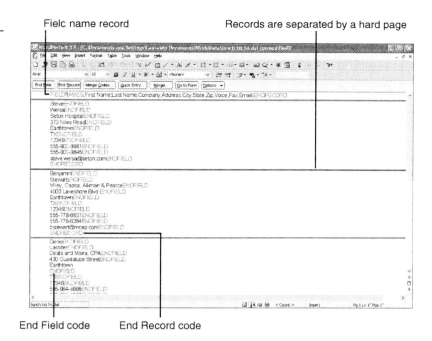

End Field code   End Record code

Take a look at the figure and notice how each field is on a line by itself and ends with an End Field code. Each record ends with an End Record code, followed by a hard page, shown by the double horizontal line in the figure. The hard page that follows each End Record field ensures that when you merge, each record is on a page by itself.

Creating Form Files

If you've gotten this far, take heart—you're in the home stretch! Creating the form file is the easy part, and if you've already typed the document, you're almost finished. An existing document can be turned into a form file in seconds. You just insert the merge codes and save the document. Voilà! It's ready for a merge.

If you create the form file from scratch, this is where you want to set up all the formatting for the merged documents. You definitely don't want to put punctuation or formatting codes in the data file; otherwise, it is duplicated over and over again.

If you want to convert an existing document to a form document, open it now. Otherwise, create a new document and type any text that you need to precede the information that will be inserted during the merge.

To create a form file

1. Choose **Tools**, **Merge (Shift+F9)** to open the Merge dialog box (refer to Figure 14.1).
2. Click **Form Document** to open a drop-down list of options (see Figure 14.8).

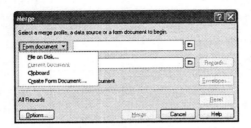

FIGURE 14.8
You can convert the current document into a form document, or you can create a form document from scratch.

3. Choose **Create Form Document**. If you already have the form document open, click **Use File in Active Window** in the Data File Source dialog box. Otherwise, choose **New Document Window** to create the form document from scratch. The Associate Form and Data dialog box appears (see Figure 14.9).

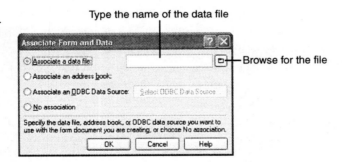

FIGURE 14.9
You can specify a data file or other data source to use with this form document in the Associate Form and Data dialog box.

4. Type the name of the data file in the **Associate a Data File** text box, or click the **Files** icon to search for the file. If you haven't created the data file yet, or you don't know where it is, choose **No Association**.
5. Click **OK**. WordPerfect adds the Merge feature bar at the top of the document (see Figure 14.10). This document is now marked as a form document.

The only difference between a form document and a regular document is that a form document contains merge codes. A merge code acts as a placeholder for the information that will come in from the data file. For example, you insert a merge field code for the Name field into a form document. When you merge the form document with the data file, the data from the Name field replaces the Name merge code. The result is a personalized letter, not a document full of merge field codes.

FIGURE 14.10
The Merge feature bar is included in every form document and data file that you create.

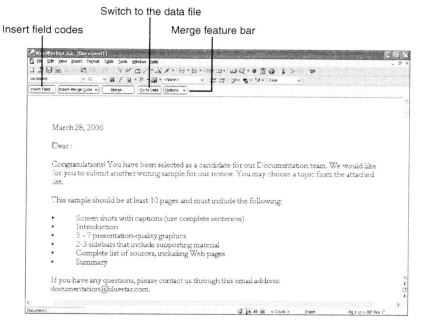

Remember that punctuation marks, spaces, blank lines, and any formatting that you want applied to the text is done in the form file. If you added commas, periods, or extra spaces to the data in the form file and in the data file, you will get duplicates in the merge results.

1. Position the insertion point where you want to insert the first piece of information. For example, in a typical mail merge, you insert the name and address information at the top of the letter.
2. Click the **Insert Field** button on the Merge feature bar. The Insert Field Name or Number dialog box appears (see Figure 14.11). The field names (or numbers) in the associated data file appear in the Field Names list box.
3. Double-click a field name to insert it in the document at the location of the insertion point, or select the field name and choose **Insert**. WordPerfect inserts the field name (or number) in parentheses, preceded by FIELD (see Figure 14.12).

note

If you associated a data file in step 4 on the previous page, that file is now tied to this form file. Whenever you need to edit the data, just click the **Go to Data** button on the Merge feature bar. WordPerfect opens the data file in another window and switches you to that window. To go back to the form document, click the **Go to Form** button in the data file window.

FIGURE 14.11
Select a field name to insert in the Insert Field Name or Number dialog box.

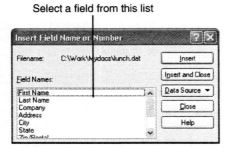

Select a field from this list

FIGURE 14.12
Merge codes are displayed in a different color to make them easier to see in the text.

First Name merge code

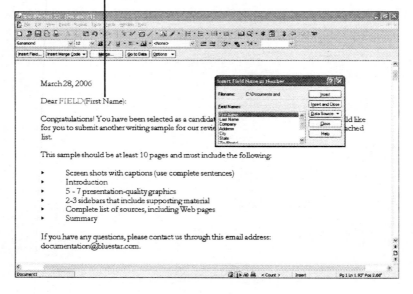

4. Continue inserting field names until you complete the form document. Be sure to include the necessary spaces, commas, or other punctuation between field names.

5. Click **Close** to close the Insert Field Name or Number dialog box. Figure 14.13 shows a sample letter with the mailing address and salutation field codes.

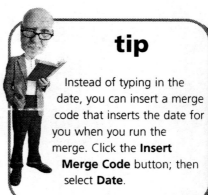

tip

Instead of typing in the date, you can insert a merge code that inserts the date for you when you run the merge. Click the **Insert Merge Code** button; then select **Date**.

The most straightforward use of the Merge feature is to set up a mail merge, where you are merging a letter with a list of addresses. It's important to emphasize that the Merge feature can be used for much more. An invoice or billing statement could be merged with a database file. A loan application, where the same information is plugged into a thousand different places, could be generated in a merge with spreadsheet data as a data source. Or maybe someday you will need to create 300 "Hello…My Name Is" labels for your high-school reunion. There are infinite possibilities.

FIGURE 14.13
The mailing address block and salutation will be filled in with information from the data file.

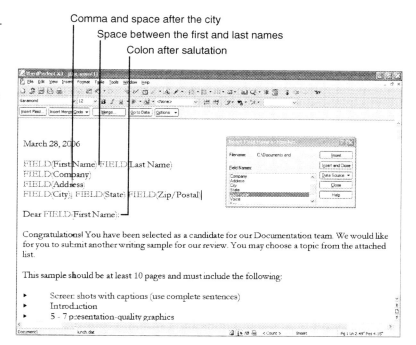

Merging the Data and Form Files Together

Now that you've got a form document and a data file, you're ready to go! If the form document or data file is open, you can click the **Merge** button on the Merge feature bar. Otherwise, choose **Tools**, **Merge**, **Merge** (**Shift+F9**) to open the Merge dialog box (see Figure 14.14).

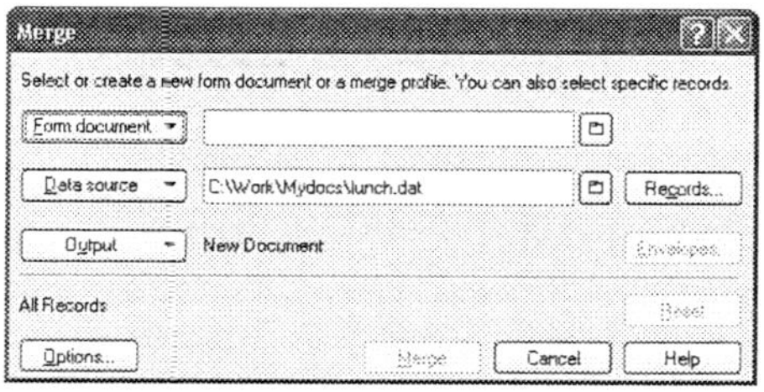

FIGURE 14.14
You can select a form document, a data file, and the output location in the Merge dialog box.

Your dialog box selections will vary depending on what files you have open:

- If you click the Merge button from the form document, Form Document is set to Current Document.
- If you associated the form document with a data file, the name of that file appears next to the Data Source button.
- If you click the Merge button from the data file, the name of the file appears next to the Data Source button.
- If the data file is already associated with a form document, the name of that document appears next to the Form Document button. Otherwise, you will need to type the filename next to **Form Document** or click the **Files** icon to search for the file.
- If you aren't running the merge from either document, you see a blank text box next to Form Document and Data Source.

In any case, you need to fill in the blanks by typing the names of the files or clicking the **Files** icon to search for them. By default, Output is set to New Document. You can also set the merge to create the results in the current document.

To change the output setting, click the **Output** drop-down list arrow to see the other three options:

- **Printer**—Sends the output directly to the printer.
- **File on Disk**—Creates a file and places the output in the file.
- **Email**—Sends the output via electronic mail.

When you have everything filled in, click **Merge**. WordPerfect matches up the field names/numbers in the form file and the field names/numbers in the data file and inserts the information into the form. When a merge is complete, the insertion point is always on the last line of the last page, so don't panic if you don't see the letters right away. Figure 14.15 shows the results of a mail merge.

Congratulations, you just completed a merge! The document onscreen at this point is the result of the merge. Under most circumstances, you wouldn't need to save this document. Think about it for a minute: You can always merge the two files again, and saving the result would be like saving the information twice. At this point, you will probably print the results. When you are finished, close the file without saving.

Setting up a merge might seem like a lot of work at first, but if you consider how much time you would spend creating a separate document for each individual, it's time well spent. I should also point out that you can reuse the data file over and over again, so once you've created that file, you don't have to repeat those steps.

Unfortunately, the results of a merge might not turn out the way you had planned. Don't worry; with just a few minor adjustments, you can sort things out. First, take a good look at the results and see whether you can detect a pattern. Is the state where the city should be? Are all the last names missing, or just one or two? When you're ready to proceed, close the merge results document without saving.

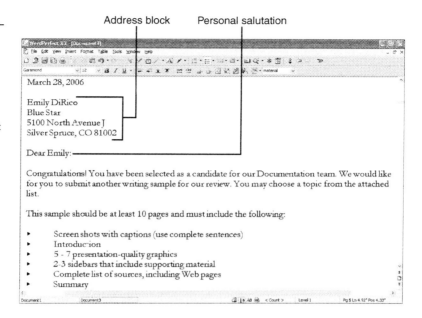

FIGURE 14.15
WordPerfect pulls information from the data file, inserts it into the form document, and creates a new set of documents.

If you're having the same problem over and over, start with the form document. Make sure you have the right field codes in the proper places. If you need to change a field code, select and delete the code, and then reinsert it. You can just save your changes and try the merge again.

If the problem occurs just in one or two entries, go straight to the data file and take a look at the records giving you trouble. Make sure the right information is in the correct field. You might have actually typed the state in the city field by accident. Save your changes and try the merge again.

Creating Envelopes

If you are working on a group of letters, you will need envelopes or labels for them. Envelopes can be created during a merge so that everything is generated together. For labels, you will need to create a label form document and merge that form with the data file in a separate merge.

To generate envelopes during a merge

1. Open the form document for the merge.
2. Choose **Tools**, **Merge** (**Shift+F9**) to open the Merge dialog box.

3. Click **Envelopes**. WordPerfect opens an envelope form document. If necessary, type the return address (or leave it out if your envelopes are preprinted).
4. Press **Ctrl+End** to move down to the mailing address block. If necessary, delete the text in the mailing address block.
5. Click the **Insert Field** button to open the Insert Field Name or Number dialog box.
6. Double-click a field name (or number) to insert the field code. Include all the necessary spacing and punctuation between the fields (see Figure 14.16).

FIGURE 14.16
Creating the envelope during a merge has an advantage: WordPerfect creates the envelope form document and integrates it into the merge process.

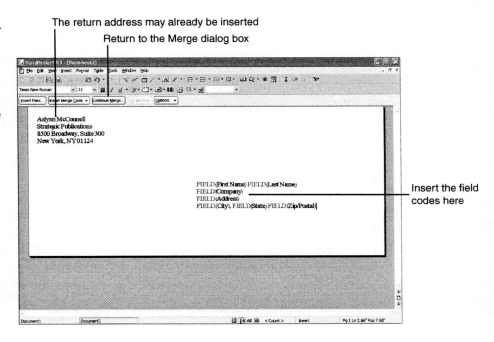

7. Click **Continue Merge** when you're finished. The Merge dialog box appears.
8. If necessary, specify a form document, a data file, and an output location.
9. Click **Merge**.

Creating Labels

Creating labels isn't integrated in the merge process, so you will need to create a labels form to use with the data file. It doesn't take long—just a few minutes to locate the correct label definition.

To create labels during a merge

1. If you've already defined the label form, you can skip to step 4. Otherwise, in a blank document, choose **Format**, **Labels** to open the Labels dialog box (see Figure 14.17).

FIGURE 14.17
You can choose label definitions for both laser-printed and tractor-fed printers in the Labels dialog box.

Select a label definition

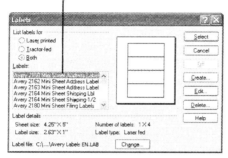

note

Just because your label isn't listed in the Labels box doesn't mean that the definition doesn't exist. Check the layout (such as 3 columns by 10 rows) or the dimensions, and compare them to the definitions in the list. You will probably find an exact match (or at least a close approximation).

2. Click **Laser Printed** or **Tractor-fed** to narrow down the list, and then select the label definition that matches your labels.

3. Click **Select** to insert the definition in the document.

4. Choose **Tools**, **Merge** to open the Merge dialog box.

5. Choose **Form Document**, **Create Form Document**, **Use File in Active Window** to display the Associate Form and Data dialog box.

6. Specify a data source, and then click **OK**. The Merge feature bar appears in the label document.

7. Click the **Insert Field** button to open the Insert Field Name or Number dialog box.

8. Double-click a field name to insert it into the label. Be sure you include all the spacing and punctuation between the fields.

caution

If every other label is blank, there is an extra page break at the bottom of the label in the form file. Close this document without saving and switch back to the label form document. Position the insertion point at the end of the address and press **Delete** until only one label is displayed. Try the merge again.

9. When you're finished inserting field codes, click **Close** to close the Insert Field Name or Number dialog box. Figure 14.18 shows a completed label form.

FIGURE 14.18
This form document is actually a sheet of labels, which will be filled in during the merge.

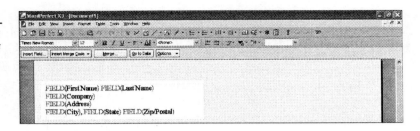

10. Click the **Merge** button on the feature bar to open the Merge dialog box.
11. Verify the data source and output location, and then click **Merge** to create the labels.

Creating Fill-in-the-Blank Forms

A typical form has a series of blanks that you need to fill in. The blanks are labeled so you know what should be entered. Electronic forms work the same way. The items that don't change are the titles and labels, so they are "fixed." The rest of the form is set aside for individual responses, which are variable.

A form document can be designed with merge codes that stop and wait for the user to type in the variable information. You can even create a message that explains what the user should be typing at this point. After the information has been entered, the merge moves on to the next code.

The Merge feature is used to fill in the form. The difference is that you merge data using the keyboard rather than a data file. Existing documents can be converted into fill-in-the-blank merge forms in just minutes.

> **tip**
> You can create a sheet of identical labels with the Merge feature. Create the label form and type the text of the label. Choose **Tools**, **Merge**. In the Merge dialog box, be sure that Form Document is set to Current Document (choose **Form Document**, **Create Form Document**, **Use File in Active Window**). When the Associate Form and Data dialog box opens, click **No Association**, then click **OK**. Make sure Data Source is set to None. If you want to use the current document, click **Output** and then click **Current Document** (otherwise, the merge will create the sheet of labels in a new document in a separate window). Click **Options**. Type the number of labels on the page in the **Number of Copies for Each Record** text box. Choose **OK**, then choose **Merge**.

To create a fill-in-the-blank form

1. If you've already created the document, open it now. Otherwise, type the titles and labels that won't change. Figure 14.19 shows a fax cover sheet with the labels and the company name typed in. This is the information that doesn't change.

FIGURE 14.19
A fax cover sheet is a good candidate for a fill-in-the-blank merge form.

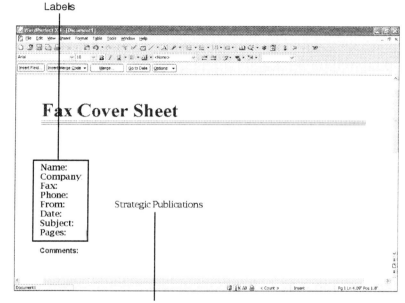

2. Choose **Tools**, **Merge** to open the Merge dialog box.
3. Click the **Form Document** button and choose **Create Form Document** from the drop-down list.
4. Click **Use File in Active Window** in the Data Source dialog box.
5. In the Associate Form and Data dialog box, click **No Association**.
6. Click in the document where you want to insert the Keyboard code.
7. Click the **Insert Merge Code** button, and then choose **Keyboard** to open the Insert Merge Code dialog box (see Figure 14.20).

FIGURE 14.20
Type the message that you want to appear in the Insert Merge Code dialog box.

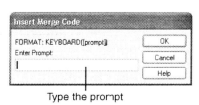

8. Type the prompt text that you want to appear, and then click **OK** to insert the Keyboard code in the form. This is the message that will pop up when the user runs the merge.
9. Repeat steps 6–8 to insert any other prompts for this form document. Figure 14.21 shows a form document with five Keyboard codes that prompt for the heading information.

FIGURE 14.21
The Keyboard code includes the message text in parentheses.

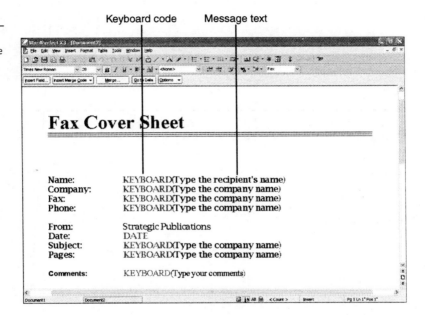

10. When you're ready to fill in the form, click the **Merge** button on the Merge feature bar.
11. Verify the location of the data file (if there is one), the form document, and the output; then click **Merge**. When a keyboard command is encountered, the merge pauses and displays the prompt message (see Figure 14.22). When the message box is displayed, the insertion point is positioned right where the Keyboard code was, so this is where you will enter the information. You will enter the text directly into the document, not into the message box.

> **tip**
> You can get the best of both worlds by combining a typical merge of a data file and form document with the flexibility of a fill-in-the-blank form. Just include keyboard codes in the form document where you want the user to type the information. The rest of the fields can be filled in from the data file.

CHAPTER 14 USING THE MERGE FEATURE

12. Type the requested information, and then click the **Continue** button on the Merge feature bar to continue the merge.

When you are finished entering information for all the keyboard codes, the merge process stops. The message box and the merge toolbar are cleared off the screen. At this point, you can either save or print the document.

FIGURE 14.22
The prompt message that you type is displayed in a window at the bottom of the screen.

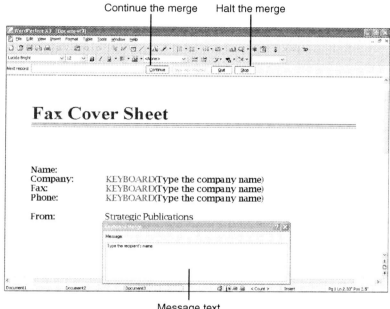

The Absolute Minimum

This chapter is the first in a section of chapters that explain how to use some of WordPerfect's automation tools. The chapter explains how to use the Merge feature to generate a batch of letters, envelopes, labels, and forms.

- You learned how to create a data file with the information that you want to insert into the form document.
- You learned how to create form documents from existing documents and from scratch.
- When you were finished creating the data file and the form document, you merged the two together.
- Envelopes can be created as a part of the original merge operation; labels are created in a separate merge.
- The Keyboard merge code can be used to create fill-in-the-blank forms, complete with messages to prompt the user.

In the next chapter, you will learn how to use the Address Book to keep track of names, addresses, and other personal information. You will also learn how to use the Address Book as the data source in a merge.

IN THIS CHAPTER

- Learn how to create and maintain address books.
- Learn how to add, edit, and move/copy address book entries between address books.
- Learn how to rearrange address book entries to make it easier to locate information.
- See how easy it is to work with the Outlook and WordPerfect Mail address books in WordPerfect.
- Learn how to route documents to multiple reviewers.
- Understand the importance of address books as a data source in a merge operation.
- Discover how to import and export address books.

USING THE ADDRESS BOOK

Everyone I know has an address book of some sort. Mine is battered and torn from years of use. Instead of buying a new book and rewriting all the information, I decided to create my address books in WordPerfect. It's much easier to edit an electronic address book than it is a written copy. Plus, I can use the address book information in a merge, so I can have WordPerfect print the labels for my holiday cards.

One of the most exciting features in WordPerfect X3 is the ability to use the Microsoft Outlook address book. If you've been using Outlook as your contact information manager, you will be pleased to know that you can use that information in a mass mailing, to print labels and envelopes, and to route documents for review.

The Address Book

The Address Book is included with the Standard, Professional, and Student & Teacher editions of WordPerfect Office X3, and most of the OEM versions of WordPerfect X3. You will also have it if you received the WordPerfect Productivity Pack with your new computer.

The Address Book is tightly integrated with WordPerfect. You can keep track of any type of information: phone and fax numbers, addresses, email addresses, birthdays, personal greetings, job titles, assistant and supervisor names, and so on. You can then use this information with the Merge feature to broadcast documents and email messages.

In WordPerfect X3, you have a choice. You can either use the WordPerfect address books, or you can use your Outlook address book. What this means is that if you already have Outlook on your system and you've been adding information to the Contacts list, you can use that in WordPerfect. Because you will be using Outlook to edit and update the contact information, you can skip to the Outlook section in this chapter and go from there.

If you received a copy of WordPerfect with a new computer, you might not have access to the Address Book, which is actually a separate program (formerly known as CorelCENTRAL). Not all OEM versions include it because it's the manufacturer's choice to include on their OEM CDs or not. If you are interested in using the WordPerfect Address Book, or the Outlook address book with WordPerfect, you can upgrade to the Standard or Professional editions of WordPerfect Office X3. Contact Corel at 1-800-77COREL for more information.

On the other hand, if you don't have Outlook on your system, the WordPerfect address books are a great place to keep your contact information. If you will take the time to enter the information, you will find that you can manipulate it in many different ways. The next several sections discuss creating and editing entries in the WordPerfect Address Book.

Starting the WordPerfect Address Book

I want to start with the WordPerfect Address Book and cover the Outlook integration later. It will be easier to follow along if your system acts and looks like the system used in the figures. For this reason, I'm going to ask that you turn off the Outlook integration so that when you open the address book, you will see the WordPerfect Address Book.

To turn off Outlook integration, choose **Tools**, **Settings**, **Environment**. If necessary, remove the check mark next to **Use Outlook Address Book/Contact List**. Now, let's open the WordPerfect Address Book dialog box and get familiar with it.

To start the Address Book

1. Start WordPerfect.
2. Choose **Tools, Address Book**. The WordPerfect Address Book dialog box appears (see Figure 15.1).

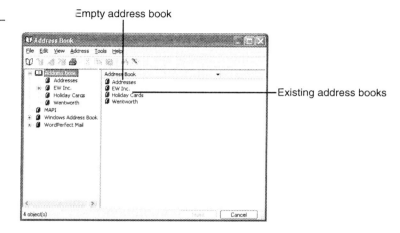

FIGURE 15.1
An empty address book called Addresses is automatically created, so you can start adding entries right away.

Adding Entries to an Address Book

You have a blank address book, just waiting for you to add some entries. For now, let's assume that you don't have the information in another file, or another address book, and you have to enter the entries from scratch. I'll explain how you can bring information in from other sources later.

To add an entry to an address book

1. If you have not already opened the Address Book dialog box as above, do so now by choosing Tools, Address book.
2. Select the address book to which you want to add. (Figure 15.2 shows several different types of address books and different types of entries to give you an idea of how the different types of entries will look in the address book window.)

3. Click the **Create a New Address Entry** button on the toolbar. The New dialog box appears (see Figure 15.3).
4. In the New dialog box, select a type of entry to create:

   - **Person**—This is the most comprehensive entry you can create. There are six tabs where you can organize the information: General, Personal, Address, Phone/Fax, Business, and Security.
   - **Organization**—This is a subset of the Person record, with three tabs: Address, Phone/Fax, and Security.

- **Resource**—You can maintain records on your company resources by identifying the name and type of the resource, the owner, the main phone number, the category, and comments. A resource might be a conference room, projection unit, videoconferencing equipment, or laptop.
- **Group**—You can create a group of address book records to make it easier to broadcast messages and general correspondence.

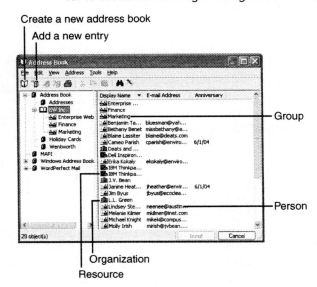

FIGURE 15.2
You can create four different types of address book entries: person, organization, resource, and group.

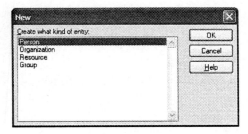

FIGURE 15.3
Select the type of entry you want to create from the New dialog box.

Depending on the type of entry you select, a blank record opens for you to fill in. Figure 15.4 shows the Properties dialog box for the Person category on the General tab. Type the information in the fields, pressing the **Tab** key to move to the next field and **Shift+Tab** to move back a field. To enter data in additional fields, click the tabs along the top of the dialog box.

FIGURE 15.4
The Person Properties dialog box has multiple tabs to organize the information.

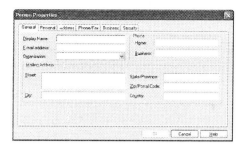

Creating New Address Books

The Address Book is designed to store a wide variety of information on individuals, organizations, resources, and groups. You can create books with contact names for each project you are involved in. Another address book might be created for your holiday greetings address list, yet another for the names of the children in your child's classroom. The possibilities are as varied as the people who use it.

To create new address books in the WordPerfect Address Book application window

1. Choose **File**, **New** or click the **Create a New Address Book** button (**Ctrl+N**) on the Address Book toolbar. The New Address Book dialog box opens (see Figure 15.5).

FIGURE 15.5
You can create several different types of address books.

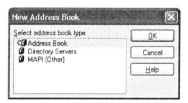

2. Select the type of address book that you want to create:

- **Address Book**—You can create an address book that can be imported into and edited in CorelCENTRAL, which was included with earlier versions of WordPerfect Office.

- **Directory Servers**—The WordPerfect Address Book lets you connect to and open directory server address books using Lightweight Direct Access Protocol (LDAP).

- **MAPI (Other)**—You can access MAPI-compliant (Messaging Application Programming Interface) address books on your computer. For example, if you've created an address book in a MAPI-compliant application, such as Microsoft Outlook or Novell GroupWise, you can open and edit it in the WordPerfect Address Book.

Depending on the type of address book you select, you will see other dialog boxes in which you can specify a name and other properties for the new address book. When you are finished, the new address book is created and the name appears in the left pane.

Working with Address Book Entries

Creating an address book and typing in the entries is only half the battle. Someone has to maintain the information, right? Those pesky clients keep changing their cell phone numbers and email addresses, so you have to stay on top of things to keep your information current. Thankfully, working with address book entries is a breeze in WordPerfect. You have many options for editing, deleting (be careful here), moving and copying records between books, printing entries, and searching for information.

To edit an address book entry

1. Double-click the person, organization, or resource entry in the list to edit the information, or select the entry and then click the **Edit an Address Entry** button.
2. Make your changes.
3. Click **OK** to save the changes or **Cancel** to discard the changes.

If you don't need an address book, or a single address book entry, you can delete it. To delete address book entries

1. Select one or more entries. Use the **Shift** key to select consecutive entries, or the **Ctrl** key to select entries scattered throughout the list.

2. Click the **Delete an Address Entry** button, or press **Delete** on the keyboard. You can also right-click the selection and choose **Delete**.
3. Click **Yes** to confirm the deletion or **No** to bail out and keep the entry.

> **caution**
> Be very, very careful when you delete records in an address book. No Undo feature can restore an entry that you've deleted in error. The same is true for deleting an entire address book. The only way to recover an accidentally deleted address book is if you can restore the files from a backup. Consider this one more reason to back up regularly so that a recent copy of your address book is secure.

To move entries to another address book

1. Select the entries in the list.
2. Click and drag the selected entries over to an address book in the left pane, as seen in Figure 15.6.
3. When the correct address book is highlighted, release the mouse button to move the entries.

FIGURE 15.6
Clicking and dragging address book entries is a quick way to move entries to another book.

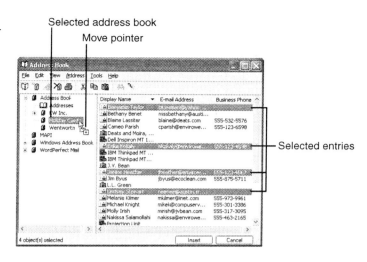

To copy entries to another address book

1. Select the entries.

2. Choose **Edit**, **Copy**, or right-click the selection and choose **Copy**.
3. Open the other address book.

4. Choose **Edit**, **Paste**, or right-click in the right pane and choose **Paste**.

You can print the current record, selected records, or all the records. The records will print with the same fields displayed in the Address Book window. If you want to print something else, you need to customize the columns in the right pane and then print.

To print address book entries

1. Select one or more records.

2. Click the **Print** button on the toolbar (**Ctrl+P**) to open the Print dialog box.
3. Make the necessary selections; then click **Print**.

To search for text in address book entries

1. Click the **Search for Specified Text** button, or choose **Edit**, **Find** (**Ctrl+F**) to open the Find dialog box.

> **tip**
>
> Your contact information is a priceless resource and should be protected. Depending on the number of contacts and the sensitivity of the information, it might be critically important that you back up your address books. A good time to do this is right after you make changes to the entries. To back up your address books, use the Import/Export Expert to export the books. You can only export one book at a time, so plan on repeating the steps for each address book.

2. Type the text you want to search for.

3. Click **OK**. If records are found that contain the search text, the dialog box expands and the records are listed below the Find text box (see Figure 15.7).

FIGURE 15.7
Type the text you want to search for in the address book entries in the Find dialog box.

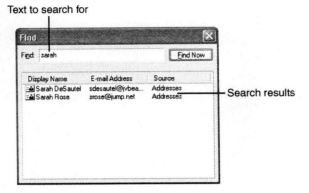

To send an email message to a contact

1. Select an address book entry.

2. Choose **Tools**, **Send Mail** or click the **Send Mail** button to start composing a mail message. If there is an email address in the selected record, it's automatically inserted into the message.

3. Finish creating the message, and then send it as you normally would.

Customizing the Address Book Window

The default display settings in the Address Book window might not be very useful to you, so you might be looking for a way to alter the display to make it easier to find information. You can do this in several ways: You can change the column headings and display different fields, or you can sort the records to group certain records together. You can also set a filter and specify what criteria must be met for a record to be displayed.

To change the fields (columns) displayed in the records list

1. Right-click a column heading to display the Columns dialog box. A list of all the fields appears (see Figure 15.8). These settings can vary among address books.

2. Place a check mark next to each of the fields that you want to see listed. These settings "stick" with the address book, so you can customize the display of fields for each address book.

FIGURE 15.8

Mark the fields that you want displayed in the record list in the Columns dialog box.

Sorting address book records is one way to group related records together. After they are grouped together, you can quickly select them and work with the records as a group. For example, you might want to work with only those records in a certain state. Sorting in ZIP Code order can help you organize your records by region.

To sort the address book records

1. Click the column heading for the field by which you want to sort. You can now select the sorted records for printing, email, or merging. For example, you can print labels in ZIP Code order if you sort the records by ZIP Code before selecting them.

2. Click the column heading again to reverse the sort (ascending to descending and vice versa). The arrow on the column heading shows you which direction the sort is done.

If you have an especially large address book and you want to be able to view only a certain group of entries, such as everyone at CompanyABC, you need to filter the entries. *Filtering* means that you tell the address book to show only the entries that include specific criteria, such as a company name like CompanyABC. The rest of the entries in your address book seem to "disappear" when the entries are filtered; however, they are all still in the address book. They are just not being displayed. After you finish viewing the specific entries for CompanyABC, you can remove the filter and all your entries will be visible again.

To set a filter for address book records

1. Choose **View**. **Filter** to display the Filter dialog box (see Figure 15.9).

2. Click the first drop-down list arrow and choose a field. These fields are the column heading names, and you are choosing the one that you want the entries to be filtered by.

3. Click the operator button between the list box and the text box. Until you change it, the button has an equal sign on it.

FIGURE 15.9
Specify the criteria that must be met for the record to be displayed in the list in the Filter dialog box.

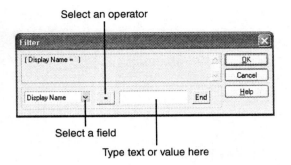

4. Select an operator from the list. The operators are used to narrow down the list. For example, you can filter out all the records with a `ZIP Code of Greater Than 53600`.

5. Type the text or value that you want to use as a filter in the text box, and then click **OK**. To continue the example in step 4, you would enter `53600` as the ZIP Code value. The program refreshes the list and displays only those records that meet the criteria.

> **caution**
> After you apply a filter, it stays there until you remove it. If you apply a filter and then close the Address Book, when you reopen it, the filter is still in place. You won't see a full list of records until you remove the filter. To switch back to the full list, choose **View, Remove Filter**.

Integrating with Outlook and WordPerfect Mail

WordPerfect X3 offers some improvements to integration with Microsoft Outlook address books. You can now use entries in the Outlook address book for document routing and review, printing labels and envelopes, and merge operations. As mentioned earlier, you must make a choice. You can either work with the entries in the WordPerfect address books or the Outlook address book, not both at the same time.

From the names, you would think that Outlook and Outlook Express were the same type of application. They are not. Outlook is a personal information manager and Outlook Express is an email/news reader. They both have address books, but they are completely separate from each other. You can work with both address books in WordPerfect, using two different methods.

You will be able to open the Outlook Express address book in the WordPerfect Address Book. The entries will appear in the Contacts folder under Windows Address Book. The Outlook address book is opened when you activate Outlook integration.

Opening the Outlook Address Book

When you're ready to work with the Outlook address book, you will need to "turn on" Outlook integration. To switch back to the WordPerfect address books, you have to turn Outlook integration back off.

To enable Outlook integration

1. In the WordPerfect window, choose **Tools**, **Settings** (**Alt+F12**).
2. Click **Environment**.
3. Click the **Use Outlook Address Book/Contact List** check box to activate this feature.
4. Choose **OK**, and then **Close** to return to the document.

When you enable the Outlook integration, Outlook "takes over" the address book. When you open the address book, you will get the Outlook Address Book dialog box. The WordPerfect address books are not available at this point.

> **caution**
>
> To integrate with the Outlook address book, WordPerfect must be able to interface with that application. The Microsoft Windows standard for electronic messaging is called MAPI. Microsoft limits the contacts available under MAPI to those that contain an email address or fax number. For this reason, only the entries that have an email address or fax number will appear in the Outlook Address Book dialog box. If you don't have the information, enter a space or "dummy" character in the field. Incidentally, Microsoft also controls what is placed in the Display Name field.

To open the Outlook address book/contact list

1. Choose **Tools**, **Address Book**. The first time you use the Outlook address book, you will have to specify a profile in the Choose Profile dialog box (see Figure 15.10).

FIGURE 15.10
After you identify your profile, the Outlook Address Book will open when you choose Tools, Address Book.

2. Either select a profile from the drop-down list or choose **OK** to use the default profile. The Outlook Address Book dialog box appears (see Figure 15.11).

FIGURE 15.11
The Outlook Address Book dialog box shows the entries in alphabetical order.

Opening the WordPerfect Mail Address Book

WordPerfect Mail is a new application included with the Standard and Professional editions of WordPerfect Office X3 and as a separate application. WordPerfect Mail is a full-featured, easy-to-use application that provides email, calendar, and contact management. It includes innovative filing capabilities, outstanding spam protection, and search functionality that performs at lightning speed.

WordPerfect Mail has an address book that you can use to maintain your contact information. You can open the WordPerfect Mail address book in WordPerfect so you can select records for document routing, merge operations, envelopes and labels, and any other occasion where you need to use contact information. Although you can open the WordPerfect Mail address book in WordPerfect, you won't be able to edit or delete the entries. If you try to do this in WordPerfect, you'll see an error message that says "Functionality not supported." You'll need to do your maintenance tasks in WordPerfect Mail.

When you're ready to work with the WordPerfect Mail address book, you will need to disable Outlook integration first. Because you'll be opening the WordPerfect Mail address books in the WordPerfect Address Book dialog box, you'll be able to use the WordPerfect and WordPerfect Mail address books together, but not at the same time as the Outlook address book.

To disable Outlook integration

1. In the WordPerfect window, choose **Tools**, **Settings (Alt+F12)**.
2. Click **Environment**.
3. Disable the **Use Outlook Address Book/Contact List** check box.
4. Click **OK**, and then click **Close** to return to the document.

To open the WordPerfect Mail address book/contact list

1. Choose **Tools**, **Address Book**.
2. Click **File**, **Open**, and then click the **Other** button.
3. Choose **Personal Address Book**.

When the process is complete, you will have a folder labeled WordPerfect Mail that contains a personal address book (see Figure 15.12). The entries from your WordPerfect Mail address book can be found in this address book.

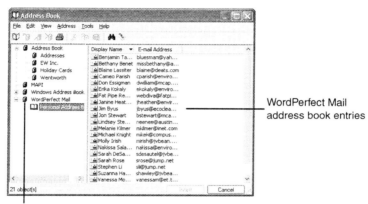

FIGURE 15.12
The WordPerfect Mail address book can be opened in WordPerfect and accessed when you need that contact information.

Routing Documents

WordPerfect has always had powerful tools for reviewing and comparing documents. Document routing was introduced in WordPerfect 12. You can email a document (as an attachment) to multiple reviewers. Each reviewer opens the attachment, makes her changes/comments, and closes the document. The document is then routed to the next person on the list. When the document has been reviewed by everyone on the list, it is sent back to you.

In WordPerfect X3, you are now able to select reviewers from the WordPerfect address books (including the WordPerfect Mail address book) in addition to the Microsoft Outlook address book. You will need to be using Microsoft Outlook 2000 or newer to use the contact information in Outlook.

To create a routing slip

1. Choose **File**, **Document**, **Routing Slip**. The Routing Slip dialog box appears (see Figure 15.13).
2. Type a subject in the Subject text box.
3. (Optional) Type a message in the Message text box. This is a great place to leave instructions for the reviewers.

FIGURE 15.13
Build a list of reviewers and give them instructions in the Routing Slip dialog box.

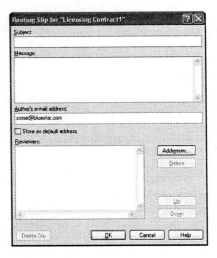

4. If necessary, modify your email address in the Author's Email Address text box.

5. Click **Addresses** to start creating a list of reviewers. The Add Reviewers dialog box with the Outlook contact list is shown in Figure 15.14). Your Add Reviewers dialog box might look different if have a different version of Outlook on your system, or if you are using the WordPerfect address books.

FIGURE 15.14
The Add Reviewers dialog box displays a list of contacts from which to choose.

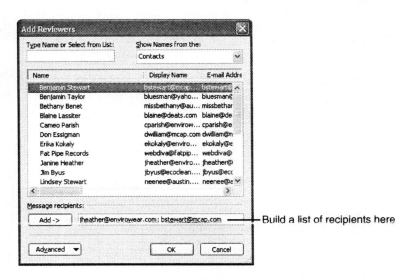

6. Select the reviewer(s) in the list. Remember, you can click the first name, and then hold down the **Ctrl** key to select the others.

7. Click the **Add** → button to add the selected names to the **Message Recipients** list box.

8. Click **OK** to return to the Routing Slip dialog box.
9. If you need to rearrange the reviewer names, select a reviewer name and then choose **Up** or **Down**. The document will be sent out to the reviewers in the order they appear on the Routing Slip, so this is an important step.
10. Click **OK**.

To give you an idea of what happens next, a reviewer will double-click the attached document in her email application. She will type her name and choose a color for her text changes to appear in. After she is done with her changes, she can either save the document and send it later, or she can send it on to the next reviewer. Each reviewer can see the names of the other reviewers and their colors, so she can figure out who made what changes. A reviewer can edit additions made by other reviewers, but she will not be able to edit or undo previous deletions.

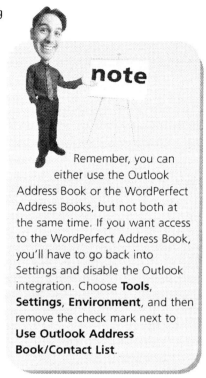

Remember, you can either use the Outlook Address Book or the WordPerfect Address Books, but not both at the same time. If you want access to the WordPerfect Address Book, you'll have to go back into Settings and disable the Outlook integration. Choose **Tools**, **Settings**, **Environment**, and then remove the check mark next to **Use Outlook Address Book/Contact List**.

Using Address Books with Merge

The Address Book is tightly integrated into WordPerfect (and other suite applications), and it's well suited for tracking all sorts of contact information. When you use the Merge feature to produce personalized letters, you can select records directly from the WordPerfect address books or the Outlook address book. If you maintain comprehensive address books, you might never create a data file again.

Associate a Form File with an Address Book

When you create a form document, you can associate the form with an address book rather than a data file. In this case, you will be able to associate one of the WordPerfect address books or the Outlook address book. See Chapter 14, "Using the Merge Feature," for more information on working with data files.

To associate a form file with an address book

1. Choose **Tools**, **Merge**.
2. Click **Data Source**, and then select **Address Book**.
3. Click the drop-down list arrow to display a list of available address books (see Figure 15.15).

FIGURE 15.15
Select an address book to merge with a form file from the list of address books on your system.

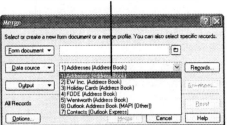

Edit an Association to an Address Book

If you need to switch to another address book, or if you created the form document with one address book and you want to switch to another, you can edit the association.

To edit an association to an address book

1. Open the form file.
2. Click the **Go To Data** button on the **Merge** feature bar.
3. Click the **Data Source** drop-down arrow and choose one of the address books from the list.
4. Click **Close**. You should see an updated list of field names in the **Insert Field** list, so you can revise the field names in the form file.

Importing and Exporting Address Books

If you want to use an address book that you created in another application, you will need to export the book into a common file format, such as ASCII, and then import it into WordPerfect. Conversely, you might want to export your address books from WordPerfect so that you can use them in another program.

Unfortunately, detailed steps for every type of import or export operation is beyond the scope of this book. However, the following list of general concepts for importing and exporting should get you moving in the right direction:

- **Using the Import/Export Expert**—Corel designed this expert to walk you through the process of importing and exporting information. You can import address books from Corel Address Book 8 (.abx), text file format (.csv, .txt), and Outlook 97/98/2000/XP. You can export to text file format (.csv, .txt) and Outlook 97/98/2000/XP.
- **Importing a merge data file**—If you want to add names and addresses that you have stored in a merge data file to an address book, you can convert the merge data file into a text file and import the text file into an

address book. If you created the data file as a table, you can open and save the file as text without making any changes. Open the data file; then choose **File, Save As**. In the Save As dialog box, choose **ASCII (DOS) Delimited Text** from the **File Type** drop-down list, and then save the file. Now, you can import this .txt file directly into the address book. See Chapter 14 for more information on creating data files.

> **caution**
> The location of the address books varies with different versions of WordPerfect, so the general rule is that you should export your books before you upgrade. After you have installed the newer version, you can import the address books from the previous version. This isn't always necessary, but it's almost foolproof.

- **Importing spreadsheet and database files**—You can use information from spreadsheet programs, such as Quattro Pro or Excel, or database programs, such as Paradox or Access in WordPerfect. First, save the file as an ASCII text file, which you can import directly into the Address Book. During the import process, you will be able to "map," or match up, the field names from the ASCII text file with the Address Book field names, so you can be sure that the information from the text file is inserted in the right places.

- **Importing other address books**—In most cases, you will be able to export addresses from another address book (such as Outlook Express) into an ASCII (or comma-delimited) text file, which can be imported directly into a WordPerfect Address Book. During the import process, the field names used in the other address book will be listed next to the fields in the WordPerfect Address Book. After you've matched up the field names, you can import the data.

- **Exporting to an ASCII text file**—If you want to use WordPerfect Address Book data in another program or in an earlier version of WordPerfect, the universally accepted format is ASCII. After you've exported an address book to a text file (*.csv, *.txt), you can open, or import, the .txt file in another application.

The Absolute Minimum

- In this chapter, you learned how to use the WordPerfect Address Book application to keep track of contact information.
- You learned how to create an address book and how to add entries to it.
- You saw how easy it is to edit and delete entries and to move and copy entries between address books.
- You learned how to sort and filter the address book entries to locate exactly what you need.
- When you activate Outlook integration, you will be able to work with the entries for a mass mailing, printing envelopes and labels and document routing.
- Address books can be used as a data source for a merge, so you learned how to associate a form file with an address book.
- Techniques for importing and exporting address books were covered so that you can bring everything into WordPerfect.

In the next chapter, you will learn how to use templates to automate document production and to ensure consistency throughout company documents.

IN THIS CHAPTER

- Learn how to open a template and how to customize the WordPerfect default template.
- Understand how important it is to back up your default template before you make any changes.
- Download and install bonus template files from the Corel websites.
- Convert existing documents into templates to automate your document production.
- Start the WordPerfect OfficeReady browser to preview and open additional templates.

WORKING WITH TEMPLATES

Every document that you create in WordPerfect is based on a template. Up to this point, you've been using the wp13us.wpt template (for the U.S. version of WordPerfect), which is the default template in WordPerfect and contains all the default settings for new documents. The default template is blank except for the initial settings. If you want to change the settings for all new documents, you edit the default template. From then on, all new documents will have those settings.

New templates are created as fill-in-the-blanks documents containing formatting, layout, and standard blocks of text, so all you have to do is provide the content. WordPerfect X3 includes some templates to help get you started.

Using WordPerfect's Templates

A nice collection of templates is included with WordPerfect Office X3, and more templates are available in the WordPerfect OfficeReady Solution Packs. You might not have to create your own for quite a while, if ever. When you do venture out and create your own template, you will be able to convert any of your existing documents into templates.

Most of the WordPerfect templates have a companion PerfectExpert project that guides you through the process of filling in the template. Rather than opening a template just as you would any other document, you select the project that you want to work on. The template is opened in the document window, and the PerfectExpert panel opens on the left side of the screen. You simply click the project buttons and choose from a list of options to alter the style, add other elements, and fill in the important text.

To create a new document based on a WordPerfect template

1. Choose **File**, **New from Project** (**Ctrl+Shift+N**). The PerfectExpert dialog box appears (see Figure 16.1).

FIGURE 16.1
You choose the PerfectExpert project that you want to use in the Corel PerfectExpert dialog box.

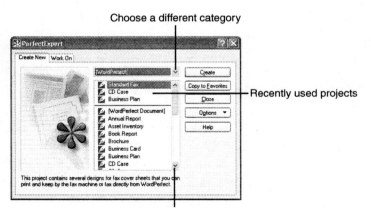

Choose a different category

Recently used projects

Scroll down through the list

2. If necessary, click the **Create New** tab to display the list of templates.
3. Scroll through the list of projects and double-click the one you want to run. You will see a PerfectScript message box asking if you want to disable macros in this document.
4. Click the **Enable Macros** button to run the macros in the template.

If you don't see the project you want, click the category drop-down list arrow at the top of the project template list and choose another category. Select WordPerfect for a list of all the WordPerfect Office X3 templates.

Some of WordPerfect's templates require personal information. If you, or anyone else, haven't filled that in yet, you will be prompted for it the first time you open a project template that uses the personal information.

Filling in Personal Information

Many project templates require personal information (such as a name, company, address, and fax number), which you can type in once and have WordPerfect insert for you whenever it's necessary. If this information hasn't been created yet, you are prompted for it when you open a template that uses it (see Figure 16.2).

When you click **OK**, the Address Book dialog box opens, with a list of available address books. You need to be able to select an address book entry that contains your personal information. If you haven't already created this record, do it now. Refer to the section titled "Creating a New Address Book Entry" in Chapter 15, "Using the Address Book," for the steps to create a new, personal information entry.

> **caution**
>
> On the previous page, you're using a template that came with WordPerfect Office X3, so you can be relatively sure that it's safe. If you get the message in step 3 when you are using a template that didn't come from a trusted source, you should choose **Disable Macros** to disable the macros. The template will probably not work correctly—this is to be expected. You should check into the sender of that template and assure yourself that it came from a respected source before you run the macros in it. The reason for extreme caution is that viruses can hide themselves in macros. By disabling the macros in a template, you are protecting your system from marauding macro viruses.

Select the entry in the list, and then click **Insert**. That's it—you're done. This entry becomes the default for all the templates. In many offices, computers are shared, so users need to select their own personal information entry in the Address Book.

FIGURE 16.2

This message appears if you haven't created a personal information entry in the Address Book.

To select a different personal information entry

1. Choose **File**, **New from Project** to open the PerfectExpert dialog box.
2. Click the **Options** button.
3. Choose **Personal Information**. A message box appears and identifies the current personal information entry.
4. Click **OK** to open the Address Book dialog box, where you can select another personal information entry.

The Disable Macro Message

Before the project template opens, you might see a PerfectScript macros message box that explains there are macros in the document, and if you don't know the source of the document, you might want to disable the macros. A macro is like a small program that you can create to repeat your actions. Some macros are malicious because they contain computer viruses, which can wreak havoc on your computer system. For this reason, it's a good idea to disable macros in documents that do not come from trusted sources.

If you're using one of the templates that shipped with WordPerfect, or a template from a trusted source, you can click **Enable Macros**; you don't want to disable the macros. However, if you are unsure of the source, it's best to click **Disable Macros** to disable the macros. Granted, the results won't be the same, but it's better to be safe than sorry.

> **caution**
> Under no circumstances should you enable the check box that turns off the PerfectScript macros message box. In the battle against computer viruses, the capability to disable macros in a document is a fundamental tool. Turning off this message box removes your ability to choose to disable or enable the PerfectScript macros.

Using the PerfectExpert Panel

When you open a template that has a companion PerfectExpert project, the PerfectExpert panel opens next to the template (see Figure 16.3). The buttons in the PerfectExpert panel give you options for customizing the template by choosing from the available variations.

FIGURE 16.3

PerfectExpert projects combine templates and a PerfectExpert panel to guide you through the process of creating the document.

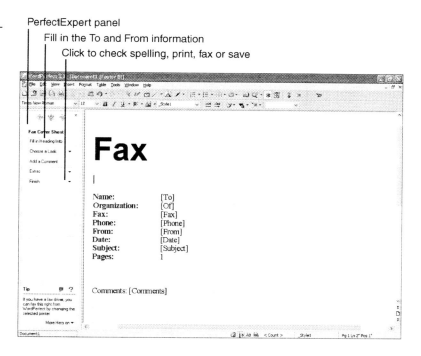

Now you can start building the document by clicking the buttons in the PerfectExpert panel. For example, in the Fax project shown in Figure 16.3, click the **Fill in Heading Info** button to open the Fax Cover Sheet Heading dialog box, where you can type all the information (see Figure 16.4). Remove the check mark next to any item that you don't want on the fax cover sheet. Click the drop-down list arrows to choose items that you've already used in these fields. Otherwise, type the information in the text boxes.

> **caution**
>
> In some cases, the PerfectExpert panel doesn't appear with the template. To manually display the PerfectExpert panel, choose Help, PerfectExpert.

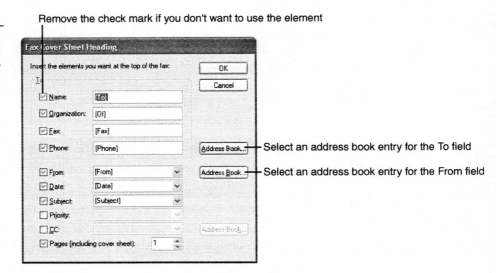

FIGURE 16.4
After you type the information in the Fax Cover Sheet Heading dialog box, WordPerfect places it in the proper place in the template.

Customizing WordPerfect's Templates

Every document you create from scratch is based on the default template (unless you specifically select a different template). Some of the default settings are listed in Table 2.1 in Chapter 2, "Creating, Saving, and Printing Documents." The default template can be customized to suit your preferences. For example, if you want 1.25-inch margins, specific tab settings, and the Century Schoolbook 12-point font, you can make these changes to the default template so that they are in place for all new documents. The other WordPerfect templates can also be edited and customized to your preferences. For example, if you like everything about the fax cover sheet template except the small footer line, edit the template and take it out. Add your company logo to the templates for instant business forms!

Backing Up the Default Template

The default template contains a lot more than initial settings. It contains the majority of your customization efforts (such as custom toolbars, menus, and keyboards), so it is particularly important that you make a backup copy of the file before you make changes.

Before you start renaming template files, be sure you close WordPerfect. When you are finished with the backup, restart WordPerfect. To make a backup copy of your default template

1. Search for the default template file—wp13US.wpt—for the U.S. version. Change the "US" to the two-letter abbreviation for your language.
2. When you find the file, rename it to wp13usold.wpt.

If the changes that you make to the default template cause any problems, you can go back to using the original default template by renaming or deleting the new template and renaming the old template back to its original filename. In other words, you delete the wp13US.wpt that you have created and then rename your original default template, wp13USold.wpt, back to wp13US.wpt. This would "reinstate" the original default template.

> **caution**
> Depending on how your system is set up, you might not be able to find the default template file. In some cases, the folder that holds that file is marked as hidden and won't be included in the search. You need to turn on the display of hidden files and folders to include them. In Windows Explorer, choose **Tools**, **Folder Options**. Click the **View** tab. The list box has an option labeled Hidden Files and Folders. Select the **Show Hidden Files and Folders** option. Click **OK**, and try the search again.

Editing the Default Template

If you routinely use settings other than the defaults, you can place these settings in the default template. The next time you create a new document, the new default settings will be in place. Be sure to make a backup copy of the default template before you make any editing changes to it. If something goes wrong, you can revert to the previous copy.

Follow these steps to edit the default template:

1. Choose **View**, **Reveal Codes** to turn on Reveal Codes.
2. Find the Open Style: DocumentStyle code at the top of the document.
3. Double-click the code to open the Styles Editor (see Figure 16.5).

FIGURE 16.5
Use the Styles Editor menus and toolbars to customize the initial document style, and then save them to the default template.

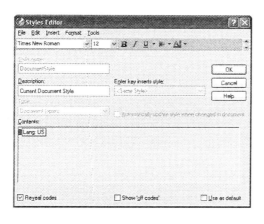

4. Using the menus in the Styles Editor, make the necessary changes, and then place a check in the **Use as Default** check box.
5. Click **OK**. You will see a message box asking whether you want to apply the document style to new documents as they are created.
6. Click **Yes** to save your changes to the default template.

If you find that your changes haven't worked out the way you wanted, and you made a backup copy of the template before you started editing, you can revert to the previous copy of the default template. Refer to the previous section, "Backing Up the Default Template," for more information.

Editing the WordPerfect Templates

WordPerfect's project templates are designed so that you can use them right away. They are generic enough to work in most situations, especially when time is more important than personalization. However, when you're ready to customize the templates, you can revise a template as easily as you revise any other document.

To edit a template

1. Choose **File**, **New from Project**. If necessary, click the **Create New** tab.
2. Select a template from the list. If you don't see the templates, open the category drop-down list and choose **WordPerfect**.
3. Click the **Options** button and select **Edit WP Template** from the list. The template opens in a document window, and the Template toolbar is displayed on top of the property bar (see Figure 16.6).

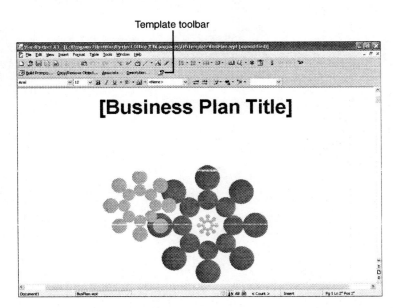

FIGURE 16.6
You can edit a template just as you would any other document.

4. Revise the template as you would any other document.

5. When you're finished, click the **Close** button to close the Template Editor. A confirmation message box appears.

6. Click **Yes** to save the template.

Earlier in the chapter, you learned how to edit the default template by modifying the DocumentStyle in the Styles Editor and saving the changes to the default template. This method works smoothly for items that you want to add to the template, but if there is something that you want to remove, or if you want to make some adjustments, you're better off editing the default template through the PerfectExpert dialog box.

To edit the default template

1. Choose **File**, **New from Project** to open the PerfectExpert dialog box.

2. Click the category drop-down list arrow and select **Custom WP Templates**. A list of customized templates appears in the list box (see Figure 16.7).

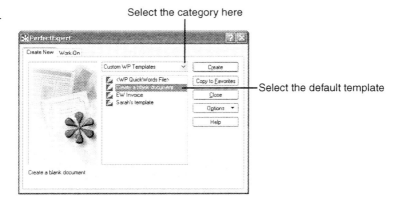

FIGURE 16.7
The templates that you create are stored in the Custom WP Templates folder.

3. Select **Create a Blank Document**.

4. Click the **Options** button and select **Edit WP Template**.

5. Use the menus, toolbars, and property bars to make your changes, just as you would in any other document.

Here's an example for you: If you want all your new documents to start out with a 12-point Century Schoolbook font and .75-inch margins on all sides, you can make those selections here and save them to the default template. Bear in mind that any changes you make here will affect all new documents, so be careful of the formatting and codes that you add.

Downloading and Installing Templates

Shortly after the release of WordPerfect Office 2002, Corel announced that it would be making additional templates and projects available in a free download. These templates, which were written for WordPerfect 10, will work just fine in WordPerfect X3.

This news is especially welcome to users of Productivity Pack and Trial versions, which do not contain the same set of templates as the other WordPerfect Office X3 editions. Academic products are discounted, and OEM products are included free with computer systems from large computer manufacturers such as Dell, Inc. Because the customer doesn't pay the retail price, some of the goodies are left out.

You'll be saving the downloaded template files to the `\wordperfect office X3\languages\en\template` folder under the `\program files` tree.

Templates and projects can be downloaded from `www.officecommunity.com/AppLogic+FTContentServer.html` in the Download Gallery section (see Figure 16.8). Click the **Templates & Projects** link at the top of the page, then click **WordPerfect**. To download a template or project zip file, click the **[download]** link. When you are prompted, save the file to the Template folder that you noted earlier.

You can also download them from Corel's FTP site at `ftp://ftp.corel.com/pub/WordPerfect/wpwin/10/english/templates`. To download a template, click the name of the template you are interested in. This opens that template's folder on the FTP server. Within each template's folder is a file named `Template and Project-Read Me.htm`. This file contains detailed information about installing the templates in WordPerfect.

Also on the FTP site, a zip file called `WP 10 Temp` contains all the template files so that you can download the whole collection at one time. Within each template category folder is also a `README` file with instructions for installation. There is a `thumbnail` folder in each category, containing a GIF file that shows you what each created project form might look like. If you download a zip file, extract the template files (.wpt and .ast) to the `\wordperfect office X3\languages\en\template` folder under the `\program files` tree. Now, you're ready to add them into WordPerfect.

FIGURE 16.8
OfficeCommunity's Download Gallery has a complete set of downloadable templates that will work with WordPerfect X3.

To install downloaded templates

1. Choose **File**, **New from Project** to open the PerfectExpert dialog box.
2. Click the **Options** button, and then select **Refresh Projects** from the list. Click **Yes** to confirm.

On my system, the downloaded templates were stored in a WordPerfect 10 category, so if you don't see the new templates in the list, open the drop-down list of categories and select WordPerfect 10.

When you open one of the WordPerfect 10 templates, you might see a message stating that the PerfectExpert resource file couldn't be found. I've ignored it and not suffered any consequences.

Converting an Existing Document to a Template

Creating a template from scratch is definitely a last resort. Other options are much faster. First, you can convert an existing document into a template. You're bound to have a handful of "form" documents that you use over and over. Fax cover sheets come to mind, but so do supply requests, time sheets, network maintenance bulletins, expense reports, newsletters, equipment checkout sheets, and so on.

Second, you can revise an existing template and then save your changes as a new template. You can use as your starting point one of your own templates or one of the templates that comes with WordPerfect, and then just make the necessary adjustments. Refer to the section "Editing the WordPerfect Templates," earlier in the chapter, for the steps.

To create a template from an existing document

1. In a blank document, choose **File**, **New from Project**.
2. Click the **Options** button and select **Create WP Template** from the list. A blank template opens in the document window, and the Template toolbar is displayed at the top of the screen.
3. Click the **Insert File** button (or choose **Insert**, **File**) to display the Insert File dialog box.
4. Select the filename for the existing document, and then click **Insert**.
5. Delete all the text that varies for each document. In other words, turn the document into a form, where there are blank spaces for the information that changes. The text that stays the same stays in the document. Make any other necessary revisions.
6. Click the **Close** button when you're finished.
7. Click **Yes** when you're asked whether you want to save the template. The Save Template dialog box appears (see Figure 16.9).

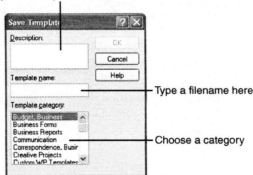

FIGURE 16.9
In addition to naming the templates, you can create a description for the template and choose a category to store the template in.

8. In the **Description** text box, type a descriptive name to appear in the template list.
9. Type a filename in the **Template Name** text box. Don't type an extension—WordPerfect assigns the .wpt extension to templates so they can be recognized as templates and not as documents.
10. Choose the category where you want the template stored in the **Template Category** list box.
11. Click **OK** to save and close the template.

Working with WordPerfect OfficeReady Browser

In addition to the standard WordPerfect templates discussed earlier, version X3 comes with the WordPerfect OfficeReady (WPOR) Browser, which is bundled with 40 extra templates that you can use in WordPerfect, Quattro Pro, and Presentations. The name "browser" just means you can use the program to organize and preview templates in a big window, as you might do in an Internet browser.

Because the WPOR Browser is a separate mini-program, you start it either from an icon on the desktop (if you have one) or from the Windows Start menu. To use the Start menu, choose **Start**, **(All) Programs**, **WordPerfect Office Ready**, **Start WordPerfect OfficeReady** to display the WordPerfect OfficeReady dialog box (see Figure 16.10).

FIGURE 16.10
The WordPerfect OfficeReady Browser provides a high-resolution preview of the OfficeReady templates, so you can quickly locate the template that you need.

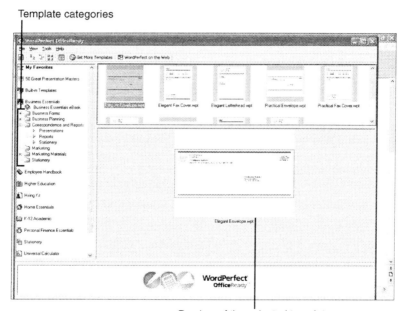

The browser's preview feature lets you quickly locate the template that you need by providing a high-resolution preview of the OfficeReady templates. The templates have been grouped into categories (Academic, Business Forms, Personal Finance, Home Essentials, Marketing Materials, and so on), so you don't waste time hunting for the right file.

When you find the template you want, you can double-click on it to launch the application (WordPerfect, Quattro Pro, or Presentations) and open the template. From there, you just fill in the blanks. In no time at all, you'll have a professionally designed document, ready to email, fax, or print.

To download additional solution packs, click the **Get More Templates** button. This opens the page for downloading solution packs for WordPerfect OfficeReady. Some solution packs are available for free download; others can be purchased. As of this writing, 11 solution packs are available for purchase: Business Essentials, Employee Handbook, Business Plans, Hiring Kit, Home Essentials, Personal Finances, K-12 Academic, Higher Education, Stationery, 50 Great Presentation Masters, and Universal Calculator.

The WPOR Browser (and associated templates) is not included with the WordPerfect Productivity Pack and the OEM copies. However, you can download the WPOR Browser from www.wordperfect.com/templates/. Note that the browser/templates package is only compatible with WordPerfect versions 12 and X3.

The Absolute Minimum

In this chapter, you learned how to use templates to speed up the creation of frequently used documents. Templates are extremely popular in settings where consistency across documents is particularly important.

- You learned how to use the WordPerfect templates to create frequently used documents.
- The default template, which contains all the initial settings for new documents, can be edited and adjusted for your preferences.
- Any WordPerfect template can be edited so that you can add your company logo or any other customization to personalize them for your business.
- Additional template projects are available online. You learned where to download them and how to add them to the list of templates in the PerfectExpert dialog box.
- Existing documents make the best templates because most of the work is already done. You saw how easy it is to convert a document into a template.

In the next chapter, you will learn how to write your own macros to speed up repetitive tasks. You will also learn how to use the macros that come with WordPerfect. Most importantly, you'll get step-by-step instructions to create three sample macros.

IN THIS CHAPTER

- Learn what a macro is and how it can save you time.
- Learn how to play macros that someone else has written.
- Gain an understanding of the variety and usefulness of macros that come with WordPerfect.
- Learn how to create your own macros and edit them to make minor changes.
- Create three sample macros that you can use right away.

CREATING AND PLAYING MACROS

Macros are different from the other automation features in WordPerfect. The macro language is powerful. With a few exceptions, anything you can do in a document can be done in a macro. The nice thing about macros is that you don't have to learn the macro language to write your own macros.

And one more thing: You might have heard about macro viruses infecting computers and causing all sorts of problems. Rest assured that WordPerfect macros are more secure and less vulnerable to viruses than Microsoft products. It's complicated to explain, but it has to do with the fact that when you open a document in WordPerfect, only the text is recognized. WordPerfect simply ignores any macros or executable code that might be attached.

What Is a Macro?

Stop and think for a minute: How much of your time is spent doing repetitive tasks? Do you create the same types of documents every week? Do you type the same address block all day long? Do you repeat the same series of steps over and over again, setting up formatting for your documents? Are you responsible for maintaining a consistent appearance in company documents? If you answered "yes" to any of these questions, you will *love* the Macro feature.

A macro can be created to perform a series of steps. Those steps might take you several minutes to complete manually, but when you play the macro, the process takes only seconds. And equally important, every time you play the macro, the exact same steps are done. This means that the results are consistent and accurate.

Let me use a popular analogy to explain how a macro works. A camcorder records video and sound on a videotape or a memory card. You can turn on the recorder, record the video, and then turn off the recorder. The video that you recorded is there for you to access when you play back the tape. The same is true for creating a macro, except instead of recording video, you record actions taken on a document. You turn on the Macro Recorder, record your actions, and then turn off the Macro Recorder. Whatever you do between turning on the Macro Recorder and turning it back off is recorded in a macro.

Don't skip this chapter because you think only techies write macros. A macro can be simple: type a signature block, insert a page number, change to a different font, and so on. A macro can also be complex. Some macros ask questions and assemble documents based on the answers.

If you're lucky, your firm maintains a standard set of macros for everyone's use. If this is the case, all you need to know is how to run them; so let's start there. I'll explain how to create your own macros later in the chapter.

Playing Macros

If someone else has written macros for you, you will need to know where they are stored so that you can play them. Actually, you don't have to know *exactly* where they are because you will have an opportunity to browse for them. The macros that come with WordPerfect are stored in the default macro folder.

The locations of the default macro folder and the supplemental macro folder are specified in Settings. Choose **Tools**, **Settings (Alt+F12)**. Click **Files**, and then click the **Merge/Macro** tab. You will see locations for the Default Macro Folder and the Supplemental Macro Folder in the middle of the dialog box. If you need to change the location, click the **Files** icon at the end of the text box to browse for the folder. The supplemental macro folder is generally used as a method for gaining access to macros stored on a network. Your network administrator will be able to give you the location of the folder.

CHAPTER 17 CREATING AND PLAYING MACROS 315

Before you play a macro, be sure that everything is in place first. If you are running a macro to add page numbers to a document, for example, you need to open the document first. Likewise, if the macro acts on selected text, select the text before you run the macro. Finally, if the macro creates a new document, you should start in a blank document.

To play a macro

1. Choose **Tools**, **Macro**, **Play** (**Alt+F10**) to open the Play Macro dialog box (see Figure 17.1).
2. Double-click a macro, or select it and click **Play**.

If the macro "hangs," you will have to cancel it manually. Press the **Esc** key to cancel the macro. A message box appears stating that the user canceled the macro.

When you open the Play Macro dialog box, the contents of the default macro folder are displayed by default. If the macro you are looking for is stored in another folder, you will need to navigate to that folder. The name of the default macro folder can be found in Tools, Settings, Files on the Merge/Macro tab.

FIGURE 17.1
The shipping macros are stored in a WordPerfect subfolder of the PerfectScript folder.

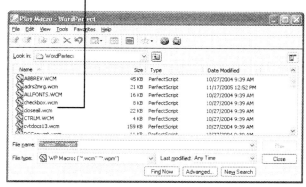

Double-click a macro file to play it

Running WordPerfect's Shipping Macros

WordPerfect ships with a collection of macros that are helpful both to use and to examine if you want to become familiar with the PerfectScript macro language. In a later section, I'll show you how to edit macros, so you can open any of the shipping macros and see how they were written.

- **Abbrev.wcm**—Opens an Abbreviations dialog box, where you can select a QuickWord and expand it in a document. The dialog box stays open so that you can expand multiple QuickWords without opening the QuickCorrect dialog box each time.

- **adrs2mrg.wcm**—Opens an Address Book to Merge dialog box, where you can choose an address book and then create a merge data file from the entire address book or just from selected records. This macro creates a text data file with a field name record at the top of the file.

- **Allfonts.wcm**—Searches for all the fonts installed for the current printer and generates a list of the fonts along with a short sample of text. Depending on the number of fonts you have installed, it might take a few minutes to generate the list. Also, your printer might not have enough memory to be able to print the list.

- **checkbox.wcm**—Creates a check box that you can click to insert an "x" in the box and click again to remove the "x." The check box is created as hypertext, so it will show up underlined and blue.

- **closeall.wcm**—Displays a Close All Documents dialog box, where you can selectively save open documents before they are closed. If documents are unnamed, you can specify a name for the documents in the dialog box. A Save check box lets you decide which documents should be saved before they are closed.

- **ctrlm.wcm**—Displays the PerfectScript Command dialog box, where you can select, edit, and insert macro commands in a macro. You don't have to open the Play Macro dialog box to select this macro. Just press **Ctrl+M** in the document window.

- **cvtdocs13.wcm**—Opens the WordPerfect Conversion Expert dialog box, where you can choose to convert a single file, a folder, or a folder and its subfolders to several different WordPerfect formats. File output formats include WordPerfect 13, 12, 11, 10, 9, 8, 7, 6, 5.1, and HTML.

- **DCConvert.wcm**—Converts WordPerfect drop cap characters (that is, the first whole word is a drop cap) to a drop cap character that is Microsoft Word compatible (that is, a number of characters drop cap).

- **endfoot.wcm**—Converts all the endnotes in a document (or just those in selected text) to footnotes. You must be outside the footnote/endnote area to run this macro.

- **Expndall.wcm**—Expands all the QuickWords in the document. You might use this if you work with documents with complex QuickWords. You might decide to turn off Expand QuickWords as you type them and then expand them all at once with this macro.

- **Filestmp.wcm**—Opens the File Stamp Options dialog box, where you can choose to insert the filename or the filename and path into a header or footer. If the document has not been named when you run this macro, a filename code is placed in the header or footer. When you save and name the file, the filename (and the path) shows up in the header or footer. If you select **Change Font**, a Font Properties dialog box appears so that you can select the font (or font size) you want to use for the file stamp.

- **flipenv.wcm**—Displays an Envelope Addresses dialog box, where you can type the return address (unless you've already selected a personal information entry in the Address Book) and a mailing address. You also can select a mailing address from the Address Book. After you fill in the address information, you can choose an envelope size. The macro creates the envelope, flipping the envelope 180 degrees so that it is upside down. This macro was created because some printers have trouble printing text within 1/4 inch of the top-left corner of an envelope, but they don't have a problem printing it within 1/4 inch of the lower-right corner. If you have one of these printers, this macro enables you to print the return address closer to the edge of the envelope.

- **Fontdn.wcm**—Reduces the font size by two points. If you select text before running the macro, only the selected text is affected; otherwise, the change takes place at the insertion point and remains in effect until you change the size again.

- **Fontup.wcm**—Increases the font size by two points. If you select text before running the macro, only the selected text is affected. Otherwise, the change takes place at the insertion point and remains in effect until you change the size again.

- **footend.wcm**—Converts the footnotes in the entire document (or just in selected text) to endnotes. You must be outside the footnote/endnote area to run this macro.

- **Longname.wcm**—This macro is for everyone who got around the DOS 8.3 filename by creating descriptive names in document summaries. This macro converts those descriptive filenames into long filenames, which can have up to 255 characters. When you run this macro, a Convert to Long Filenames dialog box appears. You can either type the name of the drive and folder where the files are stored, or you can click the **Files** icon to open the Select Folder dialog box. Select the file(s) that you want to convert in the Select Files to Rename list, and then click **OK**. When the macro is finished, a record of the changes is created in a blank document.

- **Parabrk.wcm**—Displays a Paragraph Break dialog box, where you can choose a symbol or graphic to display at every paragraph break. The symbol or graphic is centered on the blank line between paragraphs.

- **pleading.wcm**—Displays the Pleading Paper dialog box, where you can choose from a variety of options to generate a legal pleading paper.
- **prompts.wcm**—Opens Prompt Builder, which helps you create prompts for your templates. You can create messages that help guide the user along in using the template. You must be editing a template (other than your default template) before you can run this macro.
- **reverse.wcm**—Displays the Reverse Text Options dialog box, where you can choose a color for the text and a color for the fill (or background). If you've selected text, you can place the reverse text in a text box. If you've selected table cells, the dialog box is a little different. You choose from three table-oriented options: Center Text, Lock Cell, and Header Row.
- **saveall.wcm**—Displays the Save Open Documents dialog box, which is similar to the Close All Documents dialog box. It works the same way: If you want to save a document, place a check mark next to the filename. If necessary, you can change the filename and path before saving the file.
- **Savetoa.wcm**—Saves the current document and then copies the file to a disk in drive A. If you haven't named the document yet, you will get the opportunity to do so. When you name the file, don't worry about switching to drive A or typing a: in the path—all you need to do is name the file and the macro saves it to drive A.
- **tconvert.wcm**—Displays the Convert Template dialog box, where you can type the name of a template that you want to convert for use in WordPerfect X3. If you can't remember the name (or the location) of the template file, click the **Files** icon to search for it.
- **uawp13en.wcm**—According to the documentation, this macro is used by the PerfectExpert. You must not delete this file from the macros folder, so don't even think about getting rid of it!
- **wp_org.wcm**—Creates a basic organization chart that you can start filling in immediately. You get the same results that you would if you chose **Insert**, **Graphics**, **Draw Picture** to open the Presentations/Draw editing screen and then chose **Insert**, **Organization Chart** and selected the first **Single** option in the Layout dialog box. Note: You will need Presentations X3 on your system to run this macro.
- **wp_pr.wcm**—Opens an outline from a WordPerfect document in Presentations as a slide show. You can run the macro whether you have an outline in the document or not, but Presentations will have a hard time figuring out what to put on the slides with a regular document. The document is saved as pr_outln.wpd. Note: You will need Presentations X3 on your system to run this macro.

Creating Macros

When you create your first macro, try to remember that you don't have to do it perfectly the first time. You can keep recording the macro over and over until you get it right. You can also edit a macro and make some adjustments to it rather than re-recording.

Before you get started, grab a pen and jot down a rough sequence of events you need to go through so that you don't forget anything. For example, if you want to create a macro to insert a signature block, write down the closing that you prefer, make a note about the number of blank lines you want to allow room for a signature, and then jot down all the elements you want to include beneath the written signature.

You can record a macro in a blank or an existing document. It's more efficient to create the macro the next time you need to perform a certain series of steps because you can create the macro and accomplish your task at the same time.

To record a macro

1. Choose **Tools, Macro, Record (Ctrl+F10)**.
2. Type a name for the macro in the **File Name** text box. A macro is automatically saved with the *.wcm* extension, which identifies it as a macro file. By default, new macros are created in the default macro folder.
3. If necessary, choose a location for your macro from the **Save In** drop-down list.
4. Click **Record**. The Macro feature bar is displayed underneath the property bar (see Figure 17.2). The recorder is now on, so you're ready to start recording your actions.

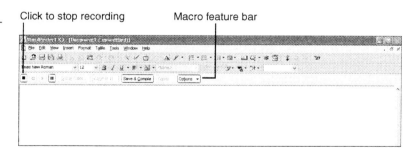

FIGURE 17.2
The Macro toolbar has buttons to help you record and edit macros.

5. Type the text, use the menus and toolbars, go through the dialog boxes, and make your selections. The macro records all your actions, whether you use the keyboard or the mouse. The only exception is that you have to use the keyboard to position the insertion point in the document window.

6. When you're finished, click the **Stop the Macro Play or Record** button. The Macro feature bar disappears, and you are returned to a normal document window. The actions you took while you created the macro have been performed on the document, so you might or might not want to save those changes.

To run the macro, follow the steps detailed previously in the "Playing Macros" section.

You can insert a pause in a macro so that someone can type something in. When you are at the point in your macro where you are ready for user input, click the **Pause While Recording/Executing a Macro** button (on the Macro toolbar). At this point, you can either type something and click the button again, or just click the button again to move past the pause. When you run the macro, the macro pauses and waits for input. When you press **Enter**, the macro resumes.

The Pause feature is powerful and easy to use. It greatly extends the power of a macro to automate any number of tasks. For example, you could pause to type in a new margin setting or to type an author name in a header. The fax cover macro in the following section uses the Pause command to pause for user input.

Editing Macros

This book is written for those who have very little experience with word processors. You might be thinking, "Editing macros doesn't exactly sound like something a beginner would do, does it?" What if I told you that for simple changes, it isn't much different from editing a document: Would you be interested?

You can open a macro file just as you would any other document. If all you want to do is delete an extra blank line or revise some of the text, you open the macro file and make your changes in the document window using the same techniques you use in documents. In most cases, it's faster to edit a macro than it is to create it again.

To edit a macro

1. Choose **Tools**, **Macro**, **Edit**.
2. Double-click the macro to open it in the document window (see Figure 17.3). The macro shown in the figure inserts a signature block.

FIGURE 17.3
You can edit macro files in the document window.

Take care not to delete the first line—it is important information for the macro to run correctly. Here are some basic editing tricks:

- To delete a blank line (hard return), select **HardReturn ()**; then press **Delete**.
- To insert an extra blank line, type **HardReturn()** on a blank line. If you press Enter, you will just insert a blank line in the macro; you won't insert a Hard Return code.
- When revising the text, be sure you don't delete the quote marks on either side of the text. If you accidentally delete one, type it back in.

When you're finished making changes, click the **Save & Compile** button to save your changes. Click the document **Close** button to close the macro file.

Recording Several Sample Macros

The best way for you to learn how to write macros is to "just do it." So, the following sections contain the steps to create three sample macros. Even if you don't think you will ever use the macros, take a few minutes and create them anyway. You will learn a lot about the way macros work.

Creating a Signature Block Macro

A typical signature block is two lines down from the last line of a letter. A signature block generally contains a person's name, followed by four blank lines (or enough room for a signature), the person's title, and other identifying information. This might include an email address or direct line phone number.

You can create this macro in a blank document or, if you prefer, you can position the insertion point at the end of a letter. You can kill two birds with one stone by creating your macro and inserting a signature block in the letter at the same time.

To create the sample signature block macro

1. Choose **Tools**, **Macro**, **Record**.
2. Type the name `sigblock` in the **File Name** text box; then click **Record**.
3. Press **Enter** two (or three) times to insert two blank lines between the last line of the letter and the closing.
4. Type `Sincerely,` or `Warm regards,` or whatever closing phrase you prefer.
5. Press **Enter** four (or five) times to insert four blank lines.
6. Type your name; then press **Enter**.
7. Type your title; then press **Enter**.
8. Type your email address or phone number; then press **Enter**.

9. Click the **Stop Macro Play or Record** button (**Ctrl+F10**) to stop recording the macro.

When you stop recording, the macro file is saved. Refer to Figure 17.3 to see what a typical signature block macro looks like when you open it for editing.

Now, open a blank document and run the macro you just created. Don't blink—if you do, you might miss seeing the macro run. Some macros run so quickly that it might seem as though the results appear out of thin air.

Creating a Document Identification Footer

This sample macro creates a footer that appears on every page of the document. The filename and location will be inserted against the left margin of the footer, in an 8-point type. This type of document identification is popular, especially when you share documents on a company network. Anyone who receives a copy of the document knows where it can be found on the network.

To create a document identification footer

1. Choose **Tools**, **Macro**, **Record**.
2. Type the name `idfooter` in the **File Name** text box; then click **Record**.
3. Choose **Insert**, **Header/Footer**.

CHAPTER 17 CREATING AND PLAYING MACROS

4. Choose **Footer A**; then click **Create**.
5. Click the **Font Size** drop-down list arrow and choose **8**. If you want, change the font as well by clicking the **Font** drop-down list arrow and choosing a new font.
6. Choose **Insert, Other, Path and Filename**.
7. Click the **Close** button on the Header/Footer toolbar.

8. Click the **Stop Macro Play or Record** button on the Macro feature bar. Figure 17.4 shows the `idfooter` macro.

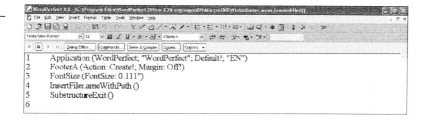

FIGURE 17.4
This macro inserts a footer with the filename and path in 8-point text.

Now, open a document that you have already created. Run the `idfooter` macro to add a footer with the path and filename for the document. Switch to Page View (View, Page) and scroll down to see the new footer. Don't worry—you don't have to save the changes—this is just so that you can test your new macro.

Creating a Fax Cover Sheet

This sample macro creates a fax cover sheet with the headings and the date automatically inserted. This macro pauses for user input when appropriate. When the macro pauses, the user types in the necessary information, then presses Enter to move on. A horizontal graphic line is inserted between the headings and the comment area.

To create the fax cover sheet macro

1. Choose **Tools, Macro, Record**.
2. Type `faxcover` in the **File Name** text box; then click **Record**.
3. Change the font size to **36** point. If you want, change the font as well by clicking the **Font** drop-down list arrow and selecting a new font.
4. Type `Fax Cover Sheet`.
5. Change the font size to **12**. If necessary, choose a different font as well.
6. Press **Enter** five or six times to insert blank lines.
7. Type `To:`; then press the **Tab** key once.

8. Click the **Pause While Recording/Executing a Macro** button on the Macro feature bar.
9. Click the **Pause While Recording/Executing a Macro** button again to move past the pause.
10. Press **Enter** twice to insert a blank line.
11. Type Fax:; then press the **Tab** key once.
12. Click the **Pause While Recording/Executing a Macro** button on the Macro feature bar.
13. Click the **Pause While Recording/Executing a Macro** button again to move past the pause.
14. Press **Enter** twice to insert a blank line.
15. Type Date:; then press **Tab**.
16. Press **Ctrl+D** to insert today's date.
17. Press **Enter** twice to insert a blank line.
18. Type From:; then press **Tab**.
19. Type your name; then press **Enter** twice.
20. Type Fax:; then press **Tab**.
21. Type your fax phone number; then press **Enter** four times.
22. Choose **Insert, Line, Horizontal Line**.
23. Press **Enter** three times.
24. Type Comments:; then press **Enter** twice.
25. Click the **Stop Macro Play or Record** button on the Macro feature bar. Figure 17.5 shows the faxcover macro.

CHAPTER 17　CREATING AND PLAYING MACROS　325

FIGURE 17.5

This macro uses the Pause command to create a fill-in-the-blanks fax cover sheet.

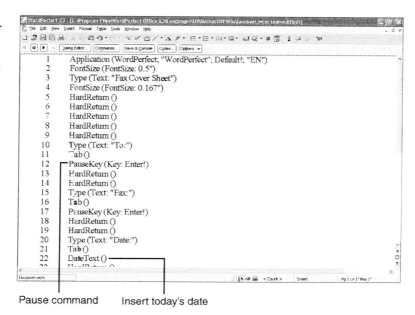

This macro creates the fax cover sheet shown in Figure 17.6.

FIGURE 17.6

This fax cover sheet was created with the faxcover macro.

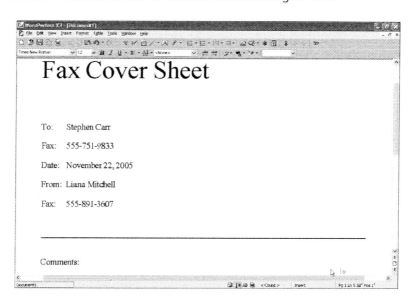

As you can see from these three sample macros, macros can help make you more efficient. They can also improve consistency in companywide documents. Any task that you can do in WordPerfect can be re-created in a macro, so the possibilities are endless. The next time you find yourself repeating the same series of steps for the second or third time, ask yourself if this is a good candidate for a macro.

The Absolute Minimum

In this chapter, you learned how to use the Macro feature to create macros for your repetitive tasks.

- You learned how to play macros that someone else has written.
- You learned about the variety of macros that are included with WordPerfect X3.
- You saw how simple it is to create your own macros.
- You also learned some basic editing techniques so that you can make minor changes instead of recording the macro all over again.
- Finally, you created three sample macros to give you an idea of how quick and easy it can be to create powerful macros for everyday use.

In the next chapter, you will learn how to use WordPerfect's legal tools.

IN THIS CHAPTER

- Put together a table of contents.
- Build a table of authorities or bibliography.
- Use the Document Map feature to navigate through lengthy documents.
- Use the Review Document feature to mark each reviewer's revisions and to allow the author to accept or reject those revisions.
- Compare two versions of a document and let WordPerfect add revision marks.
- Use WordPerfect's pleading experts to create cases, produce pleading documents, and publish pleadings to EDGAR.
- Use the new Save Without Metadata feature to strip out sensitive or confidential information.

Using WordPerfect's Legal Tools

WordPerfect has always had legal-specific tools. In fact, during the early days of PC-based word processors, WordPerfect dominated the market by a large margin. The legal industry demanded a certain feature set, and WordPerfect gave it to them. As time passed and user requests mounted, more and more tools were added. At one time, there was a separate Law Office Edition that contained a collection of pleading tools to simplify the process of preparing pleading documents. These pleading tools have been incorporated into WordPerfect X3.

Most of the topics in this chapter are used extensively in the legal field, but some of them, such as the Table of Contents and the Document Map, are utilized on long documents that anyone might create. Likewise, reviewing and marking up documents might sound like something only an attorney would do, but actually, anyone who collaborates on documents and needs to be able to incorporate everyone's changes into one document will use the Document Review features.

Creating a Table of Contents

A table of contents is a standard addition to long documents to make them easier to navigate. In most cases, the table of contents contains a list of the headings and subheadings in the document. You can have up to five different levels in a table of contents, so you can actually include four levels below a main heading.

The steps to create a table of contents are simple:

1. Mark the entries.
2. Define the table.
3. Generate the table.

Also, before we get started, let me point out a great timesaver that you will use throughout this chapter. The Legal toolbar has buttons that you can use to open dialog boxes. Instead of three menu commands, you can click one button. To turn on the Legal toolbar, right-click the WordPerfect toolbar, and then choose **Legal** from the list.

Marking the Entries

When you mark an entry for a table of contents, you are telling WordPerfect what you want to appear in the table, as well as where you want it to appear. All you have to do is select the text and pick the level of the table where you want it to appear. Let me give you an example: A main heading would be Level 1, the first subheading would be Level 2, the second subheading would be Level 3, and so on. Figure 18.1 shows a three-level table of contents.

FIGURE 18.1
Each subheading is indented underneath the higher heading/subheading.

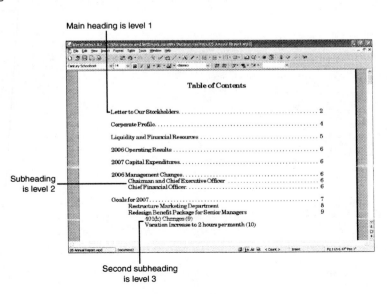

To mark text for a table of contents

1. Locate the text that you want included in the table of contents.
2. Turn on Reveal Codes (**View**, **Reveal Codes** or **Alt+F3**). This is important because you don't want to accidentally include codes that might affect the way the entry looks in the text. A bold code, for example, would cause the table of contents entry to appear bold.
3. Using the mouse or the keyboard, select the text that you want to appear.
4. Choose **Tools**, **Reference**, **Table of Contents** to open the Reference Tools dialog box (see Figure 18.2). You can also click the **Table of Contents** button on the Legal toolbar (right-click a toolbar, and then choose **Legal** to view the Legal toolbar).

> **tip**
>
> You can eliminate the step of marking your headings if you use WordPerfect's built-in heading styles. WordPerfect's heading styles have table of contents marks built-in. Simply apply the heading style Heading 1 to the main headings, Heading 2 to the first subheading, Heading 3 to the next subheading, and so on. See "Using WordPerfect's Heading Styles" in Chapter 9, "Using Styles for Consistency," for more information.

FIGURE 18.2
The Reference Tools dialog box can be anchored to the top or bottom of the screen. Just click and drag it to where you want to anchor it.

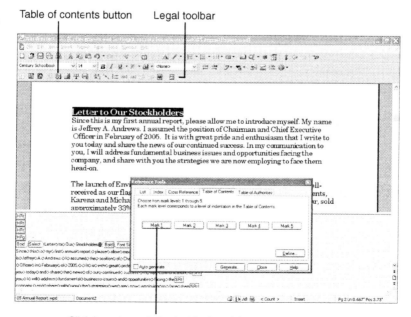

5. Click **Mark 1** to mark the selected heading for the top level in the table of contents. WordPerfect inserts paired codes around the heading to mark the text (see Figure 18.3).

FIGURE 18.3
The pair of Mark Text codes surround the text that you want to appear in the table of contents.

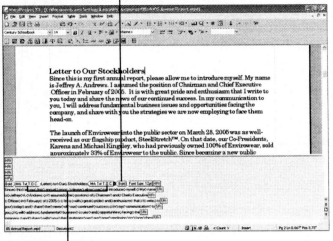

The Bold code is outside the table of contents codes

Mark Text codes surround the text that will appear in the table of contents

6. Continue selecting the headings, chapter names, or sections of text that you want in the table.
7. When you're finished, choose **Close** to exit the dialog box.

Defining the Table

That's it! The hard part is over! Marking text definitely takes the most time—the rest of the process will seem like a piece of cake! The next step to creating a table of contents is defining the table—essentially, creating a blank page, typing a title, and telling WordPerfect exactly where you want the table to start.

To define a table of contents

1. Create a blank page where you want the table of contents to appear.
2. Type `Table of Contents` at the top of the page, and then adjust the font size if you like. If you want to center the title, press **Shift+F7** at the beginning of the line.

> **caution**
> You must be careful when you mark entries for a table of contents. If you accidentally include a font size code or an attribute code, the text in the table will appear differently from the rest of the entries. If you accidentally included codes between the `Mrk Txt T.O.C.` codes, the best thing to do is delete the Mark Text codes, reselect the text, and mark the text again.

3. Click (or press Enter a few times) where you want the first table of contents entry to appear.

 4. Choose **Tools**, **Reference**, **Table of Contents** to open the Reference Tools dialog box (refer to Figure 18.2).

5. Choose **Define** to open the Define Table of Contents dialog box (see Figure 18.4).

FIGURE 18.4
Select the number of levels and the format for the entries in the Define Table of Contents dialog box.

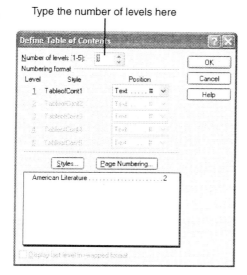

Type the number of levels here

6. Type the number of levels (or click the spinner arrows) in the **Number of Levels** box that you want to include in the table. When you do this, the dialog box will expand and show you how those levels will be formatted. Page numbers can be used, or not. Dot leaders and parentheses can also be used to separate the text from the page number.

7. Choose **OK** to define the table. WordPerfect inserts a [Def Mark] code in the document. You will see the message <<Table of Contents will generate here>> (see Figure 18.5). WordPerfect will remove that when you generate the table.

8. If you're ready to generate the table, click **Generate**; otherwise, click **Close** to exit the dialog box.

9. In the Generate dialog box, click **OK** to generate the table.

FIGURE 18.5
The dummy text is replaced by the actual table of contents when you generate the table.

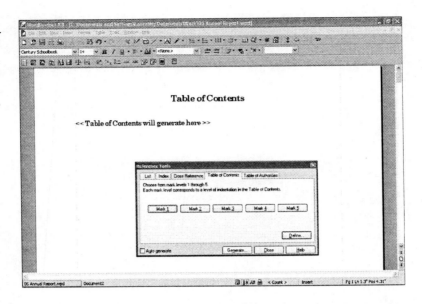

That's the quick way to set up a table of contents. If you are so inclined, you can customize the table by selecting a different format for the entries. For example, you might decide to format the first level entries with dot leader page numbers and the second level entries with page numbers in parentheses. In the Define Table of Contents dialog box, open the Position drop-down list next to each level and choose the preferred format. Figure 18.6 shows a five-level table of contents with each of the five options chosen: no numbering, page number with text, page number separated by parentheses, page number without dot leaders, and page number with dot leaders.

FIGURE 18.6
Five different format options can be applied to five levels of a table of contents.

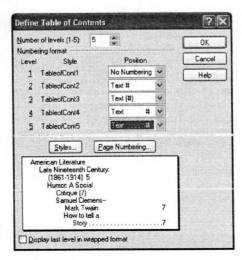

Generating the Table

When you generate a table of contents, WordPerfect runs through the document and grabs the text that you've marked for the table of contents. It inserts that text into the table of contents page and adds the page number where the text was found. WordPerfect does what you tell it to do so if the entries are incorrect, you will need to go back through and review the entries between the Mrk Txt T.O.C. codes.

To generate the table

1. Choose **Tools**, **Reference**, **Table of Contents** to open the Reference Tools dialog box (refer Figure 18.2).
2. Choose **Generate** to display the Generate dialog box. You can also click the **Generate button** on the Legal toolbar.
3. Click **OK**. After a brief pause, the completed table of contents appears onscreen (see Figure 18.7).

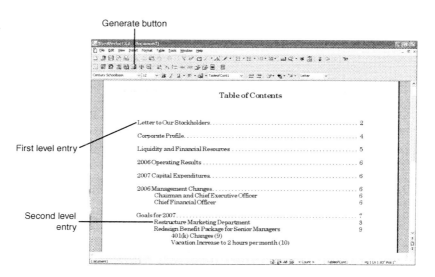

FIGURE 18.7
This table of contents uses a different page numbering style for the first and second levels.

Creating a Table of Authorities

A table of authorities is like a table of contents for a legal document. It lists the *authorities*—which are the legal references to other cases, statutes, rules, citations, regulations, amendments, and so on—that appear in a legal brief. Keep in mind that you can use the Table of Authorities feature to create a bibliography for any document that requires identification of sources.

The steps to create a table of authorities are almost identical to the steps to create a table of contents. You mark the entry, define the table, and generate it. Authorities are grouped into categories, so you end up marking entries for a certain category rather than a certain level. A table of authorities is divided into sections; each section contains one category.

Let me give you an example: You are creating a table of authorities for a brief that contains case citations, statutes, and amendments. The case citations will be in one section, the statutes in another, and the amendments in a third section. There is no limit to the number of sections you can define.

Before you start marking the text, take a minute to sketch out a rough draft of the table (or bibliography) to get an idea of how many sections you will need and what they will be called.

Marking the First Authority

When you mark an entry for a table of authorities, you are telling WordPerfect *what* you want to appear in the table and *where* you want it to appear. The difference between a table of authorities and a table of contents is how you mark the entries. In most cases, the items you are including in a table of authorities appear several times in the document. This is different from a table of contents, which have entries that appear only once in the document.

For this reason, the marking method was reworked to make it easier to mark multiple entries. The first time you mark an entry, you create what is called a "full form." Full form implies that this entry contains the text that you want to appear in the table. The next time you mark this entry, you use what is called a "short form," which is an abbreviation for the full form. Marking the second and subsequent entries is a breeze thanks to the short form. All it takes is three clicks to mark multiple entries: one click in the text, one click to select the short form, and one click to mark it.

To mark text for a table of authorities

1. Locate the text that you want included in the table of authorities. In addition to the document text, you can mark entries in footnotes, endnotes, graphic boxes, and captions.

2. Turn on Reveal Codes (**View**, **Reveal Codes** or **Alt+F3**). This is important because you don't want to accidentally include codes that might affect the way the entry looks in the text. A bold code, for example, would cause the table of authorities entry to appear bold.

3. Using the mouse or the keyboard, select the text that you want to appear.

4. Choose **Tools**, **Reference**, **Table of Authorities** to open the Reference Tools dialog box (see Figure 18.8). If the Reference Tools dialog box is already open, just click the Table of Authorities tab. Or, click the **Table of Authorities** button on the Legal toolbar (right-click a toolbar and choose Legal).

FIGURE 18.8
The first time you mark an entry will take a bit longer than marking subsequent entries.

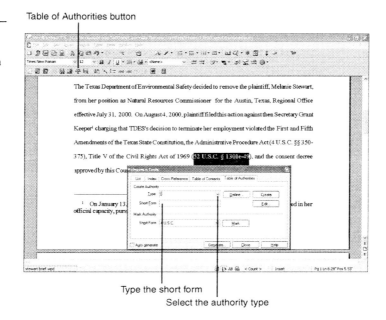

5. Either type a name or select an authority type in the **Type** drop-down list.
6. Edit the selected text in the **Short Form** text box, or just type a short abbreviation. You will use this shortcut to mark subsequent entries.
7. Choose **Create**. The Table of Authorities Full Form editing window appears with the text that you selected for the entry (see Figure 18.9).

FIGURE 18.9
When you create a full form, you can modify the text so that the entry in the table differs from the entry in the text.

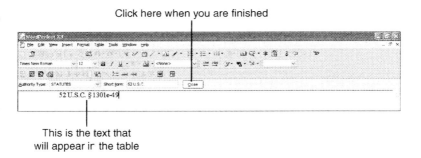

8. Edit the text so that it looks exactly the way you want it to appear in the finished table. You can add or remove font attributes, indent text, add returns, and so on.

9. When you are finished, click **Close**. A set of `ToA: Full Form` codes are inserted around the text. The code contains the section name and the short form text, so you can review entries in Reveal Codes.

note

If you later edit a table of authorities entry, the text in the full form won't be updated. You must update the full form to update the entry. To edit the full form, click the **Edit** button in the Table of Authorities tab of the Reference Tools dialog box. Select the full form in the list, and then click **OK**. When the Full Form Editing window appears, make the necessary changes, and then click **Close** to switch back to the document.

Marking Subsequent Authorities

After you mark the first authority and define exactly how you want it to appear in the table, you can continue marking the other entries with the short form. It's very quick, so you will see how your efforts to create the full forms pays off.

1. Move to the second occurrence of an authority. Use the Find feature if your document is long.

2. Click in the authority/text. Notice that you don't have to select it again.

3. Open the Reference Tools dialog box by choosing **Tools**, **Reference**, **Table of Authorities** if it is not already open.

4. Open the **Short Form** drop-down list and choose the short form (see Figure 18.10). You can also type the short form in directly.

FIGURE 18.10
Marking with the short forms is quick. Just click in the entry text and choose a short form from the list.

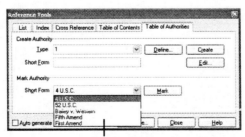

Choose a short form from this list

5. Choose **Mark**. A ToA: Short Form code is inserted in the authority text.
6. Continue marking the rest of the authorities. Remember, you don't have to select the text to mark it with a short form.
7. When you're finished, choose **Close** to exit the dialog box.

The last short form that you used is shown in the Short Form text box, so it's easy to continue marking subsequent occurrences of an authority. Just click in the authority, and then choose **Mark**. You might also consider using Find to quickly search for and mark all the occurrences of a particular authority.

Defining the Table

Just as you did for a table of contents, you have to create a page for the table of authorities. You probably want these entries on a page by themselves, with headings for each section. After you define the sections, you will be ready to generate the table.

To define a table of authorities

1. Create a blank page where you want the table of authorities to appear.
2. Type **Table of Authorities** at the top of the page. Adjust the font size if you like. If you want to center the title, press **Shift+F7** at the beginning of the line.
3. Click (or press Enter a few times) where you want to define the first table of authorities section.
4. Type a title for the section and then move down to the next line.
5. If necessary, choose **Tools**, **Reference**, **Table of Authorities** to display the Table of Authorities tab of the Reference Tools dialog box.
6. Choose **Define** to open the Define Table of Authorities dialog box (see Figure 18.11).
7. Select the section that you want to define from the list.
8. Choose **Insert**. You will see the dummy text <<Table of Authorities will generate here >>. That will be replaced with the table of authorities when generated.
9. Repeat steps 4–8 to define the location of each remaining section.

You can customize the format of a particular section to meet stated guidelines. Simply select the section in the Define Table of Authorities dialog box and choose **Edit**. Make your selections in the Edit Table of Authorities dialog box.

FIGURE 18.11
When you define a table of authorities, you have to define where each section will be placed.

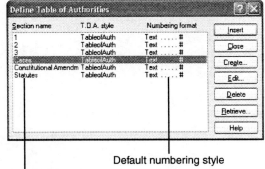

Select the section you want to define — Default numbering style

Generating the Table

When you've marked all the entries and defined the location for each section's entries, you're ready to generate the table. WordPerfect will search through the document for each entry and place it in the appropriate section of the table of authorities along with the page number where the entry was found.

If you publish a document that contains a table of authorities to PDF, WordPerfect will convert the marked headings and subheadings into entries that display as numbered bookmarks in the PDF document.

To generate the table

1. Choose **Tools**, **Reference**, **Table of Authorities** to display the Table of Authorities options.

2. Choose **Generate** (**Ctrl+F9**) to open the Generate dialog box. You can also click the **Generate** button on the Legal toolbar.

3. Click **OK**. After a moment, the completed table of authorities appears onscreen (see Figure 18.12).

> **caution**
> If you've accidentally typed a short form incorrectly, or if you have a short form that doesn't have a corresponding full form, you will get an error message when you generate the table. The problem entry will be preceded by an asterisk in the first section of the table so that you can see which entries need repair. If an incorrect short form has been used, delete the short form code and reinsert it. If the full form is missing, find the first occurrence of the authority, delete the full form, and then re-create it.

CHAPTER 18 USING WORDPERFECT'S LEGAL TOOLS **339**

FIGURE 18.12
In a table of authorities, the entries are organized into categories.

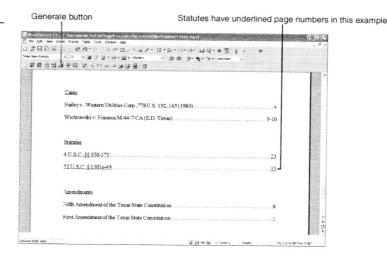

Using Document Map to Navigate Long Documents

The Document Map, a feature first introduced in WordPerfect 11, is the perfect companion to the table of contents and table of authorities features. Document Map builds a roadmap of your document using table of contents, table of authorities, or index markers. You can then navigate through the document by clicking the entries in the document map.

To display the document map

1. Open a document that contains markers for either a table of contents, table of authorities, or an index.
2. Choose **View**, **Document Map** (**Alt+Shift+M**) to display the document map. You can click a marker in the list to jump to that text in the document (see Figure 18.13).
3. If necessary, choose a marker type from the **Reference Markers** list box to display only specific entries.
4. If you prefer a tree view, click the **Turn On Tree View** button.

note

Anyone who is using a "light" version of WordPerfect can stop here. To provide an economical choice to budget-minded consumers, some of the advanced features were removed—specifically, the Review Document feature, the Document Compare feature, and the legal tools, which are covered in the rest of this chapter. If you need these features, take advantage of the upgrade pricing to upgrade to the Standard or Professional editions of WordPerfect Office X3. Visit wordperfect.com for more information on the different editions of WordPerfect Office X3.

5. If you make any changes to the reference markers, click the **Refresh the Document Map** button to update the document map.

 6. Click the **Close** button to close the document map.

FIGURE 18.13
The Document Map offers a convenient method to navigate through a lengthy document.

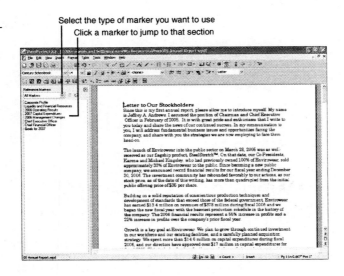

Reviewing Documents

The Internet has become the world's virtual post office—it seems as though everyone has an email address. Collaborating with people all over the world is as simple as attaching a file to an email message and distributing it. Keeping track of revisions becomes a nightmare when you get a handful of people working on the same document.

The Document Review feature can be used by both reviewers and the document's author. First, a reviewer uses Document Review to insert revisions. Then, you (as the author) use the Document Review feature to locate every revision, no matter how small. Each reviewer has a unique color, so revisions can be traced back to the person who made it. You (as the author) can accept or reject each individual change because you retain the ultimate control over the document.

Making Comments As a Reviewer

When someone sends a document to you for comments, you are considered the *reviewer*. You will have your own color, so your changes will appear in a different color than the rest of the text. This way, your changes can easily be distinguished from those other reviewers.

To review a document

1. Choose **File**, **Document**, **Review** to display the Review Document dialog box (see Figure 18.14).

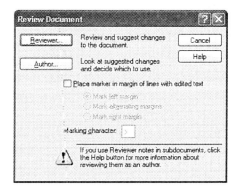

FIGURE 18.14
You can use the Document Review feature as the author or as a reviewer.

2. Choose **Reviewer**. A Reviewer property bar appears at the top of the document (see Figure 18.15).

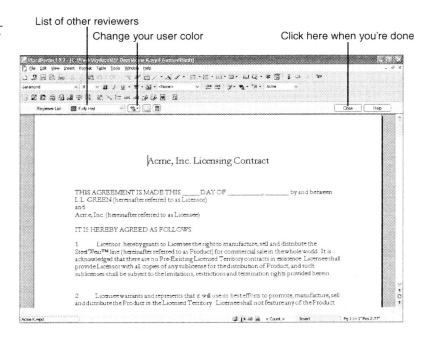

FIGURE 18.15
Your unique user color appear on the Set Color button on the Reviewer property bar.

List of other reviewers
Change your user color
Click here when you're done

3. You might see a dialog box that asks for your username and user initials. Go ahead and type your name and initials, and then click **OK**.

4. (Optional) If you want to change your color, click the **Set Color** button and then choose another color from the palette.

5. Make your revisions to the document. If you insert text, it appears in your user color. Deleted text appears in your user color with a line running through it to indicate deleted text.

6. When you're finished, click the **Close** button on the Reviewer property bar.

> **note**
> If a document has already been saved with revision marks, the Review Document dialog box appears automatically when you open the document. Choose **Cancel** if you don't want to use Document Review.

Responding to Comments As the Author

As the document's author, you have complete control over which revisions are made and which are discarded. As you review a document, each revision is selected. You can accept or reject each change individually, or you can accept or reject all the changes at once.

To review a document as the author

1. With the reviewed document open, choose **File**, **Document**, **Review**.

2. In the Document Review dialog box, choose **Author**. The property bar you see now is different from the one you saw as a reviewer. This property bar contains buttons for accepting and rejecting the revisions (see Figure 18.16).

3. The first revision is automatically selected in the text. Use the following buttons on the Author property bar to review the document:

> **note**
> You can edit revisions made by other reviewers, but you can't edit text that has been deleted by another reviewer. The only way to release that text is to review the document as the author and reject the deletion. Also, you *can* review a document as the author, even if you aren't the true author. The Reviewer and Author options are just two ways to use the feature.

- **Turn On or Off the Margin Markings That Have Been Made in the Document**—Toggles the display of margin markers on and off.

- **Display Annotations in Normal Text Color**—Turns off the display of the reviewer colors.

- **Select the Previous Annotation**—Jumps to the previous revision.

- **Select the Next Annotation**—Jumps to the next revision.

- **Insert the Currently Selected Annotation into the Text of the Document**—Accepts the revision.

- **Inserts All Annotations into the Document Text**—Accepts all revisions at once.

- **Deletes the Currently Selected Annotation**—Rejects the revision.

- **Deletes All Annotations from the Document Text**—Rejects all revisions at once.

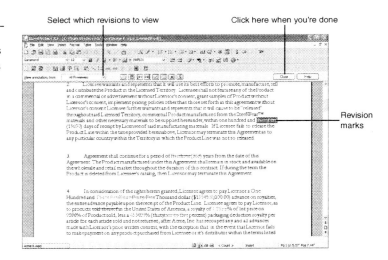

FIGURE 18.16
The Author property bar has different buttons than the Reviewer property bar.

4. If you change your mind about a revision, click the **Undo** button to reverse the action.

5. Click **Close** when you're finished.

Here's a situation that won't amuse you when it happens. Let's say that you are reviewing a document and, all of a sudden, your changes disappear. The revision marks are gone and your changes look just like regular text. What happened?

You've accidentally closed the property bar—in essence, turning off the Document Review feature. This can also happen if you are reviewing the document as an author. Don't panic; your changes are still there. Choose **File**, **Document**, **Review** and sign on as before.

Comparing Documents

Despite all the advantages that electronic file transfers can bring, you might be reluctant to distribute your documents electronically because of the possibility of accidental (or intentional) changes being made to the text. Even if you instruct someone to review the document using Document Review, there is no guarantee that she will do it. Only by comparing the reviewed document to the original can you be sure that no unauthorized changes were made.

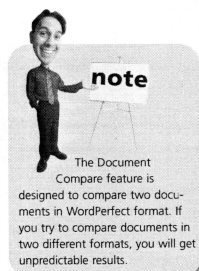

The Document Compare feature is designed to compare two documents in WordPerfect format. If you try to compare documents in two different formats, you will get unpredictable results.

Highlighting Changes in a Document Automatically

The Document Compare feature compares two copies of a document and inserts revision marks for you. If text has been added, it is displayed in redline; if text has been deleted, it is copied back into the document as strikeout text. Redline text can appear differently when printed, but onscreen the text is red. Strikeout text has a line through the middle of it.

To compare two documents

1. Open the reviewed copy of the document.
2. Choose **File**, **Document**, **Compare** or click the **Document Compare** button on the Legal toolbar. The Compare Documents dialog box appears (see Figure 18.17).

FIGURE 18.17
You can opt to insert revision marks, and then switch to reviewing the document as the author.

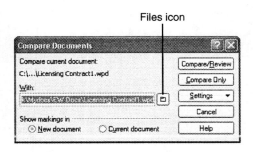

3. The name of the open document is shown in the **With** text box. Type the name of the original copy of the document, or click the **Files** icon to browse for it.

4. Choose **Compare/Review** to compare the two documents, and then review the document as the author, or choose **Compare Only** to compare the two documents and insert revision marks.

When a Compare Only process is complete, a Document Compare Summary page is created at the top of the document (see Figure 18.18). Scroll down past this page to read through the document. Text that has been inserted is shown in red; text that has been deleted appears with strikeout applied to the text.

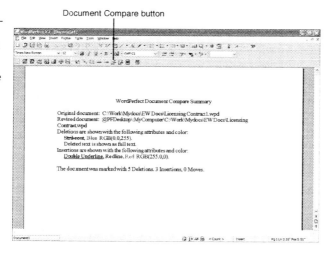

FIGURE 18.18
The summary page gives you a snapshot of the differences in the two documents.

Applying Redline and Strikeout Manually

If, for some reason, you prefer to insert revision marks manually, you can certainly do so with font attributes. Both the redline and strikeout attribute can be applied to sections of text.

To apply redline or strikeout manually

1. Select the text that you want to mark.
2. Choose **Format**, **Font** (**F9**) to open the Font Properties dialog box (see Figure 18.19).
3. Place a check mark next to the **Redline** or **Strikeout** check box.
4. Click **OK**.

  You can also use the **Redline** and **Strikeout** buttons on the Legal toolbar to apply redline and strikeout to selected text.

FIGURE 18.19
You can insert revision marks manually by applying redline and strikeout attributes to selected text.

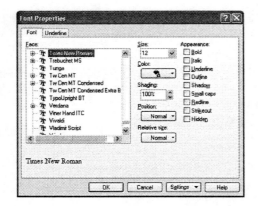

Removing Revision Marks

Whether you use the Compare Document feature to insert revision marks or you do it manually, you will be pleased to know that WordPerfect will strip out the revision marks for you.

To remove revision marks in a document

1. Choose **File**, **Document**, **Remove Markings** or click the **Remove Markings** button on the Legal toolbar to display the Remove Markings dialog box (see Figure 18.20).
2. Choose one of the options to remove the redline/strikeout text.

FIGURE 18.20
WordPerfect can remove redline marks and strikeout text in one step.

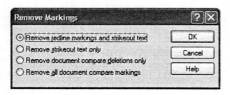

Creating Pleading Documents

Generally speaking, a pleading is every legal document filed in a lawsuit, petition, motion, or hearing. They set out the facts and legal arguments which support that party's position. Pleadings are required by state or federal statutes and court rules to be in a particular form and format: typed, signed, and dated with the name of the court, title and number of the case, and contact information for the attorney or person acting for him/herself included. In other words, pleading documents are created for virtually every type of case and must follow a strict set of formatting rules.

WordPerfect's pleading tools have evolved from a simple macro to create pleading paper to a full set of pleading creation experts that guide you through the entire process. To accomplish the first step of creating a pleading, you need to create a case.

Creating and Editing Cases

Before you can start producing pleading documents, you have to set up the cases. New cases can be created from scratch, or you can create cases based on an existing case. When case information changes, it's a simple matter to update the case.

To create a new case

1. Choose **Tools**, **Legal Tools**, **Pleading Expert Filler**, or click the **Pleading Expert Filler button** on the Legal toolbar. The Pleading Expert Filler appears (see Figure 18.21).
2. Click **Next** to move to the Case Selection section (see Figure 18.22).
3. Enable the **New Case** option and type a name for the case in the **New Case Name** text box.
4. Click **Next** to move to the Select Court section.

> **note**
>
> The Legal Tools—Pleading Paper, the Pleading Expert Designer, the Pleading Expert Filler, and Publish to EDGAR—are not installed during a typical installation. If you don't have a Legal Tools option on your Tools menu, they haven't been installed yet. Insert the CD to run the Setup program. Choose **Change Which Program Features Are Installed**, click the plus sign next to WordPerfect Office X3 (if necessary), and then click the plus sign next to WordPerfect. Click the button next to **WordPerfect Legal Tools** and choose **This Feature Will Be Installed on Local Hard Drive**. Choose **Next**, and then **Begin**. Click **Finish** to close the wizard.

FIGURE 18.21
The Pleading Expert Filler walks you through the process of creating and editing cases.

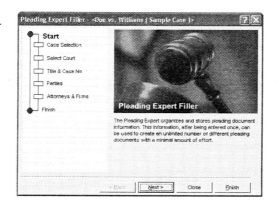

5. Select the pleading style that you want to use and type the judge's information.
6. Click **Next** to move to the Title & Case No. section.
7. Enter the relevant information here, and then click **Next** to move to the Parties section.
8. Select which parties are involved and enter the name(s) of the appellee(s) and appellant(s).
9. Click **Next** to move to the Attorneys & Firms section.
10. Enter the contact information for the attorney(s).
11. Click **Next**, and then **Finish**. WordPerfect generates the pleading document (see Figure 18.23).

> **tip**
>
> If you just need to whip up a quick pleading document, you can do this with a pleading macro. Either click the **Pleading** button on the Legal toolbar, or choose **Tools**, **Macro**, **Play** (**Alt+F10**) and double-click **pleading.wcm** in the list. Make your selections in the Pleading Paper dialog box, and then click **OK** to create the blank pleading paper.

FIGURE 18.22
In the Case Selection section, you can create new cases and edit existing cases.

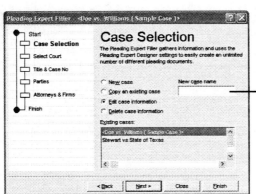

Type a new case name here

When you need to edit a case, you do so through the Pleading Expert Filler. Keep in mind that you can create new cases based on existing cases. You will save yourself some time entering the contact information.

FIGURE 18.23
The completed pleading document has all the information you typed in, in the correct place and in the correct format.

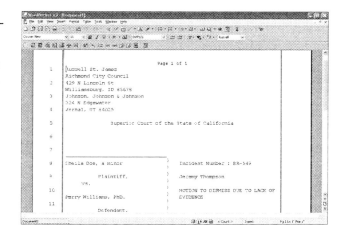

To edit an existing case

1. Choose **Tools**, **Legal Tools**, **Pleading Expert Filler**, or click the **Pleading Expert Filler** button on the Legal toolbar. The Pleading Expert Filler appears (refer to Figure 18.21).
2. Click **Next**, and then select the case you want to edit from the **Existing Cases** list.
3. Click **Next** to start working through the different sections, making your changes as necessary.

All the steps necessary to complete a pleading are listed on the left side of the Pleading Expert Filler. You can click any of the items in the list to jump to that particular section.

Creating and Editing Pleading Styles

The preceding steps illustrate the creation of a pleading document using one of the two built-in styles. Specifically, Style 1 was used, with some modifications, to create the document shown in Figure 18.23. You can create your own pleading styles and select them from the list.

Creating your own custom pleading styles is a key piece of the puzzle, and it has been completely automated to save you time. The Pleading Expert Designer walks you through the entire process.

To create a new pleading style

1. Choose **Tools**, **Legal Tools**, **Pleading Expert Designer**, or click the **Pleading Expert Designer button** on the Legal toolbar. The Pleading Expert Designer appears (see Figure 18.24).

FIGURE 18.24
The Pleading Expert Designer walks you through the process of creating your own pleading styles.

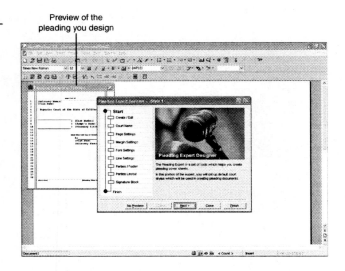

2. Click **Next** to move to the Create/Edit Pleading section (see Figure 18.25).

FIGURE 18.25
Select a style to edit, or type a new style name to create a new style in the Create/Edit Pleading section.

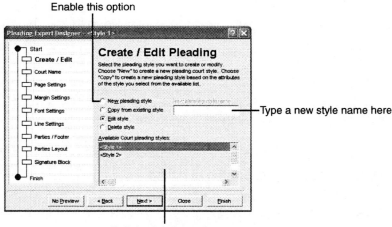

3. Follow the prompts in the Pleading Expert Designer to complete the pleading style. Notice that as you work, the preview window is updated to show you how your pleading documents will look.

The new pleading styles that you create with the Pleading Expert Designer show up in the Select Court section of Pleading Expert Filler so that you can select them when you create or edit cases.

Publishing Pleadings to EDGAR Format

Many courts are requiring electronic filing of pleadings. A standard format was developed—the Electronic Data Gathering, Analysis, and Retrieval (EDGAR) system format. To send a pleading electronically, it must be in EDGAR format with the appropriate document header file attached. WordPerfect will publish a pleading to EDGAR, but it's up to you to create the header file (in ASCII Text format).

note

The steps to create a pleading style are listed on the left side of the Pleading Expert Designer. If you are making only a few changes, click any step to go directly to it.

To publish a pleading to EDGAR

1. With the pleading open, choose **File**, **Save As**.
2. Type a name for the file in the **File Name** text box. This name should be different from the original pleading.
3. Open the **File Type** drop-down list and choose **EDGAR**.
4. Click **Save**.

If you save a document in EDGAR format, that document cannot be restored to a WordPerfect file. You will have to edit the original pleading document and save it to EDGAR format again. The good news is, that prevents multiple versions of a document: one in WordPerfect format and another in EDGAR.

tip

You can also save a pleading in EDGAR format with the EDGAR button on the Legal toolbar. Clicking the EDGAR button opens the Save As dialog box with the EDGAR format already selected. Just type a new name for the file and choose **Save**.

Saving Documents Without Metadata

Metadata is invisible information that is attached to every WordPerfect file in the form of undo/redo history, reviewers' notes, document summary information, hidden text, and comments. The Undo/Redo history contains information that has been cut, copied, or deleted. Reviewers' notes, hidden text, and comments can contain information that you do not want to share.

WordPerfect X3 introduces a new feature to ensure that you'll never get caught with confidential or sensitive information in your documents. The new Save Without Metadata feature makes it simple to remove all metadata from a document, without the need to purchase or download an additional utility.

To save a WordPerfect document without metadata

1. Choose **File**, **Save Without Metadata** to display the Save Without Metadata dialog box (see Figure 18.26).

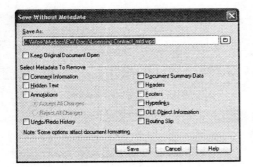

FIGURE 18.26
When you save a file, you can choose a different file format from the File Type drop-down list.

2. Click the **Browse** icon to locate the drive and folder where you want to save the document.
3. WordPerfect will automatically add _mtd to the end of the filename to identify that the file does not contain metadata. If necessary, make adjustments to the filename, but leave the _mtd alone.
4. Enable the **Keep Original Document Open** check box. (If the check box is not enabled, the original document will close and the metadata-free version will remain open.)
5. In the Select Metadata to Remove section, enable the appropriate check boxes to specify which metadata elements you want removed from the document.
6. Click **Save**.

The Absolute Minimum

In this chapter, you learned how to

- Create a table of contents by marking the entries, defining the table, and generating the table.
- Create a table of authorities that lists the sources for a legal document or research paper.
- Turn on Document Map and navigate through complex documents by the table of contents, table of authorities, or index markers.
- Review a document and insert revision marks, and then review the document as an author and either accept or reject revisions.
- Compare two documents and add redline and strikeout text automatically wherever a revision was made.
- Create and edit cases, produce pleading documents, create and edit pleading styles, and publish pleadings to EDGAR.
- Save documents without metadata to avoid revealing sensitive or confidential information.

This is the last chapter. You made it all the way through! Congratulations! You are now a confident, successful WordPerfect user.

Index

A

Abbrev.wcm macro, 316
Acquire Image command (Graphics menu), 226
Add command (Spell Checker), 95
Add Reviewers dialog, 292
Address Book (Outlook)
    documents, routing, 291-293
    mail merges, 293-294
    MAPI, 289
    opening, 289
    WordPerfect Address Book integration, 280
    WordPerfect Mail Address Book integration, 290
Address Book (WordPerfect). *See also* **Mail Address Book (WordPerfect)**
    contacts, emailing to, 286
    customizing, 286
    Directory Server, 283
    entries
        adding, 281-282
        backups, 285
        copying, 285
        deleting, 284
        editing, 284
        filtering, 287-288
        Group entries, 282
        moving, 284-285
        Organization entries, 281
        Person entries, 281
        printing, 285
        Resource entries, 282
        searching, 285
        sorting, 287
    importing/exporting, 294-295
    mail merges, 293-294
    mailing addresses, entering onto envelopes, 82
    MAPI, 283
    new address books, creating, 283
    Outlook integration, 280, 289-290
    software support, 280
    starting, 280
    View menu, 287
Address Book command (Tools menu), 281, 289
Address Book to Merge dialog, 316
Adobe Acrobat Reader, publishing documents to PDF files, 254
adrs2mrg.wcm macro, 316
Advanced tab (Print dialog), 66
aligning
    paragraphs
        center alignment, 118
        changing tab type, 123
        clearing tabs, 122
        editing tab settings, 124
        flush right alignment, 118
        moving tabs, 124
        restoring tab settings, 124
        setting tabs, 121-123
    text
        Block Protection, 130
        center alignment, 118
        Conditional End of Page, 131
        flush right alignment, 118
        Justification feature, 118-121
        line spacing, 128
        paragraph spacing, 129
        tabs, 121-124
        tables, 178, 182
        Widow/Orphan Protection, 130
All justification, 120
Allfonts.wcm macro, 316
announcements, creating, 137
antonyms, finding, 98
Append to Doc button, 83
application file icons, 38
art. *See* **images**
ASCII text files, exporting to address books, 295
Associate a Data File text box (Associate Form and Data dialog), 266
Associate Form and Data dialog, 266, 273
asterisks (*), 181, 202
At Least option, 181
attachments, sending documents as, 68
Author property bar (Review Document dialog), 342-343
authorities (tables of), 333-338
Auto Replace command (Spell Checker), 95
Auto-Suggest Filename feature, 29
automatic backups, 22
automatic proofreading features, 92
Autoscroll button, 26
Available Border Styles list box (Page Border/Fill dialog), 150

B

Back Tab option (Indent feature), 126
Background palette, 188
Backspace key, 24
backups, 42
    Address Books entries, 285
    automatic backups, 22
    default templates, 302-303
    Timed Document Backup feature, 30
Barcode button, 82
bibliographies, 333-338
bitmap graphics, 226
blank documents, opening, 8-9, 22
Block Protect feature, 130
blue screen (WordPerfect 5.1 Classic mode), switching to, 60
bold text, 72, 182
Border Style button (Graphics property bar), 230
Border/Fill command, 149-151, 185-187
borders
    deleting, 231
    graphics, 230-231
    page borders, 149-151
    tables, 188
Box Border/Fill dialog, 232

Box Fill button (Graphics property bar), 232
browse buttons, 25, 248
Browse By button, 25
browsers (WPOR), 309-310
bullets
 bulleted lists, 200-204
 menu items, 92
 numbered lists, 202-204
 QuickBullets, 110
Bullets & Numbering dialog, 200-202, 206

C

Calculate dialog, 190
calculations
 formulas, 191-194
 functions, 193-194
 QuickSum, 189-190
callout shapes, drawing, 240
CapsFix option (Format-As-You-Go), 110
cases (pleading documents), creating/editing, 347-349
Cell command, 176
Cell tab (Table Format dialog), 181-183
cells
 attributes, formatting, 181-183
 calculations, 183
 defined, 171
 diagonal lines, 183
 fill patterns, 187-188
 formulas, displaying, 191
 joining, 175-176
 locking, 183
 QuickSum formulas, 190
 splitting, 176
 two-part information, entering in, 183
Center command (Justification menu), 120
Center tabs, 121
centering text, 118-120, 137
checkbox.wcm macro, 316
checked menu items, 92
checked toolbars, 12
Checking Styles dialog, 97
Choose Profile dialog, 289
Classic mode, 59-62
Clear All Tabs option (Tab QuickMenu), 122

clearing tabs, 122-123
clip art, 221-222
Clip Properties dialog, 247
Clipboard, 244-246
Clipbook (Corel), 245-247
Close All Documents dialog, 316
Close button, 33, 235
Close command (File menu), 235
Close option (Find and Replace feature), 104
closeall.wcm macro, 316
closed object shapes, drawing, 238-239
codes
 deleting, 105
 finding and replacing, 105-106
Codes dialog, 105-106
collating print jobs, 65
Column tab (Table Format dialog), 178-179
columns
 adding, 174
 deleting, 175
 formatting, 178-179
 pages, adding to, 137
 QuickSum formulas, 190
 separator lines, 173
 tabular columns, converting to tables, 195
 width, adjusting, 172-174
Compare Document dialog, 344
Compatibility setting (Publish to PDF dialog), 254
Compatibility toolbar, 33
Conditional End of Page feature, 131
contacts (WordPerfect Address Book), emailing, 286
Contents tab (Help Topics dialog), 15
Contour option (text wrap), 229
conversion filters, 44, 250-253
Conversion Utility dialog, 44
Convert command (Table menu), 195-196
Convert File Format dialog, 253
Convert Template dialog, 318
converting
 documents, 44
 file formats, 225, 250-253
 files, 44
 ordinal text to superscript, 110

tables to other formats, 196
tabular columns to tables, 195
templates to documents, 307-308
Convert: Table to Text dialog, 196
Convert: Text to Table dialog, 195
Copy button, 54, 244
Copy command (Edit menu), 47, 54
Copy Formula dialog, 192
Copy To button, 47
Copy To Folder command (Edit menu), 47
copying
 Address Book (WordPerfect) entries, 285
 documents, 47
 files, 47
 formulas, 192
 text, 53-54, 244-247
copyrights, Internet images, 227
Corel FTP site, downloading templates, 306
Corel Knowledge Base tab (Help Topics dialog), 16
Corel on the Web command (Help menu), 16
CorelCENTRAL. *See* Address Book (WordPerfect)
cover sheets (faxes), 323-326
Create a New Address Book button, 283
Create a New Address Entry button, 281
Create command (Table menu), 170
Create Data File dialog, 260-261
Create Graphics Line dialog, 219-220
Create New button, 83
Create WP Template command (Options menu), 308
ctrlm.wcm macro, 316
Custom Line command (Line menu), 219-220
Custom Page Numbering dialog, 140
Custom WP Templates command (Options menu), 305
Customize Settings dialog, 61
customizing
 Address Book (WordPerfect) entries, 286
 styles, 162-163

table of contents, 332
templates, 302-305
views, 37-38
WordPerfect 5.1 Classic mode, 60
Cut button, 54, 244
Cut command (Edit menu), 47, 54
cvtdocs12.wcm macro, 316

D

data files
creating, 260-261
data, entering/importing, 263-264
editing, 264
fields, 260
form files, merging with, 270
formatting, 262
records, 260
Data Source button (Merge dialog), 270
database files, importing, 295
Date/Time command (Insert menu), 24
dates (modification), listing files by, 41
DCConvert.wcm macro, 316
Decimal Align tabs, 121
default document settings, 22
default folders, 39
default macro folder, 314
default styles, customizing, 162-163
default tab settings, clearing/restoring, 122-124
default templates, 302-304
Define Table of Authorities dialog, 337
Define Table of Contents dialog, 331
delay codes, inserting/editing, 147-149
Delete an Address Entry button, 284
Delete command, 49, 175
Delete key, 24
Delete Structure/Contents dialog, 175
Deletes All Annotations From the Document Text button (Author property bar), 343

Deletes the Currently Selected Annotation button (Author property bar), 343
deleting
Address Book (WordPerfect) entries, 284
borders, 231
codes, 105
columns, 175
documents, 49
files, 49
first-line indents, 127
folders, 49
formatting codes, 87
lines from lists, 203
page borders, 151
page breaks, 135
QuickWords entries, 114
Reveal Codes, 87
revision marks, 346
rows, 175
table lines, 187
tabs, 122-123
text, 23-24, 107
Demote button (Outline Property bar), 207, 210
Desktop command (Send To menu), 245
Details view, 37
diagonal lines, adding to cells, 183
Dictionary, 100-101
Directory Server address books, 283
disabling. *See* turning on/off
Display Annotations in Normal Text Color button (Author property bar), 343
Display Settings dialog, 60
Distance dialog, 145
distorting images, 224
dividing rows across pages, 181
Document Compare, 344-346
document identification footer macros, 322-323
Document Initial Font dialog, 141
Document Map, 339
Document Review feature, 340-343
documents
announcements, creating, 137
backups, 30, 42

blank documents, opening, 8-9, 22
bullets, 110
closing, 33-34
comparing, 344-346
converting, 44, 307-308
copying, 47
date/time, inserting, 24
default settings, 22
deleting, 49
Document Map, 339
Document Review, 340
emailing, 67-69
envelopes, creating, 81-83, 271-272
faxing, 66-67
file formats
conversion filter installation, 252-253
incompatible file formats, 253
supported file formats, 250-251
file icons, 38
folders, creating/deleting, 46-49
fonts, synching with page numbers, 141
footers, 322-323
form documents versus standard documents, 266
formatting
Block Protection, 130
bold, 72
Conditional End of Page, 131
fonts, 73-76
italics, 72
open codes, 87
paired codes, 86
printing formatting codes, 88
Reveal Codes, 86-87
underline, 72
Widow/Orphan Protection, 130
forms, creating, 274-276
graphics, 215
bitmap graphics, 226
borders, 230-231
fill patterns, 232-233
images, 220-227
layering, 240-241
lines, 216-220
shapes, 236-240
sizing handles, 218, 222-224
text boxes, 228
vector graphics, 226
watermarks, 233-235
wrapping text around, 229

DOCUMENTS

guidelines, hiding, 10
help, 11-15
indentation, 110
insertion points, 9, 25-27
invitations, creating, 137
labels, creating, 272-274
layouts, previewing, 66
line spacing, 128
lists, 199
   adding items, 203
   adding/deleting lines, 203
   bulleted lists, 200-201, 204
   editing, 203
   numbered lists, 202-204
   turning on/off bullets, 203
   turning on/off numbering, 203
macros, 313-326
margins, 77-80
Merge feature, 259
   data files, 260-261, 264
   envelopes, 271-272
   fill-in-the-blank forms, 274-276
   form files, 265-269
   labels, 272-274
   Merge dialog, 269-270
   troubleshooting problems, 270
metadata, saving without, 351
moving, 47
multiple documents
   opening, 37, 62
   printing, 65
   switching between, 63
naming, 34
navigating in, 24-27
opening
   converting on open, 44
   multiple documents, 37, 62
   Open File dialog, 36
outlines, 199, 205
   adding items to, 207-208
   collapsing/expanding, 210
   creating, 206
   editing, 207-210
   Outline property bar, 207
   outline styles, 211-212
   promoting/demoting items, 210
   rearranging items in, 208-210
pages
   borders, 149-151
   delay codes, 147-149
   headers/footers, 142-146
   Make It Fit feature, 152
   page breaks, 134-135
   page numbers, 138-142
   paper size and orientation, 135-136
   subdividing, 136-137
   suppressing formatting, 146
paragraph spacing, 129
pleading documents, 346
   creating cases, 347-348
   creating styles, 349-351
   editing cases, 348-349
   publishing in EDGAR format, 351
previewing, 28, 64
previous documents, opening, 36
printing
   collated copies, 65
   entire document, 28
   multiple pages, 66
   Print Preview, 28, 64
   selected text, 66
   specific pages, 66
   unprintable zones, 80
proofreading
   Dictionary, 100-101
   Find and Replace feature, 103-106
   foreign languages, 101-103
   Format-As-You-Go feature, 109-110
   Grammar-As-You-Go feature, 92
   Grammatik, 96-98
   QuickCorrect, 107-114
   QuickWords, 112-114
   Spell Checker, 94
   Spell-As-You-Go feature, 92
   Thesaurus, 98
property bars, 11
publishing, 254-255
QuickWords, inserting into, 113
renaming, 48
reviewing, 340-343, 346
routing, 291-293
saving, 29-31, 251-252
searching, 40-43
SpeedLinks, inserting, 111
spell-checking, 92-94
styles
   applying, 158
   creating, 157-161
   customizing, 162-163
   default settings, 162-163
   displaying effects, 158
   editing, 161
   heading styles, 158-159
   naming, 158
   open styles, 156
   paired styles, 156
   QuickFormat, 163-164
   QuickStyles, 157-158
   saving, 161
   Word (MS) compatibility, 160
tables. *See also* individual table entries
   of authorities, 333-338
   of contents, 328-333
   rows, 174-175
templates
   backups, 302-303
   converting documents to, 307-308
   creating documents from, 297-301
   downloading, 306
   editing, 303-305
   installing, 306-307
   wp11us.wpt, 297, 303
text
   aligning, 118, 121-124
   centering, 137
   copying, 53-54, 244-247
   cutting, 54
   dragging/dropping, 54-55
   entering, 22
   erasing, 23-24
   exporting to other file formats, 251-252
   formatting, 73
   indenting, 125-127
   moving, 53-55
   pasting, 54, 69, 244-247
   searches, 42
   selecting, 52
   symbols, 83-85
   undoing mistakes, 24, 55-56
   zooming in/out of in Print Preview, 64
toolbars, 11-12
zooming in/out, 56-58

dot leaders, 122

Double Indent option (Indent feature), 126

double-clicking mouse, text selection, 52

downloading
   Internet images, 227
   templates, 306, 310
   WPOR Browser, 310

dragging/dropping
   Address Book (WordPerfect) entries, 284-285
   lines, 218-219
   tabs, 124
   text, 54-55
   text boxes, 228

Draw Combined Shapes button (Draw Object Shapes dialog), 236-239

Draw Diagonal Line in Cell option (Table Format dialog), 183
Draw Object Shapes dialog, 237-239
drawing
    callout shapes, 240
    closed object shapes, 238-239
    line shapes, 237-238

E

EDGAR format (pleading documents), 351
Edit an Address Entry button, 284
Edit Field Names dialog, 264
Edit menu, 24, 54-56, 104-106, 244
Edit WP Template command (Options menu), 304
editing
    Address Book (WordPerfect) entries, 284
    cases (pleading documents), 348-349
    data files, 264
    delay codes, 149
    Document Review comments, 342
    form file associations, 294
    formatting codes, 87
    formulas, 192
    headers/footers, 143-144
    in-place editing, 249-250
    lists, 203
    macros, 320-321
    outlines, 207-210
    styles, 161
    tab settings, 124
    table of authority entries, 335-336
    templates, 303-305
    zoom settings, 57
electronic messaging, Outlook Address Books, 289
emailing
    Address Book (WordPerfect) contacts, 286
    documents, 67-69
Embed Fonts Using TrueDoc™ option (Save File dialog), 75
embedding data. *See* OLE (Object Linking and Embedding)
endfoot.wcm macro, 316
Envelope Addresses dialog, 317
Envelope command (Format menu), 82

envelopes, creating, 81-83, 271-272
erasing text, 23-24
Expand As Text with Formatting option (QuickWords), 114
Expndall.wcm macro, 316
exporting
    address books, 294-295
    text to other file formats, 251-252

F

fancy borders, selecting, 151
Favorites list (Help Topics), 16
faxes
    cover sheet macros, 323-324, 326
    document faxing, 66-67
field names, inserting into form files, 267-268
Field Names button, 264
file formats, saving documents as, 30-31
File menu commands
    Close, 235
    Delete, 49
    Install New Font, 73
    New, 22, 63
    New from Project, 298
    Open, 36
    Page Setup, 135-136
    Print, 28, 67
    Print Preview, 64
    Rename, 49
    Save, 29
    Save As, 31, 251
    Send To, 67
File Stamp Options dialog, 317
files
    application file icons, 38
    ASCII text files, exporting address books to, 295
    backups, 42
    converting, 44
    copying, 47
    data files
        creating, 260-261
        defined, 260
        editing, 264
        entering data in, 263-264
        fields, 260
        formatting, 262
        importing data into, 264

    merging with form files, 270
    records, 260
    database files, importing, 295
    deleting, 49
    file formats
        conversion filter installation, 252-253
        incompatible file formats, 253
        saving documents as, 30-31, 251-252
        supported file formats, 250-251
    filenames, 29, 42-43
    folders, organizing in, 46
    form files, 265-270
    icons, 38
    lists, rearranging, 38-39
    LRS files, 102
    merge data files, importing, 294
    modification date, listing by, 41
    modified files, displaying, 42
    moving, 47
    naming, 29
    publishing, 254-255
    renaming, 48
    routing, 291-293
    searching, 40-43
    type, listing by, 40
Files command (Settings menu), 30
Files Settings dialog, 30
Filestmp.wcm macro, 317
Fill in Heading Info button, 301
fill patterns, 187-188, 232-233
fill-in-the-blank forms, creating, 274-276
Filter dialog, 288
filters (conversion), 44, 250-253
Find and Replace feature, 103-106
Find dialog, Address Book (WordPerfect) entries, 285-286
Find Next option (Find and Replace feature), 104
Find Now button, 42
Find Prev option (Find and Replace feature), 104
finding
    Address Book (WordPerfect) entries, 285
    codes, 105-106
    documents, 40-43
    hard returns in rows, 180

How can we make this index more useful? Email us at indexes@quepublishing.com

Help Topics, 15
text, 103-104
first-line indents, 127
flipenv.wcm macro, 83, 317
flush right alignment, 118
Folder command (New menu), 46
folders
    creating, 39, 46
    Custom WP Templates, 305
    default folders, 39
    deleting, 49
    documents, organizing, 46
    naming, 46
    navigating, 39
    renaming, 48
    WordPerfect Office X3, 8
Font button, 82
Font command (Format menu), 74
Font Properties dialog, 76
Fontdn.wcm macro, 317
fonts
    attributes, 76
    default settings, 22
    documents, saving with, 75
    effects, selecting, 76
    font sizes, 74
    headers/footers, 144
    installing, 73
    page numbers, synching with, 141
    QuickFonts, 75
    selecting, 73-74
Fontup.wcm macro, 317
footend.wcm macro, 317
footers
    creating, 143
    editing, 143
    footer creation macros, 322-323
    formatting, suppressing, 146
Foreground palette, 188
foreign languages, selecting, 101-103
Form Document button (Merge dialog), 270
form documents versus standard documents, 266
form files
    associations (mail merges), 293-294
    creating, 265-269
    data files, merging with, 270
    field names, inserting, 267-268

Format command
    Paragraph menu, 127
    Table menu, 177-178, 182
Format menu commands
    Envelope, 82
    Font, 74
    Justification, 120
    Keep Text Together, 129-131
    Labels, 273
    Line, 118, 124
    Make It Fit, 152
    Margins, 80
    Paragraph, 127
    QuickFormat, 163
    Styles, 157, 160-161
Format Records in a Table check box (Create Data File dialog), 261
Format-As-You-Go feature (QuickCorrect), 109-110
formatting
    codes, displaying/deleting, 86-87
    data files, 262
    documents, 72-80, 86-87
    envelopes, 81
    pages
        borders, 149-151
        centering text, 137
        delay codes, 147-149
        headers/footers, 142-146
        Make It Fit feature, 152
        page breaks, 134-135
        page numbers, 138-142
        paper size and orientation, 135-136
        subdividing, 136-137
        suppressing formatting, 146
    tables, 177-188
    text
        alignment, 118
        Block Protection, 130
        Conditional End of Page, 131
        line spacing, 128
        paragraph spacing, 129
        styles, 156-164
        tabs, 121-124
        Widow/Orphan Protection, 130
forms, creating, 274-276
Formula toolbar, 191-192
formulas
    adding
        functions to, 193-194
        to tables, 191-192
    cells, displaying in, 191
    copying, 192

editing, 192
    math operators, 192
Forward button, 26
From File command (Graphics menu), 225-227
FTP site (Corel), downloading templates, 306
full justification, 120-121
functions adding to tables, 193-194

G

General tab (Publish to PDF dialog), 254
Generate dialog, 333, 338
glyphs, 239
Go Back One Folder Level button, 39
Go to Data button (Merc feature), 267
Go to Form button, 267
Grammar-As-You-Go feature, 92
Grammatik, 96-98, 103
graphics, 215
    bitmap graphics, 226
    borders, 230-231
    file icons, 38
    fill patterns, 232-233
    images, 220
        clip art, 221-222
        copyrights, 227
        distorting, 224
        file formats, 225-226
        importing, 224-227
        Internet images, 227
        moving, 223
        scanned images, 226
        sizing, 223
    layering, 240-241
    lines, 216-220
    shapes, 236-240
    sizing handles, 218, 222-224
    text boxes, creating, 228
    text wrapping, 229
    vector graphics, 226
    watermarks, 233-235
Graphics button (Graphics property bar), 241
Graphics command (Insert menu), 225

KEYBOARDS 361

Graphics property bar, 230-232, 235, 241
Group entries (WordPerfect Address Book), 282
grouping files by modification date, 41
guidelines
    hiding, 10
    margins, adjusting, 10, 78
    tables, turning on/off in, 186

H

Hanging Indent option (Indent feature), 126
hard page breaks, inserting, 134-135
hard returns, locating in rows, 180
headers/footers, 145
    creating, 142-144
    editing, 143-144
    fonts, 144
    formatting, suppressing, 146
    header rows, 181
    multiple headers, 146
heading styles, 158-159
help, 13
    Help menu, 15-18
    Help Topics, 15-16
    Microsoft Word Help, 18
    QuickTips, 11, 14
    TIDs (technical information documents), 16
Hide Family button (Outline Property bar), 207
hiding
    guidelines, 10
    hotkeys, 13
    toolbars, 11
    Workspace Manager, 9
highlighting document changes, 344-346
history lists (Thesaurus), 100
horizontal lines, 145, 216
Horizontal option (Table Format dialog), 182
hotkeys, hiding/displaying, 13
hyperlinks, creating via SpeedLinks, 111

I

Icons view, 37
idfooter macros, 322-323
Ignore Cell When Calculating option (Table Format dialog), 183
Image Tools dialog, 235
images, 220
    bitmap graphics, 226
    clip art, 221-222
    copyrights, 227
    distorting, 224
    file formats, 225-226
    importing, 224-227
    Internet images, 227
    moving, 223
    scanned images, 226
    sizing, 223
    vector graphics, 226
Import/Export Expert feature (WordPerfect Address Book), 294
importing
    address books, 294-295
    database files, 295
    images, 224-227
    merge data files, 294
    spreadsheets, 295
    text
        into merge data files, 264
        supported file formats, 250-251
in-place editing, 249-250
incompatible file formats, 253
indenting, 110, 125-127
Index tab (Help Topics dialog), 15
Insert Columns/Rows dialog, 174
Insert Field button, 267, 273
Insert Field Name or Number dialog, 267-268, 273
Insert File button, 308
Insert Image dialog, 225
Insert menu commands
    Date/Time, 24
    Graphics, 225
    Header/Footer, 143-144
    Line, 216
    Object, 248
    Outline/Bullets & Numbering, 200-206, 211
    Shapes, 237
    Text Box, 228
    Watermark, 234

Insert Merge Code button (Merge feature), 268
Insert Merge Code dialog, 275
Insert Object dialog, 248-249
Insert Page Number dialog, 141-142
Insert the Currently Selected Annotation into the Text of the Document button (Author property bar), 343
inserting
    columns into tables, 174
    delay codes, 147
    field names into form files, 267-268
    footers, 142-143
    functions into formulas, 193-194
    hard page breaks, 134-135
    headers, 142-143
    page numbers, 139-142
    QuickWords into documents, 113
    rows into tables, 174
    SpeedLinks into documents, 111
insertion points, 9, 25-27
Inserts All Annotations into the Document Text button (Author property bar), 343
Install New Font command (File menu), 73
installing
    conversion filters, 44, 252-253
    fonts, 73
    Legal Tools, 347
    templates, 306-307
    WordPerfect, 8
Internet images, importing, 227
Invalid format error messages, 44
invitations, creating, 137
italic text, 72

J – K

jaggies (bitmap graphics), 226
joining table cells, 175-176
Justification feature, 118-121

Keep Text Together dialog, 129-131
keyboards
    Backspace key, 24
    Delete key, 24

How can we make this index more useful? Email us at indexes@quepublishing.com

documents, navigating with, 26-27
hotkeys, hiding/displaying, 13
menu items, selecting, 13
Tab key, 172
text, selecting with, 52
WordPerfect 5.1 Classic mode keyboard, switching to, 61-62
keyboards tab (Customize Settings dialog), 61

L

labels, creating, 272-274
Landscape option (page orientation), 136, 262
Language dialog, 102-103
languages (foreign), selecting, 101-102
Last Modified option (Open File dialog), 42
launching. *See* opening/closing
layering graphics, 240-241
Layout Preview button (WordPerfect X3 Print dialog), 66
Left Align tabs, 121
Left command (Justification menu), 120
legal documents. *See* pleading documents
Legal toolbar (Review Document dialog)
   Document Compare, 344
   Pleading Expert Designer button, 349
   Pleading Expert Filler button, 347-349
   Table of Authorities button, 334
Line attributes option (Create Graphics Line dialog), 220
Line command, 118, 124, 216
line shapes, drawing, 237-238
lines
   custom lines, 219-220
   horizontal lines, 145, 216
   moving, 218-219
   spacing, 22, 128
   tables, formatting in, 185-187
   vertical lines, 217
links, creating
   OLE (Object Linking and Embedding) links, 248-249
   via SpeedLinks, 111

List view, 37
lists, 199
   adding items, 203
   bulleted lists, 200-204
   editing, 203
   lines, adding/deleting, 203
   numbered lists, 202-204
   toolbars list, displaying, 12
Lock Cell to Prevent Changes option (Table Format dialog), 183
Longname.wcm macro, 317
Look up command (Thesaurus), 98-100
LRS (Language Resource) files, 102

M

Macro command (Tools menu), 315
Macro Edit command (Tools menu), 320
Macro menu, 315, 319
Macro toolbar, 320-324
macros, 83, 313-326
magnifying. *See* zooming in/out
Mail Address Book (WordPerfect), 290. *See also* Address Book (WordPerfect)
mail merge feature. *See* Merge feature
mail merges, 293-294
Mail Recipient command (Send To menu), 68-69
mailing
   documents (email), 67-69
mailing addresses, envelopes, 81-82
Make It Fit dialog, 152
MAPI, 283, 289
margins, 77
   adjusting, 78-79
   changing, 10
   default settings, 22
   setting via Page Setup dialog, 80
   tables, 178
Margins command (Format menu), 80
Match menu commands, 105
math operators, 192
Memo Heading dialog, 301
Merge button (Merge dialog), 270

Merge command (Tools menu), 260, 266, 269, 293
merge data files, importing, 294
Merge dialog, 269-270
Merge feature, 259
   data files, 260-261, 264, 270
   envelopes, creating, 271-272
   fill-in-the-blank forms, 274-276
   form files, 265-270
   Go to Data button, 267
   Insert Field button, 267
   Insert Merge Code button, 268
   labels, creating, 272-274
   troubleshooting, 270
metadata, saving documents without, 351
Microsoft Word Help command (Help menu), 18
Microsoft Word mode, 9
minimum row height, specifying, 181
modification date, listing files by, 41
modified files, displaying, 42
More command (QuickMenu), 12
mouse
   documents, zooming in/out of, 57
   double-clicking, text selection, 52
   menu items, selecting, 13
   navigating documents with, 25-26
   point and click, 25
   quadruple-clicking, text selection, 52
   selecting text with, 52
   single-clicking, text selection, 52
   text, dragging/dropping, 55
   triple-clicking, text selection, 52
Move Down button, 207-208
Move to button, 47
Move Up button, 207-208
moving
   Address Book (WordPerfect) entries, 284-285
   data between programs
      Clipbook, 245-247
      conversion filter installation, 252-253
      incompatible file formats, 253
      OLE (Object Linking and Embedding), 247-250
      supported file formats, 250-251
      Windows Clipboard, 244
   documents, 47
   files, 47

images, 223
insertion points, 25-27
lines, 218-219
tabs, 124
text, 53-55
text boxes, 228
toolbars, 12
moving around. *See* navigating
multiple documents
opening, 62, 67
printing, 65
switching between, 63
multiple headers/footers, 146
multiple pages, printing, 66

N

Name a Field text box (Create Data File dialog), 261
naming
documents, 34, 48
folders, 46
QuickWords entries, 114
text styles, 158
navigating
documents, 24-27, 339
drives, 39
folders, 39
tables, 172
Network command (Clipboard menu), 246
New Address Book dialog, 283
New Blank Document button, 22, 63
New command (File menu), 22, 63
New dialog, 281-282
New from Project command (File menu), 298
Number button, 203
number of copies (Print dialog), 65
numbered lists, 202-204
Numbering command (Page menu), 139
numbers (page), 138
Custom Page Numbering dialog, 140
document fonts, synching with, 141
inserting, 139-142
Page Numbering Font dialog, 140-141
Page numbering format list, 140
Values dialog, 140
Numbers tab (Bullets & Numbering dialog), 202, 206
Numeric Format command (Table menu), 192

O

Object command (Insert menu), 248
Object(s) Back One button (Graphics property bar), 241
Object(s) Forward One button (Graphics property bar), 241
OLE (Object Linking and Embedding), 247-250
Open button, 36
open codes, 87
Open command (File menu), 36
Open File dialog, 36-39, 42
open styles, 156
opening/closing
Address Book (Outlook), 280, 289
Clipbook, 245
documents, 33-34
 blank documents, 8-9, 22
 converting on open, 44
 multiple documents, 37, 62, 67
 Open File dialog, 36
 previous documents, 36
Outlook address books, 289
QuickCorrect, 107
QuickMenu, 12
submenus, 13
toolbars, 12
WordPerfect, 8
WPOR Browser, 309
operators (math), 192
Options menu commands
Create WP Template, 308
Custom WP Templates, 305
Edit WP Template, 304
Language, 103
ordinal text, converting to superscript, 110
Organization entries (WordPerfect Address Book), 281
orientation (paper), 135-136
orphans, preventing, 130
Outline property bar, 207, 210
Outline/Bullets & Numbering command (Insert menu), 200-206, 211
outlines, 199, 205
adding items to, 207-208
collapsing/expanding, 210
creating, 206
editing, 207-210
Outline property bar, 207
outline styles, 211-212
promoting/demoting items, 210
rearranging items in, 208-210
Outlook Address Book. *See* **Address Book (Outlook)**
Oxford English Pocket Dictionary, 100-101

P

Page Border/Fill dialog, 149-150
page breaks, 134-135
Page command (View menu), 124
Page menu commands
Border/Fill, 149-151
Delay Codes, 147
Insert Page Number, 141
Numbering, 139
Page Setup, 135-136
Suppress, 146
Page Numbering button, 145
Page Numbering Font dialog, 141-140
Page numbering format list, 140
page numbers, 138
Custom Page Numbering dialog, 140
document fonts, synching with, 141
inserting in predefined positions, 139-141
inserting manually, 141-142
Page Numbering Font dialog, 140-141
Page numbering format list, 140
suppressing formatting, 146
Values dialog, 140
Page Setup dialog, 80, 135-136
Page Width option (Zoom button), 124

PAGES

pages
  borders, 149-151
  columns, adding, 137
  Conditional End of Page feature, 131
  delay codes, 147-149
  formatting
    centering text, 137
    suppressing, 146
  headers/footers, 142-146
  Make It Fit feature, 152
  margins, 77-80
  page breaks, 134-135
  page numbers, 138-142
  paper size and orientation, 135-136
  printing, 66
  rows, adding, 137
  subdividing, 136-137
paired codes, 86
paired styles, 156
paper size
  changing, 135
  default settings, 22
Parabrk.wcm macro, 317
Paragraph Break dialog, 317
Paragraph Format dialog, 127, 129
Paragraph menu commands, 127
paragraphs
  aligning
    center alignment, 118
    changing tab type, 123
    clearing tabs, 122
    editing tab settings, 124
    flush right alignment, 118
    moving tabs, 124
    restoring tab settings, 124
    setting tabs, 121-123
  indenting, 125-126
  justifying, 119-121
  line spacing, 128
  paragraph spacing, 129
Paste button, 54, 244
Paste command (Edit menu), 47, 54
Paste Special command (Edit menu), 244
pasting
  document text into emails, 69
  text, 54, 244-247
Pause While Recording/Executing a Macro button (Macro toolbar), 320, 324
pausing macros, 320

PDF (Portable Document Format), publishing documents to, 254-255
PerfectExpert dialog, 298-301
Person entries (WordPerfect Address Book), 281
Person Properties dialog, 283
personal information, adding to project templates, 299-300
pictures. *See* **images**
pixels, 226
Play command (Macro menu), 315
Play Macro dialog, 314-315
Pleading button, 348
pleading documents, 346
  cases, creating/editing, 347-349
  EDGAR format, publishing in, 351
  styles, creating, 349-351
Pleading Expert Designer button (Legal toolbar), 349-351
Pleading Expert Filler button (Legal toolbar), 347-349
Pleading Paper dialog, 318, 348
pleading.wcm macro, 318
Pocket Oxford Dictionary, 100-101
point and click, 25
portrait orientation, 135
Position on page option (Create Graphics Line dialog), 220
positioning tables, 178
previewing
  document layouts, 66
  documents, 28, 64
  shapes, 240
  templates via WPOR Browser, 309
previous documents, opening, 36
Print dialog, 28, 65-67
  Advanced tab, 66
  formatting codes, printing, 88
Print Envelope button, 83
Print Preview button, 64
printing
  Address Book (WordPerfect) entries, 285
  documents, 64-66
    collated copies, 65
    entire document, 28
    multiple pages, 66
    Print Preview, 28, 64
    selected text, 66
    specific pages, 66
    unprintable zones, 80

  formatting codes, 88
  multiple documents, 65
programs, moving data between
  conversion filter installation, 252-253
  Corel Clipbook, 245-247
  incompatible file formats, 253
  OLE (Object Linking and Embedding), 247-250
  supported file formats, 250-252
  Windows Clipboard, 244
Programs command (Start menu), 8
Promote button (Outline Property bar), 207, 210
Prompt Builder, 318
prompts.wcm macro, 318
Proofread command (Tools menu), 92
proofreading documents, 92
  Dictionary, 100-101
  Find and Replace feature, 103-106
  foreign languages, 101-103
  Format-As-You-Go feature, 109-110
  Grammar-As-You-Go feature, 92
  Grammatik, 96-98
  QuickCorrect, 107-114
  QuickWords, 112-114
  Spell Checker, 94
  Spell-As-You-Go feature, 92
  Thesaurus, 98
property bars, 11. *See also* **scrollbars; toolbars**
  Author (Review Document dialog), 342-343
  displaying, 11
  Graphics property bar, 230-232, 235, 241
  Outline property bar, 207, 210
  Reviewer (Review Document dialog), 342
  Watermark property bar, 235
Publish to PDF dialog, 254
Publish to XML dialog, 255
publishing documents
  to PDF, 254-255
  pleading documents in EDGAR format, 351
  to XML, 255
pull-down menus, 13

Q

quadruple-clicking mouse, text selection, 52
Quick Data Entry dialog, 261-264
QuickBullets option (Format-As-You-Go), 110
QuickCorrect, 85, 107
　Add Entry option, 108
　adding/deleting entries, 108
　Format-As-You-Go feature, 109-110
　QuickWords feature, 112-114
　SpeedLinks feature, 111
　symbols, 85
QuickFonts, 75
QuickFormat, 163-164
QuickIndent, 110, 127
QuickLines option (Format-As-You-Go), 110
QuickMenu, 12
QuickOrdinals option (Format-As-You-Go), 110
QuickStyles, 157-158
QuickSum, 189-190
QuickSymbols option (Format-As-You-Go), 110
QuickTips, 11, 14
QuickWords feature (QuickCorrect), 112-114
quote marks (" "), macros, 321

R

RealTime Preview, 57, 73, 121
rearranging
　file list, 38-39
　outlines, 208-210
recording macros, 319
redline text, document comparisons, 344-346
Redo command (Edit menu), 56
Reference Tools dialog, 329, 334
Refresh the Document Map button, 340
Remove Filter command (View menu), 288
Remove Markings dialog, 346

removing
　borders, 231
　lines from lists, 203
Rename command (File menu), 49
renaming
　documents, 48
　files, 48, 49
　folders, 48
　QuickWords entries, 114
reordering outlines, 208-210
Replace All option (Find and Replace feature), 104
Replace command
　Grammatik, 97
　Spell Checker, 95
　Thesaurus, 100
Replace feature
　code searches, 105-106
　Replace with Nothing option, 107
　text searches, 103-104
Replace menu commands, 106
replacing
　QuickWords entries, 113
　text
　　Dictionary, 100-101
　　Find and Replace feature, 103-107
　　Grammar-As-You-Go feature, 92
　　Grammatik, 96-98
　　QuickWords entries, 113
　　Spell Checker, 94
　　Spell-As-You-Go feature, 92
　　Thesaurus, 98
resizing
　images, 223
　pointers, 223
　text boxes, 228
Resource entries (WordPerfect Address Book), 282
responding to Document Review comments, 342
restoring default tab settings, 124
Resume command, 95-97
Reveal Codes
　deleting, 87
　Show 'Off Codes' option, 161
　turning on/off, 86-87
Reveal Codes command (View menu), 87, 105, 303, 329, 334
Reverse Text Options dialog, 318
reverse.wcm macro, 318

Review Document dialog, 341
　Author property bar, 342-343
　Legal toolbar, 347-349
　Reviewer property bar, 342
　Set Color button, 342
Reviewer property bar (Review Document dialog), 342
reviewing documents
　comments
　　changing color, 342
　　creating, 340
　　editing, 342
　　responding to, 342
　Document Review, 340
　revision marks, deleting, 346
　troubleshooting, 343
revision marks
　color, changing, 342
　creating, 340
　deleting, 346
　editing, 342
　redline text, 344-346
　responding to, 342
　strikeout text, 344-346
　troubleshooting, 343
Right Align tabs, 121
Right command (Justification menu), 120
Rotate option (Table Format dialog), 183
routing
　documents, Address Book (Outlook), 291-293
　slips, creating, 291
Routing Slip dialog, 291-293
Row tab (Table Format dialog), 179-181
rows
　adding, 174
　deleting, 175
　dividing across pages, 181
　fixed row heights, setting, 180
　formatting, 179-181
　hard returns, locating, 180
　header rows, 181
　height
　　adjusting, 180
　　setting, 179
　　specifying minimum height, 181
　pages, adding to, 137
　QuickSum formulas, 190

rule classes (Grammatik), turning on/off, 97
Ruler command
　Start menu, 8
　View menu, 79, 122

S

Save As command (File menu), 31, 251
Save As dialog, 29-31
Save button, 29
Save File dialog, 31, 75
Save Open Documents dialog, 318
Save Template dialog, 308
Save Without Metadata dialog, 352
saveall.wcm macro, 318
Savetoa.wcm macro, 318
saving
　documents
　　converted documents, 44
　　file formats, 30-31
　　saving and closing, 29
　　to other file formats, 251-252
　　without metadata, 351
　fonts with documents, 75
　text styles, 161
scanned images, importing, 226
Scrapbook dialog, 221
scrollbars, 25, 60. See also property bars; toolbars
Search for Specified Text button, 285
searching
　Address Book (WordPerfect) entries, 285
　code, Find and Replace feature, 105-106
　Dictionary, 100-101
　documents, 40-43
　files by filenames, 42-43
　Find and Replace feature, 103
　Help Topics, 15
　text via Find and Replace feature, 103-104
　Thesaurus, 98
　web searches, Yahoo! Search bar, 10
Select Language dialog, 103
Select the Next Annotation button (Author property bar), 343

Select the Previous Annotation button (Author property bar), 343
selecting
　commands in tables, 171
　fancy borders, 151
　font effects, 76
　fonts, 73-74
　foreign languages, 101-103
　menu items, 13
　page borders, 150
　text, 52, 66
Send Mail button, 286
Send Mail command (Address Book Tools menu), 286
Send To command (File menu), 67
Send To menu commands
　Desktop, 245
　Mail Recipient, 68-69
sending documents
　via email, 67-69
　via fax, 66-67
servers (OLE), 249
Set Color button (Review Document dialog), 342
Set Paragraph Number button (Outline Property bar), 207
setting
　fixed row heights, 180
　margins via Page Setup dialog, 80
　row height, 179
　tabs, 123-124
Settings command
　Language menu, 102
　Tools menu, 30, 289
Settings menu commands, 30
setup.exe program, 8
shadow cursor, insertion points, 9
shapes
　callout shapes, 240
　closed object shapes, 238-239
　glyphs, 239
　inserting, 236-237
　line shapes, 237-238
　previewing, 240
Shapes command (Insert menu), 237
shortcuts
　indenting text, 126
　symbols, entering into text, 84
　table of, 27
Show "Off Codes" option (Reveal Codes window), 161
Show Family button (Outline Property bar), 207

Show Levels button (Outline Property bar), 207, 210-211
Show/Hide Margin Markers button (Author property bar), 342
sigblock macros, 322
signature block macros, 322
single-clicking mouse, text selection, 52
Size Column to Fit feature (Table menu), 174
sizing
　column widths, 172-174
　fonts, 74
　images, 223
　paper, 135
　tables, 178
　text boxes, 228
sizing handles, 218, 222-224
Skip All command, 95-97
Skip Once command 95-97
soft page breaks, 134
sorting Address Book (WordPerfect) entries, 287
spacing
　lines, 128
　paragraphs, 129
Spacing command (Line menu), 128
Specific Codes dialog, 106
SpeedFormat, 184-187
SpeedLinks feature (QuickCorrect), 111
Spell Checker, 94-95, 103
Spell-As-You-Go feature, 92
Split Cell dialog, 176
Split command (Table menu), 176
splitting table cells, 176
spreadsheets, importing, 295
Start menu commands, 8
starting. See opening/closing
Stop Macro Play or Record button (Macro toolbar), 320-324
strikeout text, document comparisons, 344-346
styles, 156
　applying, 158
　creating, 157-161
　customizing, 162-163
　default settings, 162-163
　editing, 161
　effects, displaying, 158

heading styles, 158-159
naming, 158
open styles, 156
paired styles, 156
QuickFormat, 163-164
QuickStyles, 157-158
saving, 161
Word (MS) compatibility, 160
Styles Editor, 160-161, 303
subdividing pages, 136-137
subheadings, designating in tables of contents, 328
submenus, opening, 13
superscript, converting ordinal text to, 110
supplemental macro folders, 314
supported file formats, 250-251
suppressing page formatting, 146
switching
between multiple documents, 63
to WordPerfect 5.1 Classic mode, 60-62
symbols, 83-85, 110
synonyms, finding, 98

T

Tab key, 172
Tab QuickMenu, 122-123
Tab Set dialog, 124
Table Borders/Fill dialog, 185-188
Table Format dialog, 177-183
Table menu
commands
Borders/Fill, 185, 187
Calculate, 190
Convert, 195-196
Create, 170
Delete, 175
Format, 177-178, 182
Formula Toolbar, 191
Insert, 174
Join, 176
Numeric Format, 192
QuickSum, 190
SpeedFormat, 184
Split, 176
Size Column to Fit feature, 174
Table of Authorities button (Legal toolbar), 334
Table QuickCreate button, 171
Table SpeedFormat dialog, 184

Table tab (Table Format dialog), 177-178
tables
calculations
formulas, 191-194
functions, 193-194
QuickSum, 189-190
cells
attributes, 182-183
calculations, 183
defined, 171
diagonal lines, 183
fill patterns, 187-188
formatting, 181-182
joining, 175-176
locking, 183
splitting, 176
columns
adding, 174
adjusting width, 172-174
column separator lines, 173
converting tabular columns to tables, 195
deleting, 175
formatting, 178-179
commands, selecting, 171
converting, 196
creating, 170-171
data files, formatting, 262
formatting
borders, 188
cells, 181-183
columns, 178-179
entire table, 177-178
fill patterns, 187-188
lines, 185-187
rows, 179-181
SpeedFormat, 184-187
guidelines, turning on/off, 186
landscape page orientation, viewing in, 262
navigating, 172
positioning, 178
rows
adding, 174
deleting, 175
dividing across pages, 181
formatting, 179-181
header rows, 181
locating hard returns, 180
sizing, 178
text
aligning, 178, 182
rotating, 183
tables of authorities, 333-338

tables of contents, 329-333
tabs
back tabs, indenting text, 126
Center, 121
changing type, 123
clearing, 122-123
Decimal Align, 121
default settings, 22
dot leaders, 122
Keyboard tab (Customize Settings dialog), 61
Left Align, 121
moving, 124
restoring defaults, 124
Right Align, 121
setting, 121-123
settings, editing/restoring, 124
tabular columns, converting to tables, 195
tconvert.wcm macro, 318
technical information documents (TIDs), 16
templates
backups, 302-303
documents
converting from, 307-308
creating, 298-301
customizing, 302-305
downloading, 306, 310
editing, 303-305
installing, 306-307
wp11us.wpt, 297, 303
WPOR Browser, 309-310
text
aligning, 118-124
back tabs, 126
Block Protection, 130
capitalization, 110
centering, 137
Conditional End of Page, 131
converting to/from tables, 195-196
copying, 53-54, 244-247
cutting, 54
deleting, 107
Dictionary, 100-101
document searches, 42
documents
entering into, 22
pasting into emails, 69
dragging/dropping, 54-55
erasing, 23-24
exporting, 251-252

fonts
    attributes, 76
    default settings, 22
    font sizes, 74
    formatting, 73
    headers/footers, 144
    installing, 73
    QuickFonts, 75
    saving with document, 75
    selecting, 73-74
    selecting effects, 76
    synching with page numbers, 141
formatting, 72-76, 86-87
graphics, wrapping around, 229
indenting, 125-127
insertion points, 9, 25-27
justifying, 118-121
line spacing, 128
lists, 199
    adding items, 203
    adding/deleting lines, 203
    bulleted lists, 200-201, 204
    editing, 203
    numbered lists, 202-204
    turning on/off bullets, 203
    turning on/off numbering, 203
moving, 53-55
ordinal text, converting to superscript, 110
outlines, 199, 205
    adding items to, 207-208
    collapsing/expanding, 210
    creating, 206
    editing, 207-210
    Outline property bar, 207
    outline styles, 211-212
    promoting/demoting items, 210
    rearranging items in, 208-210
paragraph spacing, 129
pasting, 54, 244-247
proofreading
    Dictionary, 100-101
    Find and Replace feature, 103-106
    foreign languages, 101-103
    Format-As-You-Go feature, 109-110
    Grammar-As-You-Go feature, 92
    Grammatik, 96-98
    QuickCorrect, 107-114
    QuickWords, 112-114
    Spell Checker, 94
    Spell-As-You-Go feature, 92
    Thesaurus, 98
QuickCorrect, adding to, 108

redline text, document comparisons, 344-346
saving, 251-252
selecting, 52, 66
spell-checking, 92-94
strikeout text, document comparisons, 344-346
styles
    applying, 158
    creating, 157-161
    customizing, 162-163
    default settings, 162-163
    displaying effects, 158
    editing, 161
    heading styles, 158-159
    naming, 158
    open styles, 156
    paired styles, 156
    QuickFormat, 163-164
    QuickStyles, 157-158
    saving, 161
    Word (MS) compatibility, 160
symbols, 83-85, 110
tables
    aligning in, 178, 182
    entering in, 172
    rotating in, 183
    rows, 174-175
Thesaurus, 98
undoing mistakes, 24, 55-56
Widow/Orphan Protection, 130
zooming in/out, 56-58, 64

Text Box command (Insert menu), 228
text boxes, creating/sizing, 228
Thesaurus, 98-100, 103
Thumbnail view, 37
TIDs (technical information documents), 16
Tiles view, 37
time/date, inserting into documents, 24
Timed Document Backup feature, 30
toolbars. *See also* property bars; scrollbars
    checked toolbars, 12
    closing, 12
    Compatibility toolbar, 33
    displaying list of, 12
    Formula toolbar, 191-192
    hiding, 11
    Legal toolbar, 334, 344, 347-349
    Macro toolbar, 320-324
    moving, 12
    QuickTips, 11, 14

    unchecked toolbars, 12
    WordPerfect 5.1 Classic mode toolbars, turning on/off, 60
    Yahoo! Search bar, 10
Toolbars command (View menu), 11, 211
Tools menu commands
    Address Book, 281, 289
    Dictionary, 100
    Grammatik, 96-97
    Language, 102
    Macro, 315
    Macro Edit, 320
    Merge, 260, 266, 269, 293
    Proofread, 92
    QuickCorrect, 85, 107-111
    QuickWords, 112-113
    Settings, 30, 289
    Spell Checker, 94
    Thesaurus, 98
triple-clicking mouse, text selection, 52
troubleshooting
    Document Review, 343
    Invalid format error message, 44
    Merge feature, 270
    undoing mistakes, 55-56
Turn on Tree View button, 339
turning on/off
    Document Review, 343
    Grammar-As-You-Go feature, 92
    guidelines, 10, 78
    Outlook integration, 280, 290
    QuickIndent, 127
    Reveal Codes, 86-87
    rule classes (Grammatik), 97
    ruler, 79
    Spell-As-You-Go feature, 92
    table guidelines, 186
    toolbars, 11
    Widow/Orphan Protection, 130
    WordPerfect 5.1 Classic mode scrollbars/toolbars, 60
    Yahoo! Search bar, 10
two-part information (cells), 183
Type menu commands, 106

U – V

uawp13en.wcm macro, 318
unchecked toolbars, 12
Underline button, 72
underlined text, 72
Undo button, 49, 56

Undo command
  Edit menu, 24, 55-56
  Grammatik, 97
  Thesaurus, 100
Undo/Redo History command (Edit menu), 56
unprintable zones, 80
unsupported file formats, 253
upgrades
  Address Book exports, 295
  Dictionary, 101
Use Same Alignment as Column option (Table Format dialog), 182

Values dialog, 140, 142
vector graphics, 226
Vertical Line command (Line menu), 217
Vertical line/Horizontal line option (Create Graphics Line dialog), 220
vertical lines, 217
Vertical option (Table Format dialog), 183
View button, 37
View menu commands
  Document Map, 339
  Filter, 287
  Guidelines, 10, 78
  Page, 124
  Remove Filter, 288
  Reveal Codes, 87, 105, 303, 329, 334
  Ruler, 79, 122
  Toolbars, 11, 211
  Zoom, 57
views, customizing, 37-38

W

Watermark property bar, 234-235
watermarks, 146, 233-235
web searches via Yahoo! Search bar, 10
What's This button, 14
Widow/Orphan Protection, 130

width (columns), adjusting, 172-174
Word
  help, 18
  WordPerfect X3 styles, compatibility of, 160
WordPerfect 5.1 Classic mode, 9, 59-62
WordPerfect Address Book. *See* **Address Book (WordPerfect)**
WordPerfect Conversion Expert dialog, 316
WordPerfect Legal mode, 9
WordPerfect Mail Address Book, 290
WordPerfect Office X3 folder, 8
Wordperfect.com website, 10
Workspace Manager, 9, 59-62
WP 10 Temp zip files, downloading templates, 306
wp13us.wpt template, 297, 303
WPOR (WordPerfect OfficeReady) Browser, 309-310
wp_org.wcm macro, 318
wp_pr.wcm macro, 318
Wrap Text dialog, 229

X - Y - Z

XML, publishing documents to, 255

Yahoo! Search bar, 10

zip files, downloading templates, 306
zooming in/out, 56
  Page Width option, 124
  Print Preview text, 64
  specific areas, 58
  via mouse, 57
  zoom settings, 57

How can we make this index more useful? Email us at indexes@quepublishing.com

Introducing the Corel Digital Imaging product family

The Corel Digital Imaging product family enables you to get the most out of your digital photos and art.

Enhance your photos with **Corel® Paint Shop® Pro X**, transform your photos into personalized, handmade paintings with **Corel® Painter™ Essentials 3**, and manage and publish your photos with **Corel® Photo Album™ 6**.

For everything from photo editing and digital painting, to organizing image collections and creating keepsakes and crafts, the Corel Digital Imaging product family offers easy-to-use, integrated tools for everyone.

The easiest way to turn your pictures into professional-looking photos – fast!

Now it's easy to turn your photos into stunning paintings!

The easiest way to manage and share your photos. Guaranteed.

Mike Reed

Ryan Church

Greg Banning

Corel Painter Essentials 3 is based on the award winning power of Corel® Painter™ IX – the professional's choice for digital painting and illustration.

COREL

For more information, please visit
www.corel.com/digitalimaging